Buildings operate in a multitude of ways, they are structural, constructional, social, cultural and aesthetic. They modify the environment and act as mechanisms for generating, or inhibiting, social contact. This makes the question of how to research them one that is as rich as it is varied. This compilation of essays, all about one building, brings together authors each with different perspectives and methodologies. It could be considered a primer in the possible suite of approaches open to the researcher, or taken together it makes for a rare attempt to synthesise across disciplines. It gives about the best example I have seen of what a 'trans-disciplinary' approach to architectural research could look like.

Professor Alan Penn, Dean of The Bartlett, UCL, UK.

How buildings work for their occupiers and how design icons perform for their users is an imprecise and understudied field. The connections between design aspiration and their impact on people are rarely understood despite the huge capital investments that buildings command. This book brings a fresh and rigorous perspective to the field, founded in original and compelling research. It should become the bible for anyone interested in commissioning, designing and evaluating how buildings can add value to society.

Ricky Burdett, Professor of Urban Studies,
London School of Economics, UK.

Take One Building

This book evaluates how we experience and understand buildings in different ways depending upon our academic and professional background. With reference to Rem Koolhaas' Seattle Central Library, the book illustrates a range of different methods available through its application to the building. By seeing such a variety of different research methods applied to one setting, it provides the opportunity for researchers to understand how tools can highlight various aspects of a building and how those different methods can augment, or complement, each other.

Unique to this book are contributions from internationally renowned academics from fields including architecture, ethnography, architectural criticism, phenomenology, sociology, environmental psychology, and cognitive science, all of which are united by a single, real-world application, the Seattle Central Library.

This book will be of interest to architects and students of architecture as well as disciplines such as ethnography, sociology, environmental psychology, and cognitive science that have an interest in applying research methods to the built environment.

Ruth Conroy Dalton is Professor of Building Usability and Visualisation at the University of Northumbria at Newcastle. She is an architect and her research interests are on the relationship between the spatial layout of buildings and environments and how people understand, and interact in, those spaces.

Christoph Hölscher is Professor of Cognitive Science at ETH Zurich. He is a psychologist by training, and the focus of his work is at the intersection of spatial cognition and architectural design.

Take One Building

Interdisciplinary Research Perspectives of the Seattle Central Library

Edited by Ruth Conroy Dalton and Christoph Hölscher

LONDON AND NEW YORK

First published 2017
by Routledge

2 Park Square, Milton Park, Abingdon, Oxfordshire OX14 4RN
711 Third Avenue, New York, NY 10017

Routledge is an imprint of the Taylor & Francis Group, an informa business

First issued in paperback 2018

Copyright © 2017 selection and editorial matter, Ruth Conroy Dalton and Christoph Hölscher; individual chapters, the contributors.

The right of Ruth Conroy Dalton and Christoph Hölscher to be identified as the authors of the editorial material, and of the authors for their individual chapters, has been asserted in accordance with sections 77 and 78 of the Copyright, Designs and Patents Act 1988.

All rights reserved. No part of this book may be reprinted or reproduced or utilised in any form or by any electronic, mechanical, or other means, now known or hereafter invented, including photocopying and recording, or in any information storage or retrieval system, without permission in writing from the publishers.

Notice:
Product or corporate names may be trademarks or registered trademarks, and are used only for identification and explanation without intent to infringe.

British Library Cataloguing in Publication Data
A catalogue record for this book is available from the British Library

Library of Congress Cataloguing in Publication Data
A catalog record for this book has been requested.

ISBN: 978-1-4724-7114-7 (hbk)
ISBN: 978-1-138-61658-5 (pbk)

Typeset in Sabon
by Out of House Publishing

Contents

List of figures	ix
List of tables	xi
List of contributors	xii

Introduction	1
RUTH CONROY DALTON AND CHRISTOPH HÖLSCHER	

PART I
The process of design

9

1	Diamonds and sponge ALBENA YANEVA	11
2	Just how public is the Seattle Central Library? Publicity, posturing, and politics in public design SHANNON MATTERN	21
3	OMA's conception of the users of Seattle Central Library RUTH CONROY DALTON	38

PART II
The building as artefact

51

4	One-way street KIM DOVEY	53
5	A phenomenological and hermeneutic reading of Rem Koolhaas's Seattle Central Library: Buildings as lifeworlds and architectural texts DAVID SEAMON	67
6	The feel of space: Social and phenomenal staging in the Seattle Central Library JULIE ZOOK AND SONIT BAFNA	95

viii *Table of contents*

7 Seattle Central Library as place: Reconceptualizing space, community, and information at the Central Library 113
KAREN FISHER, MATTHEW SAXTON, PHILLIP M. EDWARDS, AND JENS-ERIK MAI

PART III
The library and its users 135

8 Emotional responses to locations in the Seattle Central Library 137
SASKIA KULIGA

9 Why people get lost in the Seattle Central Library 157
AMY SHELTON, STEVEN MARCHETTE, CHRISTOPH HÖLSCHER, BEN NELLIGAN, THOMAS SHIPLEY, AND LAURA CARLSON

10 Using social media to gather users' feedback of the Seattle Central Library 167
RUTH CONROY DALTON AND SASKIA KULIGA

11 Discovering Serendip: Eye-tracking experiments in the Seattle Central Library as the beginning of a research adventure 188
CLEMENS PLANK AND FIONA ZISCH

Epilogue: Drawing together the multiple perspectives of the Seattle Central Library 203
WILFRIED WANG

Index 210

Figures

0.1	The relationship between the architect, the building, and the user	4
1.1	Seattle Central Library	13
1.2	One of the architects' models of the Seattle Central Library	15
3.1	Temporary signs in the library	40
3.2	A dystopian vision of the labyrinthine qualities of Borges's Library	41
3.3	An example of a Sayeki-like anthropomorphic exploration of the world	44
4.1	Syntax and segmentarity	56
4.2	Seattle Central Library, figurative section	59
4.3	Living room, auditorium, and street entry	60
4.4	Spiral stack	61
4.5	Spatial structure	61
4.6	Diagram produced by Seattle Central Library management	62
5.1	Seattle Central Library, 2008	72
5.2	Seattle Central Library, 2008. West entry wall	75
5.3	Seattle Central Library, 2008. East entry wall	76
5.4	According to Thiis-Evensen, the wall expresses insideness-outsideness and motion, weight, and substance in three ways	77
5.5	Thiis-Evensen's four breadth themes and two building examples of each	78
5.6	Thiis-Evensen's four height motifs and two building examples of each	79
5.7	Seattle Central Library's west wall vertical expression as a sinking motif contributing to a sense of separation between inside and outside	80
5.8	The splayed entry frame of the Seattle Central Library's west wall	81
5.9	Seattle Central Library's east wall vertical expression as a rising motif	83
5.10	Seattle Central Library's east wall vertical expression as a squeezed motif	84
5.11	The east wall's inward-sloping arcade structure and entry	84
5.12	The east wall's arcade entry	85
6.1	Attending a meeting	102
6.2	Retrieving a book	104

x *Figures*

6.3	Sightseeing	107
8.1	Alphabetically sorted 76-word subset for the 'reaction card task'	141
8.2	Photographs used as an 'anchor' during the questionnaire	143
8.3	Results from the 'reaction card task'	145
8.4	Subset of six questionnaire items	148
8.5	VGA for the public spaces of the Seattle Central Library	150
9.1	Framework for predicting navigational difficulty using a three-factor model from Carlson et al. (2010)	158
9.2	Four challenges defined by the complexity and number of floors	161
9.3	Start and end locations for the navigation tasks, connected by the shortest paths	161
9.4	Select quotes from participants	162
10.1	Relationship between Web 2.0, social media, and user-generated content	171
10.2	Plans of public levels and areas of the Seattle Central Library	172
10.3	External view of Seattle Central Library	173
10.4	Example of an online review page	174
10.5	Average proportion of review content focus partitioned by geographic location of the reviewer	181
10.6	Split of positive, neutral, and negative reviews of the library by semantic theme	181
10.7	Wordles of locals' comments, split by thematic content	182
11.1	Stable space	195
11.2	Instable space	196
11.3	Two areas of interest – escalator and people in the background; test result from eye-tracking observation	197

Tables

5.1	Phenomenology and hermeneutics: some thematic and methodological commonalities	68
5.2	Phenomenology and hermeneutics: some thematic and methodological differences	69
5.3	Student responses when asked to guess what kind of building is the Seattle Central Library	71
5.4	Descriptors of the Seattle Central Library provided by at least two students	71
5.5	Examples of Yelp reports on the Seattle Central Library: users and visitors	87
7.1	A sample of responses from word association – 'architecture'	121
7.2	Reasons that people come to the Seattle Central Library with other people	123
8.1	Results from the convex space analysis and the visibility graph analysis	149
8.2	Spearman-Rho correlation matrices	151
10.1	Characteristics of different POE types	169
10.2	Mapping between Preiser's Levels of Performance categories and this study's semantic categories	176
10.3	Examples of positive and negative comment extracts for each of the five Seattle Central Library categories	177

Contributors

Sonit Bafna is Associate Professor at Georgia Tech's College of Design. He works in the area of architectural morphology addressing issues in interpretation, aesthetics, and design cognition, and developing models to explain human behavior and perception in designed environments. He is currently at work on a book titled *Imaginative Reasoning in the Shaping of Buildings*.

Laura Carlson is Professor of Psychology and serves as Vice President, Associate Provost and Dean of the Graduate School at the University of Notre Dame. Her primary research interest is in spatial language and spatial cognition. Her particular focus is on how various characteristics of the objects being described (e.g. geometric features, functional parts) and the goals of the speaker and listener impact descriptions of their spatial location. Her research has employed empirical, computational, and psychophysiological measures to investigate the way in which the objects and their spatial relations are encoded, represented, and described.

Ruth Conroy Dalton is Professor of Building Usability and Visualisation at the University of Northumbria at Newcastle. She has taught at the Architectural Association, London, the Georgia Institute of Technology, Atlanta, and the Bartlett School of Architecture, UCL. Her research interests are centred around the relationship between the spatial layout of buildings and environments and their effect on how people understand and interact in those spaces. She is an expert in space syntax analysis, architectural and spatial cognition, and pedestrian movement/wayfinding. She is passionately interested in placing the user at the centre of architectural design.

Kim Dovey is Professor of Architecture and Urban Design at the faculty of Architecture, Building, and Planning at the University of Melbourne. His research on social issues in architecture and urban design has included investigations of housing, shopping malls, corporate towers, urban waterfronts, and the politics of public space. His books include 'Framing Places: Mediating Power in Built Form' (Routledge 1999, 2008), 'Fluid City' (Routledge 2005), 'Becoming Places' (Routledge 2009), and 'Urban Design Thinking' (Bloomsbury 2016) Current research projects include those on urban place identity, creative clusters, transit-oriented urban design, and the morphology of informal settlements.

Phillip M. Edwards is an Instructional Consultant at the Center for Faculty Excellence at the University of North Carolina at Chapel Hill. He received an MS in Information (2003) from the University of Michigan School of Information, and his research interests lie in the areas of critical digital pedagogy and information literacy education. He also holds a BS in chemistry and a minor in mathematics (2001) from the University at Buffalo.

Karen Fisher is Professor at the University of Washington Information School and Adjunct Professor of Communication, and Visiting Professor at the Open Lab, Newcastle University, UK as well as Åbo Akademi University, Turku, Finland. Her focus is on how people experience information as part of everyday life, with an emphasis on the interpersonal aspects, the role of informal social settings or 'Information Grounds,' as well as the broader impacts of information and communication technologies.

Christoph Hölscher is Chair of Cognitive Science at ETH Zürich. He is a psychologist by training and the focus of his work is at the intersection of spatial cognition and architectural design. He is a leading researcher on human wayfinding in built environments, e.g. complex public buildings and urban environments. His research considers both the users of buildings and the architectural designers shaping the environments. Studies on building users include psychological testing of navigation in real-world buildings as well as virtual reality simulations, which is seen as a vital pre-occupancy evaluation tool. The overarching, applied goal of his research is to enable evidence-based design to address building usability requirements and improve our understanding of human spatial cognition.

Saskia Kuliga is an environmental psychologist and holds a master's degree from the University of Twente in The Netherlands. She is interested in human–environment interaction and is currently a doctoral student at the Center for Cognitive Science in Freiburg where she is supervised by Professor Christoph Hölscher. She investigates how building users perceive, behave, and evaluate architectural environments: her work includes wayfinding studies, the potential of unsolicited user comments for post-occupancy evaluation, studies about human and robot dynamic landmark placement, building circulation, building-user behavioural studies, and research into architectural education.

Jens-Erik Mai is Professor of Information Studies at the University of Copenhagen. He was previously at the University of Washington and the University of Toronto. His work concerns basic questions about the nature of information phenomena in contemporary society. He is concerned with the state of privacy and surveillance given new digital media, with classification given the pluralistic nature of meaning and society, and with information and its quality given its pragmatic nature.

Steven Marchette undertook his graduate research with Amy Shelton, studying the principals of human spatial memory, such as reference frame selection, as well as individual differences in the use of memory systems during navigational learning. He is particularly interested in how people establish and maintain their orientation, and how orientation must take into account the hierarchical nature of space. He is interested in complex environments such as college campuses – with rooms inside buildings and buildings placed around the campus – in which it can be quite problematic to reorient yourself.

xiv *Contributors*

Shannon Mattern is Associate Professor of Media Studies at the New School in New York. Her teaching and research address relationships between the forms and materiality of media and the spaces – architectural, urban, and conceptual – they create and inhabit. She has written about libraries and archives, media companies' headquarters, place branding, public design projects, urban media art, media acoustics, media infrastructures, and material texts. She is author of 'The New Downtown Library: Designing with Communities' and 'Deep Mapping the Media City' (both published by University of Minnesota Press) and she writes a regular column about media spaces for 'Places', a journal focusing on architecture, urbanism, and landscape.

Ben Nelligan is currently a research fellow in the Carlson Lab at the University of Notre Dame's Department of Psychology. His research focuses on how humans learn the environments around them and use this to navigate from place to place. More specifically, he is interested in understanding how environmental features, such as landmarks or the shape of buildings, and situational factors, such as stress or one's goals, interact with individual differences in how a person typically approaches navigation. He did his graduate work with Amy Shelton at Johns Hopkins University studying individual differences in how humans learn environments and how these differences contribute to success and failure of navigation.

Clemens Plank is an architect, researcher, and senior lecturer at the University of Innsbruck (Faculty of Architecture) where he supervises Design Studio and teaches architectural theory. His academic work draws strongly on neuroscientific research, pursuing a contemporary analysis of the phenomenological experience of architecture. His real-space experiments have been exhibited at Researchers Night, Innsbruck, 2005 and 2007; VLOW, Bregenz, 2008 (Winner of award vlow08 for young researchers). In collaboration with Fiona Zisch and Michael Wihart, he continues his research on novel digital technologies and environmentally responsive solutions to building design. In 2014 they founded Holon Architecture Laboratory, a platform for researchers and thinkers guided by an anthropocentric approach to architecture.

Matthew Saxton is Associate Dean for Academics at the University of Washington. He has worked as a reference librarian in academic, public, and special library environments. He teaches courses on reference work and research methods and his primary research interest is in the evaluation of information services.

David Seamon is Professor of Architecture at Kansas State University in Manhattan, Kansas. Trained in behavioural geography and environment behaviour research, he is interested in a phenomenological approach to place, architecture, environmental experience, and environmental design as place making. His books include 'A Geography of the Lifeworld' (New York: St Martin's Press, 1979); 'Dwelling, Place and Environment: Toward a Phenomenology of Person and World' (edited with Robert Mugerauer; New York: Columbia University Press, 1989); 'Dwelling, Seeing, and Designing: Toward a Phenomenological Ecology' (Albany, NY: State University of New York Press, 1993); and 'Goethe's Way of Science: A Phenomenology of Nature' (edited with Arthur Zajonc, Albany, NY: State University of New York

Press, 1998). He is Editor of the Environmental and Architectural Phenomenology Newsletter.

Amy Shelton is Director of Research at the Center for Talented Youth and Professor and Associate Dean for Research and Doctoral Programs in the School of Education at Johns Hopkins University. She holds a joint appointment in the School of Medicine and serves on the steering committees for the university-wide Science of Learning Initiative. Her research in cognitive psychology/cognitive neuroscience focuses on spatial skills, individual differences, and mechanisms of learning, couched in the broad context of understanding the characterization and needs of the individual learner. Dr. Shelton's professional orientation takes a strong basic science approach that is informed by the problems and questions of practice and application.

Thomas Shipley is Associate Professor of Psychology at Temple University. As a graduate student he studied with Robert Rescorla, Henry Gleitman, and Elizabeth Spelke. He worked as a postdoctoral researcher with Philip Kellman. He is interested in visual perception, spatial reasoning, perception action coordination, and food. His recent research has addressed the question of how human actions are recognized, including limits on the role of previous visual experience, the nature of action representations, and the importance of dynamics. Shipley is also part of the Research in Spatial Cognition group in Nora Newcombe's Spatial Intelligence and Learning Center where he is working on eye movements in mental rotation and segmentation of large spaces.

Wilfried Wang is the co-founder of Hoidn Wang Partner in Berlin with Barbara Hoidn and, since 2002, has been the O'Neil Ford Centennial Professor in Architecture at the University of Texas at Austin. He was born in Hamburg, studied architecture in London, and was partner with John Southall in SW Architects (1989–95). He was the founding co-editor of 9H Magazine (1979); with Ricky Burdett co-director of the 9H Gallery (1985–90), and director of the German Architecture Museum (1995–2000). He has taught at the Polytechnic of North London, University College London, ETH Zürich, Städelschule, Harvard University, and the Universidad de Navarra. Wang is the author and editor of various architectural mono and topographs and co-editor of the O'Neil Ford Mono and Duograph series. He is also the chairman of the Erich Schelling Architecture Foundation, adjunct member of the Federation of German Architects, foreign member of the Royal Swedish Academy of Fine Arts, Stockholm, member and deputy director of the architecture section of the Akademie der Künste, Berlin, and honorary member of the Portuguese Chamber of Architects.

Albena Yaneva is Professor of Architectural Theory and director of the Manchester Architecture Research Centre (MARC) at the University of Manchester, United Kingdom. She has been Visiting Professor at Princeton University School of Architecture and Parsons School of Design. Her research is intrinsically transdisciplinary and crosses the boundaries of science studies, cognitive anthropology, architectural theory, and political philosophy. She is the author of several books: The Making of a Building (Oxford: Peter Lang, 2009), Made by the OMA: An Ethnography of Design (Rotterdam: 010 Publishers, 2009), Mapping Controversies in Architecture (Ashgate 2012), Five Ways to Make Architecture Political. An Introduction to the Politics of Design Practice (forthcoming with

Bloomsbury Publishing, London), and editor (with Alejandro Zaera-Polo) of *What is Cosmopolitical Design?* (Routledge 2015). Her work has been translated into German, Italian, Spanish, French, Portuguese and Thai. Yaneva is the recipient of the RIBA President's award for outstanding university-located research (2010).

Fiona Zisch is an architect, researcher, and architectural lecturer at the University of Innsbruck and the University of Westminster. She is currently finishing a transdisciplinary PhD in architecture and neuroscience at University College London under the supervision of Professor Stephen Gage (Bartlett School of Architecture) and Dr Hugo Spiers (Institute for Behavioural Neuroscience). Her research interest focuses on how neural mechanisms construct our experience of space and what implications neuroscientific knowledge holds for architectural design. She uses a combination of technologies in her research, including EEG technology, laser scanning, and mobile tracking technologies. Together with Clemens Plank and Michael Wihart, she co-founded the Holon Architecture Laboratory. Her design work has been exhibited at NASA Houston, London and New York.

Julie Zook is Assistant Professor in the College of Architecture at Texas Tech University. Her research and scholarship focus on interstices between aesthetics, morphology, and society. She recently completed a dissertation investigating urban typologies through concurrent analysis of the representation of city scenes in film and the morphology of filming locations. In her consulting work, she has conducted spatial analysis and made design recommendations on urban design, healthcare architecture, and offices for a variety of client organizations.

Introduction

Ruth Conroy Dalton and Christoph Hölscher

Before starting this introductory chapter, we wanted to provide a brief comment on the scope of the book: on the whole, the parts of this edited book focus on the creative design process, the realised building (or building as artefact) or the building in use and its reception by its users. For the majority of chapters, it is clear that the relationship between the user and the building is central, being discussed either implicitly or explicitly: we are researching a building in relation to its experiential qualities. It should therefore be noted that, in terms of architectural research, this book covers little in terms of architectural history, urban or master planning, or the more structural or tectonic aspects to architectural engineering (although occasionally aspects of some of these may be touched upon). In principle, this book is intended to be used as a reference book, a compendium of case studies, or an integrated course textbook.

It seemed that there were probably two logical ways in which to start this book. The first way might consist of a scholarly discourse on the nature of architectural research; the other approach would be to tackle the more fundamental question of why we might want to research buildings and the built environment in the first place. Although we will touch upon the former topic, it is the latter question that will serve as our starting point.

So why research buildings or architecture or the built environment? For some people, they have no choice: we mandate that students of architecture must, at some point in their education, write a term paper, or papers, or even a lengthier thesis/dissertation on the topic. Researchers from a wide range of disciplines, which includes but is not confined to architecture, may find that they need to address this topic, either directly or obliquely, as part of their research. Again, they may have little or no choice but to grapple with the question of the built or designed environment. Even practising architects can find themselves needing to research the history, background, or context of a site or perhaps having to understand how an existing building functions, in order to adapt, extend, or modify it as part of their everyday professional practice. And then, of course, there are people who choose to research architecture through no reason of compulsion, but are simply driven, we would argue, by an innate curiosity about a building or its context. However, we would like to think that we are actually being somewhat disingenuous here, by separating those who *have to* do research from those who *choose* to do so, as we sincerely feel that all research, mandatory or otherwise, stems from a fundamental curiosity about the nature of the world around us. Human beings are 'pattern-seeking' creatures; we are drawn to looking for order or regularity in the world around us. Early researchers in Gestalt psychology noted that when people were presented with a seemingly, but not quite, random pattern of dots, any apparent order was immediately discerned: dots closer together were judged as being part of a greater whole/group 'entity' and series of dots that appeared to form linear alignments were considered connected and continuous, to give but two examples. We believe that this pattern-seeking instinct is ever present, in every sphere of our lives, and is bound to our innate curiosity about the world that ultimately underpins and sustains research: once we have noticed a pattern or regularity in the world, we seek to understand why it has occurred and what is its significance. This is the essence of all research.

Having spent a number of years tutoring architecture students' final year dissertations, it has become increasingly apparent that a lot of research into architecture starts not with a question, but with a building (or site, place, abstract building 'type', or work of a particular architect or practice). This innate curiosity about the world, and the drive to understand it, is frequently instigated by real-world, architectural phenomena. Statements such as, 'I want to study the Pompidou Centre'; 'I want to evaluate the Kings Cross redevelopment area'; 'I want to investigate schools for the blind/hospitals/Maggie's Centres'; 'I want to document the work of Zaha Hadid' are all typical opening statements of students. We would like to suggest that this is not simply the mark of an immature researcher who needs to be redirected to approach their investigation via a clear formulation of a research question (as useful as that can be), but rather that this is the sign of a commendable, basic research instinct. So, if starting with a building or site is a valid point of departure, then what comes next? How are researchers of, and into, the built environment expected to select the appropriate research tools with which to explore the building that their innate curiosity and laudable research instinct has prompted them to investigate?

The real-world building as research stimulus is the strength and unique approach of this book, since this book also starts from such a beginning. In our case the building is the Seattle Central Library designed by the Office of Metropolitan Architects (OMA) along with their local, Seattle-based partners, Loschky, Marquardt, and Nesholm architects (LMN). The idea behind this book is a very straightforward one, to take a single building and illustrate a range of different methods available to researchers of the built environment through their application to the same building. By seeing the range of different methods applied to one building, a prospective researcher is not only able to see how different tools can highlight different aspects of a building, and therefore inform their own choice of approach, but also how different methods can complement each other, or be combined in a 'mixed methods' approach.

There is a tale that originated in the Indian subcontinent of a number of blind men trying to describe an elephant. Each person uses their hands to touch part of the elephant and then describes what they feel: the person who is touching the leg describes the elephant as being 'tree-like', the one who touches the tail draws comparisons to a rope and the smooth tusks are likened to pipes, and so on (there are a different number of blind people and elephant body parts depending on which variation of the tale is being told). The point of the story is that no one person is wrong, and that the full picture is found by combining these different truths together. In this book, the elephant is the Seattle Central Library and there is no immediately available, over-arching 'truth', no one true way of considering or researching this building. Throughout the book, the reader will encounter as many variations of the Seattle Central Library as there are chapters and experts and methods. We can, rather irreverently, paraphrase

Introduction 3

the eminent physicist, Werner Heisenberg, who stated, 'We have to remember that what we observe is not nature in itself, but nature exposed to our method of questioning'. In our, somewhat playful, rewording of his quotation, this becomes, 'We have to remember that what we observe is not [a building] in itself, but [a building] exposed to our method of questioning'. Such a multiplicity of views of a single building is also fascinating for those of us interested in architecture; it is remarkable to note how differently a building is viewed from the perspective of an architectural critic, compared to a phenomenologist or an ethnographer.

We came to conduct our own research into the Seattle Central Library almost by chance and, in our case, the building was not our starting point. A group of international researchers decided to collaborate in order to understand the relationship between pedestrian movement or wayfinding, the design of complex buildings and spatial cognition, and we consisted of an architect, a cognitive scientist (namely the two editors of this book), plus two cognitive psychologists (and later the group expanded to include additional members from other related disciplines). Our early research discussions took place at a very abstract and theoretic level until we decided that it would help us explain and 'ground' our approach and theories if we could relate them back to a real building. One of us had heard anecdotally that the Seattle Central Library was meant to be a very confusing and disorientating building and so we began to find out more about it. At this initial stage, none of us had ever actually visited the building, but the more we found out about the building, the more it seemed an ideal setting for our collaboration. It is very easy, in this area of research, to find buildings that have little or no architectural merit and are extremely confusing to be in (just think of many large, civic hospitals). Conversely, it is possible to find examples of award-winning buildings that are exemplars of clear and comprehendible design, but rarely does 'award winning' and 'bewildering' come together in the same package. What initially struck us about Seattle Central Library was its almost schizophrenic nature: it was simultaneously 'great architecture' whilst also being 'fundamentally flawed' (the nature of this schism is explored in detail in Chapter 3, OMA's conception of the users of Seattle Central Library). The building had won major accolades and awards, whilst at the same time the internet and social media were awash with accounts of people having become lost in it and almost succumbing to panic attacks, or posting photographs of the confusing, temporary signs that the librarians were forced to improvise, shortly after the building opened (again, please refer to Chapter 3 for examples of these temporary signs). We realised rapidly that we had found our research setting, and what a rich research 'vein' it would subsequently prove to be.

Naturally, we also did what all other diligent researchers do, we found out what other people had written about the building and what other research had also been conducted into the library. In this process, we learnt, perhaps not unsurprisingly, that we were not the only academic researchers to 'discover' what an abundant source of research inspiration the Seattle Central Library would prove to be. In many respects the seed of this book had already spontaneously germinated at this point in time (this would have been around 2010–11), if only we had been sufficiently prescient to recognise it. In reality it took two field-based studies, three peer-reviewed journal papers, and a number of international talks plus many, many informal conversations with people around the world on the topic of the Seattle Central Library, until the vision of this book began to take shape. At its most simple, the initial idea of this book was to bring together these numerous studies of the building, from many different disciplines, under one cover. At a more sophisticated level, it can be seen as a roadmap of how to conduct different kinds of research into the built environment, demonstrated by being applied to a single setting, for ease of comparison between the methods.

The book is divided into three parts. The first part focuses on the design process, which covers all events, both inside the architects' offices and outside in the wider public realm (via consultation and public participation events), which took place prior to the building being opened in May 2004. The focus of the first part is intended to be more on 'process' than on 'product'. The second part is about the physical building as ultimately realised in the context of downtown Seattle. If we go all the way back to Vetruvius, and consider the Vitruvian Triad of architectural qualities, the second part of the book would be concerned with '*firmitas*' and '*venustas*', or the materiality and aesthetics of the building. This is in contrast to the final part of the book, where the focus shifts from the building to its users, or the '*utilitas*', or functionality, of the building, to complete Vetruvius's set. Naturally these parts are not always mutually exclusive: it can be challenging to talk about the design process without discussing the architects' conception of their imagined user, or to consider the materiality of a building without accounting for its functional consequences, but for the most part, the emphasis, rather than scope, of the chapter clearly places it into one of the above three parts.

The division between these chapters reflects a diagram (Figure 0.1) that we, the editors, have repeatedly used in our research and invited talks over the past ten years of our collaboration. This diagram is a circular one, which places the architect at the top of the circle, and shows how they are engaged in two parallel activities: the architect

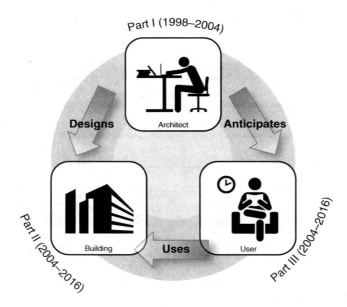

Figure 0.1 The relationship between the architect, the building, and the user. Architect icon created by Augusto Zamperlini; building icon created by Dennis Tiensvold; building user icon created by Edward Boatman, all from the Noun Project.

designs the building whilst also anticipating the actions/needs/behaviours of the end user (and this is the first part of the book); the building, in the bottom left of the diagram (and representing Part II of the book) is then used by the client/members of the public shown in the bottom right (and this is the final part of the book). Over the years we have used Figure 0.1 to illustrate why it is necessary to research all three aspects of a building: the design process and architect's intentions, the building and its context, plus the behaviour and opinions of its users in order to form a full and complete picture of 'how architecture works'. And so it is probably not at all surprising to find that this vision of how to research architecture, which has sustained and underpinned our work together, should have re-emerged so strongly in the guise of the book's structure.

Part I of the book is naturally the shortest, since it is the part concerned with the design process and, in terms of duration, covers the shortest period of time. In November 1998, the proposal for a new central library in downtown Seattle was given the green light by Seattle voters. The process of holding an international design competition, for OMA/LMN to enter and win in May 1999, and for the collaborating practices to subsequently design, build, and open the library took an impressively short period of time, namely just over five and a half years. In contrast, the library has now been in use for approximately double that period of time. We therefore have just three chapters in the first part of the book. The first of which is by Albena Yaneva, an ethnographer, who spent an extended period of time in OMA's office observing their everyday interactions and practices. Fortunately for this book, this happened to take place during the period of time in which the Seattle Central Library was being designed and so she has been able to bring a unique perspective to their design process, having been immersed in their office environment and witnessed events first-hand. For this opening chapter, she employs a classic ethnographic approach, and comments on the profound relationship between OMA's design process and their use of architectural model making. The second chapter, by Shannon Mattern, takes more of a social science, case study approach to the library, focusing in particular on the relationship between the architects, the library, and its would-be public, set against the political and social climate of Seattle around the turn of the millennium. Her particular focus is on the medium of communication between the key stakeholders. The final chapter in Part I, by Ruth Conroy Dalton, specifically investigates how, through their published material and statements, the architects appeared to consider their prospective users during the design phase. Unlike Yaneva's direct, experience-based research, these latter two chapters are based on interpretive research of primary, published sources.

Part II of the book includes four chapters and, as far as possible, is concerned with the material and aesthetic qualities of the building. This part begins with a chapter by Kim Dovey and is an examination of the claim that OMA utilises programmatic innovations which include the production of fields of social encounter, new functional juxtapositions, and forms of spatial segmentation designed to resist social reproduction and enable certain 'freedoms'. This examination, using the Seattle Central Library as a case example, utilises an adapted method of space syntax analysis filtered through a Deleuzian framework of assemblage theory.

The next two chapters in this part are both focused on the experiential qualities of the building and, although the second of these chapters by Julie Zook and Sonit Bafna is one of those that could just as easily have been placed into either the second or third part of the book, it has been presented alongside David Seamon's chapter, as they both employ, amongst other methods, a phenomenological approach. Seamon's chapter is concerned with buildings as 'Lifeworlds', or the everyday experience of being immersed in a place or location, and as 'architectural objects'. He uses the Seattle Central Library as a means to illustrate what phenomenology (the experienced building) and hermeneutics (the building as a semantically interpreted object) offer architectural research; he examines the Seattle Central Library from four different perspectives from which he procures real-world evidence via a range of research methods, including questionnaires, formal archetypes (derived from Thiis-Evensen) and a phenomenological reading based on building users' reviews and architectural critiques. This chapter serves as an excellent introduction, and comparison, to both approaches, whilst also providing a good grounding in phenomenology, preparing the reader for the next chapter. In their contribution to the book section, Zook and Bafna assess how the Seattle Central Library engages the public imagination by considering the location and distribution of potential views, exposure, and visual access to different parts of the building; this is set against the underlying strategies by which the sensory phenomena of the building are presented to the builder users. There is a pleasing balance between the two chapters by Seamon and by Zook and Bafna, namely that Seamon's chapter focuses predominantly on a phenomenological reading of the external appearance of the building whilst the Zook and Bafna chapter is concerned with the library's internal spaces, and so we are led gradually (and phenomenally) up to, in, and around the building over the course of these two chapters. Both of these chapters are interesting as they employ phenomenology as part of a mixed-method approach, contrasting the experiential qualities of the building with a range of different analytical techniques.

The final chapter in this part is by Karen Fisher and her colleagues, Matthew Saxton, Phillip Edwards, and Jens-Erik Mai. This chapter applies two primary frameworks for understanding libraries as 'place' (Oldenburg's 'third place' concept and Cresswell's five facets of place) to analyse questionnaire responses regarding the social, political, cultural, and economic meaning of the Seattle Public Central Library. This study contributes to the theories of place by adding the element of 'information' to it, comprising themes regarding information finding and seeking, life-long learning, learning resources, and learning environments. Again, this is a chapter that overlaps strongly with the final part, where the emphasis is on the user, but has been included in this part as its focus is resolutely on the concept of the library as a 'place' rather than on the user experience per se, despite the fact that it employs the elicitation of user's feedback as a method.

In the third and final part of this book, the focus shifts from the building to the building's users and how they behave in, experience, understand, and use the library. The first of these chapters is by Saskia Kuliga where she presents and discusses a set of subjective spatial experience data gathered from the Seattle Central Library in order to explore the relationship between people's emotional response to, and the spatial layout of, buildings. This chapter serves to represent an environmental psychological approach to understanding human–environment interaction, whilst also including other analytic methods to objectively understand and quantify the role played by the building. Following on from the environmental psychology approach described above, the next chapter in this part is the one that, above all others in the book, focuses on how experimental methods from fields such as psychology can be integrated into research on the built environment. This chapter, written by a group of eminent experimental psychologists, Amy Shelton, Christoph Hölscher, Thomas Shipley, and

Introduction 7

Laura Carlson along with colleagues, Steven Marchette and Ben Nelligan, sets out to discover why people get lost in the Seattle Central Library. It begins by outlining why this building appears to be a challenge for navigation and wayfinding and then illustrates how the authors tested wayfinding within the building as a case study of how to use psychological experimental methods to answer architectural research questions.

The penultimate chapter, by Ruth Conroy Dalton and Saskia Kuliga, presents a study in which unsolicited, user feedback of the Seattle Central Library was gathered from selected social media and user-review websites to determine the viability of utilising social media as a novel and unconventional approach to post-occupancy evaluation. This chapter suggests that highly valuable information is currently available from peer-to-peer networks and that this forms a new class of post-occupancy evaluation data, which is radically different to current post-occupancy evaluation paradigms and one which might be increasingly valuable as a method used by architectural researchers as well as practising architects.

The final chapter in this book, *Discovering Serendip*, by practising architect and researcher Clemens Plank and his research collaborator Fiona Zisch, presents another method, which is increasingly becoming available to architectural researchers, that of using eye-tracking technology to investigate how and what people pay attention to in the built environment. It describes an experiment using the Seattle Central Library as an empirical testing site to ask questions of, and investigate, architectural perception and to determine which areas of the library appear to draw our visual attention and why. This chapter concludes by raising important questions on the very nature of architecture and architectural research. Plank and Zisch's chapter is the perfect concluding chapter since it effectively merges the user and the building into a unified whole – a syzygy – an irrevocably yoked pair of entities, each mutually dependent on the other. It is also interesting that Plank, Zisch, and Dalton, in their respective chapters, independently focus on the concept of 'empathy' as being crucial to the understanding of the design process/performance of the Seattle Central Library and, by extrapolation, to understanding architecture in general.

So, how can you, our reader, get the most out of this book? We envisage that there are probably three main ways in which you might use this book. The first mode would be guided by your overall research focus: whether it is the design process, the building, or the user. If your research question clearly falls into one of these three categories, then the chapters contained within each individual part should serve as a good starting point and we would recommend reading these chapters in full, whilst probably dipping in and out of the other chapters, as (or if) they seem relevant to your research question. If, however, you have an idea of what kind of methodology you might wish to employ, for example, interpretive research of published sources, or questionnaires or experimental methods, then you can flick through the book, focusing primarily on those chapters employing such methods. Finally, it is, of course, our sincere wish, that for some readers, *all the chapters* will be equally of interest as, together, in the same way that the blind men described their elephant, they synergistically provide a clear and powerful insight into a very unique building. By reading this collection of chapters as a single text you will encounter one of the most comprehensive narratives of the design, realisation, and public reception of a single building ever to have been published.

Finally, having read through all of these chapters, you will hopefully be left with the conviction that, just as William Dietrich (a writer for the *Seattle Times*),

8 *Ruth Conroy Dalton and Christoph Hölscher*

commenting on the library, observed: 'Perhaps no other Seattle building has involved so many really bright people, thinking really hard, about what architecture is supposed to accomplish'. This can be paraphrased, in the context of this book, as: 'Perhaps no other... building has involved so many really bright people, thinking really hard, about what [one particular building] was supposed to, [and has/has not,] accomplish[ed]'.

Part I
The process of design

1 Diamonds and sponge

Albena Yaneva

An ethnographic glance at design

Accounting for the momentum in the practice of the Office for Metropolitan Architecture (2001–4), this chapter offers an ethnographic glance at design. It gathers small accounts of different design trajectories, reminiscent of short stories. These are narratives I told many times while working in or presenting my work on OMA, but which I never wrote down separately.[1] They are stories that deserve to be told. Written as such, they provide interpretations of the design process without drawing sequential linear storylines; nor do they rely on predictable narratives of events. Short stories, as a literary genre, revolve around the resolution of a conflict, a tension, a false assumption, an inversed expectation, and often have unexpected ironic or tricky endings. Similarly, concise ethnographic accounts rely on a fold in time and space to account for the distinctive features of design in this office; image patterns evoke a sense of the reality of design. The different stories follow often unconnected projects and events. Nevertheless, their sequence provides an extended story arc, progressing through accumulation. The common feature of all stories is that they all account for the nature of design invention; the latter is not reduced here to an abstract concept of creation or construction. Instead, I tackle it as something that resolves into concrete actions and practices: in collective rituals, techniques, habits, and skills ingrained by training and daily repetition, in reuse of materials and recycling of historical knowledge and foam chunks. It is also a very fragile process – when a building is in the making and as long as it exists as a scale model, its existence is very tentative, very frail. At any moment in the design process it can live or it can die, it can merge into something else, it can be reused, recollected. That is, a view of design as constituted from the inside; it stems from the experience of making.[2]

Diamonds and sponge

On a September afternoon in 2002 I had arranged to meet Erez, an architect at OMA, for an interview. We decided to meet downstairs on the first floor – the only place we could have a discussion uninterrupted by other designers or project emergencies. Ole's (another architect at OMA) glass office was another quiet space for uninterrupted discussions, but it was occupied at the time. I somehow preferred also the first-floor interviews because as soon as I entered its tranquil and well-organized spaces, rhythmically ordered by better-arranged tables of models, I was immediately transported to the office future, an immediate future. I liked spending time on the

12 *Albena Yaneva*

ground floor where the busy model shop opened to a larger quasi-exhibition space, where Rem used to begin his guided tours of the office. I also remember Rem showing me around on my first visit to OMA, and he was especially proud of some of the models you can only view in this space: some Prada experiments with sponge[3] and the huge models of buildings in construction like Porto or Seattle. I remember Rem calling the Prada sponge samples 'the material of modernity'. What I also recall is the strangeness of the material and Rem's pride. Sometimes, tired of the busy-bee rhythm of the seventh floor, I simply retired to the first floor to contemplate these models.

And, here was Erez, seated next to the Seattle model, feeling comfortable to be in the limelight of the interview and sharing the silent space with the models: he, like myself secretly admired most of them.

> This is a model made in 1999, it's a very conceptual thing. But you can see that these diamonds are here, it's a mesh. And they stayed until the building began to be constructed; so, this material remained throughout the process. At one point we tried some fabrics, and they stayed all the way on the model too. Another good example of this could be Prada; you see this material, sponge, over there [he points to the sponge samples]. So the Prada sponge at the beginning was a small model in sponge, which they tried to imitate. Chris worked quite a lot to develop the material that would really imitate it and present the same qualities and the same appearance. And eventually they managed to do it. It came from the model, almost in a direct line to the final thing.[4]

The connection between the so-called 'diamonds' on the Seattle model (Figure 1.1) and the diamond seismic system of the building under construction puzzled me for a while. I wanted to understand it. Erez and I looked at the Seattle diamonds together: 'Very often there is a direct connection between the material of the model and the material of the building,' states Erez. It is a literal one: 'If for instance the model has a wire mesh operating copper bottom, it's about taking that literally.'[5]

To understand how direct this connection can be, to witness how exactly the mesh of the Seattle model became a material used for the building and how the sponge as 'the material of modernity' was obtained for Prada, I shall first guide you through some related stories of material invention within the OMA practice.

Numerous stories of design at OMA emphasize how important the techniques of model making are for the shape of a building. Olga tells me, for instance, that a prevailing story in the office is the one about how the use of Perspex in model making changed the world of architecture. Later I understood that it was the OMA version of this story that excited most designers at work, namely, how the foam cutter is an invention as important as Perspex, an invention capable of changing the face of architecture. Once the transparent and easy-to-manipulate Perspex began to be used for models, this changed the face of the final buildings, claim OMA architects. The Perspex models 'show at one glance the outside and the inside'.[6] It also anticipated buildings with such properties. In the same way, the foam cutter, its angle, its speed, allow OMA designers to produce 77 curved and innovative building shapes. This particular technique triggers changes in the building design. Erez quotes another example of how the modelling guides the building design.

> **Erez:** The technique of modelling influences the design. If you build a square building, it's easier to build it out of foam. For example, the Guangzhou Opera

Figure 1.1 Seattle Central Library

House has a super-weird shape, it's a folding surface. Building this folding surface was really, really hard. So, when we develop the technique of building the model, it influences the design, because it never turns out the way you thought it would be. Then, if it's nicer it will influence the design. If it's not, you can abandon it and move on to another technique because you don't manage 'to establish beauty' as Rem says. So, it's not beautiful at first sight.

AY: And how did you manage to build it?

Erez: We built an extension to the foam cutter and we placed two guides on the sides for the foam with one wire. We really worked very hard, but we only obtained three models from it. Because we just couldn't build it. At that point we constructed it on the computer, and the final model was built from the 3-D computer file. Some outsourcing guy built it for us on the computer because we couldn't. Again it's time and knowledge. We can do it. But in the process in which the office works we need to produce something new for tomorrow morning, so to speak. So, we cannot spend three days building a model.[7]

There is a variety of elements that are to be taken into consideration in the making of a new model or shape: the restrictions of the site, the clients' fears, the programme requirements, the small budget, the community protests against the design, the protected buildings, the zoning filling, the neighbours' vulnerability, etc. This list can be extended according to the specificity of each project and its destination. Yet, what remains a common feature of all buildings to come is that they are all 'things', i.e., contested assemblies of contradictory issues. Looking at design practice, we should add another aspect that would make the 'thingly' nature of a building

14   *Albena Yaneva*

easier to comprehend.[8] There are *studio events* related to the particular performance of a design object, or the substantiation of a property of an object in time. They are embedded in the process of using particular modelling techniques or in experimentation with materials and shapes. These singular events often point to the intensity of design life at OMA. The fact that the materiality of Perspex or the specific use of the foam cutter has a certain impact on the building's shape cannot be doubted. Yet, the importance of these singular events for the building-to-be has not been entirely accounted for. Can a model fully predict in advance what the building-to-be will look like? Can architects be completely prepared for the building to come? Can the building faithfully follow its models? Both models and buildings travel and undergo changes in this process. In their attempts to move towards each other, to bring life into the studio and to re-enact it, the tentative moves of the two travellers trace a twisting trajectory interrupted or guided by studio events.

While the foam is still blue

Sitting in front of Erez that afternoon in the interview, sharing the space only with the model of the Seattle Library, I thought about the differences between the colour perception of the two office spaces. If the seventh-floor open-plan space were to be defined in colour, that would definitely be blue because of the blue foam predominantly used by OMA. As you go downward to the first floor, you start thinking about design in many other different colours. Why is that?

> The blue foam means that you do not have definition, it's going to be blue foam or metal and copper, maybe. So, that's how it could then be developed. We had three models at the beginning, they were all in foam; but they were painted – one was concrete and we sanded it until it looked like a concrete block. One was of glass and we made a pattern on it. One was made of foam, but was a structural model, so it had more transverse bars. And so those three were meant to be three kinds of representations. These models say: 'it could be concrete, it could be glass, it could be steel. Which one do you want?' The concrete was the more abstract and the more interesting in relationship to the project.[9]

From the comment above we learned from Carol, a senior architect at OMA, that blue stands for the not-yet-defined materiality of the building-to-be. On the one hand, the model can *represent* existing or intended materials – steel, concrete, glass. These are all materials that are to be taken from the catalogues. They are known and predictable. To make a model that would represent one of those materials would merely require simulating their texture or form on the model. Architects would simply say: 'OK we would like to have it in copper', and they will try to *imitate* the copper on the model. That is how architects at OMA and architects from other practices often work. On the other hand, in the process of office experimentation, some new materials and material effects can be obtained. In that case, 'architects build a scale model to look for new materials'. The material comes as a result of a studio event. And that is something so distinctive for OMA.

> Sometimes we use some materials of which we are not quite sure of how they work. We just find them attractive and we use them on the model, and then we

start developing that material. Then we call people and we discuss how we can actually achieve this sort of effect. Sometimes we just use a material that really does not exist. It may become so interesting that we say 'OK, it looks really nice, but how can we achieve this in reality?' That's why a lot of things are developed in the office. Some offices simply apply existing materials. Of course it's easier to use materials from the shelf, from the catalogue, but we can't be on the cutting edge if we do that. So, we develop our own materials, we develop new structures.[10]

The experimental effect achieved on the model is to be repeated and reproduced at building level. Take the Flick house[11] for instance. At the beginning, designers constructed a blue model and they had difficulty in considering how to make 'a material that will give the same transparent light that was seen in the mode' (see Figure 1.2 for an example of a model of the Seattle Central Library).[12] Another example is the model of the NATO headquarters.

When we did these small lines,' explains Erez, 'it was just an experiment with the model technique. Then we tried to imitate this quality of the façade; you see it

Figure 1.2 One of the architects' models of the Seattle Central Library

16 *Albena Yaneva*

over there. So, to design the real façade we tried to imitate the façade effect we first achieved on the model.

I wondered how this effect was obtained. Could it possibly be merely skilful use of the foam cutter, or something else? Erez replied quickly: 'This was all done with the foam cutter, you just do a lot of stripes, and that's all'.[13] The models test true effects, as Ole describes this process. In that sense OMA models are realistic:

> We do try to test a lot of things on models with the sense of realism, which obviously still implies different degrees of abstraction, but it really also comes down to your experience, and to your ability to learn from these things.[14]

Thus, when these randomly and locally achieved effects in the concrete situation of model experimentation, as seen on the Flick and the NATO models, are to be repeated and reproduced, slowly and gradually merging into a novel material, a new tentative design trajectory is triggered. If we follow it for a while, we are certainly able to witness how a studio event plays a part in generating the reality of a building-to-be.

A material that compels the designer can easily create a studio event.

> We work with different models, and when we try to finish one we put some materials on it. We do not look at the catalogue. Instead of going outside and finding a good material, we first look at our own. If something is compelling and looks good… you can look for up to six months for some materials that simulate whatever you put into the model. It always goes from the model to the catalogue and not the other way around.[15]

The fact that designers at OMA refuse to use the catalogue of existing materials, preferring to pick and make their own materials *in situ*, shows the extent to which the dense foam environment provides a creative milieu for a proactive design process. It allows different materials to stimulate the makers and to involve them in model making and experimentation. What follows is a 'let's do it' moment, which architects often recall in these stories of invention, especially for the emblematic Prada sponge. Erez tells the story: 'Somebody just hung more clues on the sponge and said: "Let's try to do a material that will look the same and will have this quality". And eventually we did it.' Erez continues: 'If you want this material to happen you hire a manufacturer. You have few guys who do material studies, and interesting companies that do this interesting stuff.'[16] The research on materials can be further used for other projects and purposes, not necessarily for this building.

But while designers and manufacturers desperately try to produce a material that would repeat the same effects as generated in the model making, in order to help the model get closer to the building-to-be, what happens to the building? How does the building travel to get closer to the materials and shapes generated in the studio process? How do these two travellers meet, how do their tentative moves of approaching each other draw trajectories of invention?

Diamonds and sponge 17

Under the pressure of the construction, and in front of the eyes of astonished workers and engineers in Seattle or Porto, architects constantly move back and forth between the building-under-construction and its models, comparing, correcting, and simultaneously updating them. 'In Porto, they have a model on the site, because it's such a complicated building that they can go and look at things in the model to better understand it and update it'.[17] Even the production phase is still subject to changes, argues Kunlé, another architect at OMA. 'So, if we realize that something is totally wrong at that point, we can still change the model after the building.'[18] To understand the Seattle Library, for instance, in terms of what the space would look like in three dimensions and to test the diamond seismic system installed between the platforms of the library, as well as the ramps and the fabric of w-sections on the interior of the glass and aluminium skin, the architects built up a mock-up:

> We built the curtain wall, the exterior skin to test it. We did also the book ramp. We basically did one bay of it and we went from ground level, maybe 6 feet high, just to check two different ways of rafting. And even the public was invited to examine it, including disabled people who could test whether they could actually use the wheelchairs.[19]

Models, mock-ups, and building stand side by side, and are amended and improved at the same time. This points to the existence of a specific relationship between the models and buildings, as seen under the OMA spotlight. Building and models stand together as two simultaneously present competitive arrangements in architectural design. There is no way to get out of the model without getting into the building, there is no way to get out of the building without getting into the model. The model serves as a way of seeing and envisioning the building because it 'carries a similar spirit or understanding'.[20] Every change in it, every tiny adjustment is meant to influence the building to a certain extent. As architects from OMA put it, the model is made in order to see how it affects the building.

Models and building are associated in such a way that once the architects, clients, and public see the models, they think of the building.

> The building is one moment in the process. And even if you build it, it's just one moment, because of the deadlines. But we always go on and develop it. It's endless. Maybe it also leads to something bad on some occasions. But there is no end to these things. And that's why, when you look at the CCTV and all these models, none of them is really an end product, and none of them is really a beginning, and none of them can stand for the building itself. And everywhere you keep models that look different.[21]

Thus, the direction of the whole design process is not an ultimate building: instead of beginning with models and ending up with a building in a linear, step-by-step progressive venture, design contains both models and building as two events; each of them is a moment from the becoming of the other, each of them emerges under certain conditions from the other. Both models and building are defined as two states of an active matter, two frozen 'moments' of it: one refines the other as they happily sit at the two ends of the design continuum. Rather than being a

18 *Albena Yaneva*

terminus, the building stands next to its models, coalescent or conterminous with them. That is why a composition of a few models is always kept in the office and on the construction site.

If we look more closely at the criss-cross trajectories of models and buildings at OMA, can we say what the arrow of invention looks like? Does it go from the model to the catalogue, from model effects to novel building materials, from studio events to construction reality? Or, is it perhaps the other way around? Neither the model flies towards the building in an accelerated course, nor does the building systematically respond to the demands of an experimental model. The model is not an ideal for the building to follow, nor is the building an obedient disciple of the model guidance. Neither imitates nor strictly pursues the other. The 'monster model' and the building-to-be run side by side and, in the rush they change pace, they make friends, they respond to other experimental studio events. As a model and a building refer to each other, they trace multifarious trajectories of invention.

Architecture as office enterprise

If we cannot say that the building strives to imitate the model, then we equally cannot maintain the statement that the model is a tool for generating reality. After all, what does it mean to produce realist architecture?[22] No one in the office can answer this question. Ole explains,

> I have always struggled with the term 'realistic', because I don't know if 'realistic' really implies copying any reality, since what one is dealing with is different degrees of abstraction and, as I said, different degrees of interpretation. So, in a certain sense, there is no realistic representation of anything. Architecture remains a process of translation and further definition.[23]

We can argue for the centrality of the 'the model in the studio' in OMA's design. The events in the office generate numerous effects; they introduce life into the studio. Material inventions happen as a re-enactment of studio events. Thus a building is not supposed to represent a reality 'out there'. Instead it tries to repeat, refer to, and get closer to life as enacted in the office. It is not description, but enactment that guides the design process at OMA. The fact that there is no urban life 'out there', far from the studio, has been demonstrated by all those designers who never visited the Whitney site in Manhattan but kept on designing for it, by all those who never learned Spanish but built in Cordoba, and by those who never borrowed a book from the Seattle Library, but reinvented the library typology. Designers never go 'outside'; there is no outside. Manhattan, Seattle, Cordoba are brought into the office; their life is re-enacted in studio practice. The studio constitutes their world. There is no one imaginary Reality within the walls of the office on Heer Bokelweg Street,[24] and another Reality outside, but one heterogeneous design world that generates meaning. This story tells us also something about Koolhaas that is often overlooked. It is not by chance that when he looks through the interior glass wall of the office with two doors, the entire world is 'in here'. OMA and Koolhaas treat the studio as the world, a world that is to be re-enacted in practice, a world that is to be reinvented by design.

Notes

* This chapter is a reprint from "Diamonds And Sponge" (one chapter) plus one paragraph (358 words) from Chapter 1 from Made by the Office for Metropolitan Architecture: An ethnography of design. 010 Publishers, 2009.
1 A different study of design in the making, based on rare ethnographic materials from OMA with a particular focus on the projects for the extension of the Whitney Museum of American Art in New York, was published in a separate book (Yaneva, 2009).
2 Some recent investigations on design practice have shown an attempt to tackle alternative thinking in architecture, but rely mainly on the designers' discourse rather than on the experience of designing architects (see Hubbard, 1995; Mitchell, 1996; Fisher, 2000). My study is rather inspired by architectural analyses that focus on the practices of designing architects as reflective practitioners (Schön, 1983, 1985) and on the particular translations of architectural visuals on the way to the final building (Evans, 1997, 1989).
3 Prada Sponge, Los Angeles, USA, 2004; research and development of foam material in the use of Prada Epicenter store; built.
4 Interview with Erez, November 2002, OMA.
5 Interview with Erez, October, 2002, OMA.
6 Interview with Olga, October 2002, OMA.
7 Interview with Erez, November 2002, OMA.
8 On the 'thingly' nature of buildings see Latour and Yaneva, 2008.
9 Interview with Carol, October 2002, OMA.
10 Interview with Kunlé, November 2002, OMA.
11 Flick House, Zurich, Switzerland, 2001; museum for contemporary art; commission.
12 Interview with Olga, November 2002, OMA.
13 Interview with Erez, November 2002, OMA.
14 Interview with Ole, November 2002, OMA.
15 Interview with Olga, November 2002, OMA.
16 Interview with Erez, November 2002, OMA.
17 Interview with Carol, October 2002, OMA.
18 Interview with Kunlé, 11 November 2002, OMA.
19 Interview with Carol, October 2002, OMA.
20 Interview with Ole, November 2002, OMA.
21 Interview with Erez, November 2002, OMA.
22 Koolhaas's approach is often described as realist: 'Koolhaas knows what his architecture is supposed to look like when materialized. That is, he knows his models and tries, like a realist painter, to make his buildings approach them as closely as possible. He abides by the reality that he has taken as a model, and this is why I have described his architecture as "realist" at some point' (Moneo, 2004, p. 313).
23 Interview with Ole, November 2002, OMA.
24 That is the Rotterdam address of the Office for Metropolitan Architecture.

References

Evans, R. Architectural projection. In *Architecture and its image: Four centuries of architectural representation: Works from the collection of the Canadian Centre for Architecture.* Cambridge, MA: MIT Press, 1989: 369.
Evans, R., R. Difford, and R. Middleton. *Translations from drawing to building and other essays.* London: Architectural Association, 1997.
Fisher A. Developing skills with people: A vital part of architectural education. In D. Nicol, ed., *Changing architectural education: Towards a new professionalism.* London: Taylor and Francis, 2000: 116–22.
Hubbard, B. *A theory for practice: Architecture in three discourses.* Cambridge, MA: MIT Press, 1995.

Latour, B. and A. Yaneva. 'Give me a gun and I will make all buildings move': An ANT's view of architecture. In R. Geiser, ed., *Explorations in architecture: Teaching, design, research*. Berlin: Birkhauser, 2008: 80–9.

Mitchell, M.A. Educating through building: Architects, appropriate technology and building production. In N. Hamdi, ed., *Educating for real*. London: Intermediate Technology Publications, 1996.

Moneo, R. and G. Cariño. *Theoretical anxiety and design strategies in the work of eight contemporary architects*. Cambridge, MA: MIT Press, 2004.

Schön, D.A. *The reflective practitioner: How professionals think in action*. New York: Basic Books, 1983.

Schön, D.A. *The design studio: An exploration of its traditions and potentials*. Portland, OR: International Specialized Book Service, 1985.

Yaneva, A. *Made by the Office for Metropolitan Architecture: An ethnography of design*. 010 Publishers, 2009.

2 Just how public is the Seattle Central Library?

Publicity, posturing, and politics in public design

Shannon Mattern

When they voted to tax themselves to support the overhaul of their city's library system, Seattleites expected to play a leading role in deciding how those funds would be spent – particularly in the case of the city's new Central Library.[1] Throughout the design process, the public's input was solicited and catalogued – but because the library and design team controlled both the major design decisions and the discourse surrounding that design, the public's input had only limited effect. A case study of the communication surrounding the design of the Seattle Central Library illuminates the discursive system that frames the design agenda, informs the design itself, and defines the extent of public involvement.

Introduction

Seattle of the 1990s was a city in transition – a city whose identity was bound up with its Native American heritage, its geographical splendour, and flannel shirts, but also with its status as birthplace to some of the world's largest and most successful technology, aviation, and bioengineering companies, and its distinction as home to two of the world's richest individuals. One constant, however, was the city's reputation – or perhaps even notoriety – for public process. And recently, Seattle, also famous for its great love of books, was given the opportunity to build a new downtown public library – an institution supposedly founded on the ideals of free and universal access. Colouring the public process surrounding this design project were first, a critically acclaimed, Dutch-born, internationally practising intellect-architect, and second, a climate of architectural suspicion that arose after Frank Gehry's multi-coloured blob, the Experience Music Project, appeared beneath the Seattle Center's Space Needle.

Gehry's design was only the latest in a series of unpopular public projects. In 1991, Robert Venturi's Seattle Art Museum met with a cool reception. And in the mid-1990s, Seattleites rejected Microsoft billionaire Paul Allen's offer to fund Seattle Commons, a park linking the central business district to the waterfront. In their attempts to up-date the city's architectural image, the city government, civic organizations, real-estate developers, and public institutions found that Seattleites suffered from what Douglas Kelbaugh, former member of the architecture faculty at the University of Washington, called the 'Lesser Seattle syndrome'. Local architect Mark Hinshaw (1999, pp. 26–7) explained what Kelbaugh meant:

> Architecturally, Seattle is a very reticent city. Almost as if people are afraid to make a social blunder that might offend someone. Perhaps... we've been working

so hard at becoming a cosmopolitan/commercial, cultural hub of the Pacific Rim that we've taken ourselves way too seriously. Maybe all that turgid praise in magazines like Newsweek and Fortune has given us a collective complex.

The city was indeed facing what urban historian Thomas Bender might call a 'crisis of representation': its civic identity, and the architectural representation of that identity, stood somewhere between provincialism and cosmopolitanism (Bender, 2000). Resolving this crisis was not a matter of choosing one or the other, but of finding a way to integrate the city's multiple identities. Geographer David Harvey (1998, p. 66) argues that the modern city is a ' "palimpsest" of past forms superimposed upon each other'. And he recognizes that 'shifts in the experience of space and time', like those that Seattle was undergoing, 'generate new struggles in such fields as aesthetics and cultural representation... The way a city imagines itself, represents itself, and materializes itself are not necessarily congruent' (Harvey, 1996, p. 247). These inconsistencies between Seattleites' self-images, their visual and verbal representations of themselves, and the steel, glass, and concrete representation of those identities in their physical city spark 'discursive struggles over representation' (p. 322).

Not to mention that the relative homogeneity of Seattle's demographics in the past round of investment in building civic infrastructure, which might have fostered cultural and aesthetic consensus, no longer held. In the days of Forward Thrust, a regional development programme begun in the late 1960s, minorities accounted for less than 20 per cent of the city's population, but by the 1990s, that percentage had grown to nearly 30 per cent (Kurian, 1994).[2] The city's increasing ethnic diversity can account in part for the existence of multiple publics, whose histories, interests, and perspectives varied.

Perhaps a new Seattle Central Library – the institution that, according to city librarian Deborah Jacobs, represents the 'transparency of democracy' – was Seattle's 'chance to get it visibly [and ideologically] right' (Brewster, 1998). These 'discursive struggles over representation' could be edifying and productive for the city as they are debated and resolved in the public process surrounding the library design project. A case study of this place-making process could prove instructive in uncovering the discursive variables – verbal and visual – that informed the design process, shaped the library building itself, and, most importantly, embodied in built form prevailing institutional and civic ideologies. These discursive struggles – although they may at times seem to be petty word games, visual puns, or semantic debates – are actually integral to public process: they help to set the design agenda, to determine the way people talk about design and envision 'representations of space', and to ultimately shape the function and form of the city's civic realm.

It is my contention, however, that despite the volume and robustness of public discourse in the Seattle Central Library's design review process, the public's commentary and criticism had only a limited effect on the form and character of the design. The public was indeed kept well informed throughout the process, and input, from staff and patrons, was indeed solicited, but this input resulted in only minor interior changes – such as the shifting of programmatic elements and the reorganization of floor layouts – while the core design scheme remained intact. It seemed at times that the library and the design team used public participation merely as a strategy of public management, providing a semblance of involvement and influence, but in reality excluding the public from any of the substantial decisions. The major decisions lay, perhaps rightfully so, with those who were best qualified to make them, with the experts: the architect, the library's governing body, and city librarian Deborah Jacobs.

The nature of the institution

America's public libraries are, by design, democratic and based on the principle of universal access. But how far does this right to access extend? Does it simply mean that citizens cannot be denied entry to the library building? Or does accessibility imply that every citizen has a right to contribute to the institution's ideological development and participate in determining how that institution is designed and built?

John Pastier, former *Los Angeles Times* architecture critic, argues that an urban library's architecture 'should announce that this is the city's prime public building, a place that celebrates knowledge, imagination, and self-improvement' (Pastier, 1999). According to Pastier, it is the city – not an architect or the city elites – that produces great buildings. Making great buildings is a citywide enterprise, which means that everyone is entitled to participate in the design of these civic structures.

In its own literature, the Seattle Public Library (SPL) also emphasized the representative and democratic nature of this institution. This downtown library would be a 'special civic place', the SPL asserted,

> A signature building that [would] be an enduring and instantly recognized Seattle landmark, embodying not only Seattle's civic values, but also conveying a sense of wonder, expectation and discovery. Through the unified success of its physical design and function, the new Central Library [would] both engage and express the richness of Seattle's public, cultural and intellectual life.[3]

This 'richness' implies plurality, inclusiveness, and the engagement and concrete expression of the city's diverse publics, cultures, ideals, and values. These two dense sentences also convey the complexity of the library's programme, its symbolic richness, and its active role in shaping – not only concretizing, or solidifying – Seattle's culture and values. As Pastier argued, if this building is to do all these things, it is the entire city's responsibility to make it work.

Seattle's public was welcomed into the design process even before the city knew where that library would be built. As early as 1998, when the SPL was developing its capital plan outlining the construction and renovation of the downtown and branch libraries, Jacobs met with people in their neighbourhood libraries, church basements, and local restaurants – more than 100 meetings in all – to get their input. Then, on 3 November 1998, a revised $196.4 million bond measure, believed to be among the largest of measures passed for an American urban library, was placed before the citizens of Seattle. Despite a small opposition that claimed that the proposition favoured the downtown library at the branches' expense, the bond passed with a 72 per cent majority.[4] Voters expected, in addition to a new downtown library, a doubling of the total square footage of their branch libraries. They anticipated the arrival of three brand new branches, six replacement branch buildings, and improvements of some sort for every remaining neighbourhood library.

24   Shannon Mattern

Because Jacobs needed to win citizen support for the bond measure, as well as approval of new construction in the design review process, an extensive campaign to rally public support and involvement was critical to the success of the initiative.

Seattleites, for their part, felt an even greater sense of entitlement to contribute to the development of their new library system because they were footing the bill. Public scepticism about paying the high cost of design left Jacobs with the challenge of transforming the elevated cultural ambitions of the city's cognoscenti into a beloved populist initiative. Newspaper critics played a critical role in advancing the notion that support for libraries translated into support for innovative design, arguing that, for their downtown library, Seattleites wanted more than a 'box for people and books', expecting instead 'a design to arouse emotions, shape thoughts and declare a new civic sensibility. We're not interested in the merely functional,' Casey Corr wrote in the *Seattle Times* (1999a), putatively on the public's behalf. 'We want ideas in our buildings.'

Close to a thousand people attended the public meeting at which Steven Holl and Zimmer Gunsul Frasca were eliminated from the semi-finalist round of the architect-selection process, leaving OMA and its local partners, LMN Architects, to design the downtown library. The public again packed Benaroya Hall, the city's new home for the symphony, only six weeks into the schematic design period to see how the library was taking shape. According to Jacobs, 'the Library Board and OMA/LMN had a commitment from the beginning to present early ideas publicly in order to give everyone an opportunity to comment and be involved in the process'.[5] She continues, 'It is more typical for an architect to wait until there is a more completed design before presenting anything to the public. We wanted to do things differently.' This early solicitation of public input bespoke, at least ostensibly, the SPL's commitment to public process through all stages of the design.

But, in late 1999, a small crisis erupted, generating a 'climate of distrust'. A clandestine shift of $15 million in bond money from the neighbourhoods to the downtown library was regarded by many as a 'broken promise' (Corr, 1999b). Jacobs had guaranteed the neighbourhood libraries equal representation and proportionate funding, but, when the Bill and Melinda Gates Foundation donated $20 million – $15 million of which was to fund neighbourhood library projects – library officials offset the Gates's gift by shifting $15 million in bond money from the neighbourhoods to the Central Library.[6] The branches would still receive the $68.2 million promised to them, the library asserted, but they offered an inadequate explanation as to why the Gates's contribution would replace, rather than supplement, the bond money. The Library Board, Mayor Paul Schell, and the City Council – the real decision makers – approved the shift.[7,8] And, instead of seeking public input and responding to public concerns, the library explained the funds transfer as a simple 'bookkeeping change', or a 'housekeeping measure'.[9] Even for those eventually convinced of the shift's legality, the misunderstanding bred suspicion that lingered, particularly among branch librarians and patrons, for years afterward.

By the early part of 2000, however, central librarian Jill Jean was helping to organize the roughly 550 full-time employees of the library into 37 staff work groups, each addressing a different aspect or area of the library, from the loading dock to information services to artwork.

Jacobs made clear to her staff that 'we want you to get your questions answered so you feel comfortable with the process and are able to answer questions from the public'.[10] At the same time, Seattleites were invited to join ten public work groups addressing the needs of various populations served by the library, including, among others, the business, arts, and disabled communities. These concurrent programmes for involving the public and the staff demonstrate that the client and design team recognized that this public library would have to serve multiple publics in multiple ways: it would have to work effectively as both a functional and a representative space, for both its patrons and its librarians.

The public at large reconvened periodically throughout the next two years – often numbering a thousand or more – to view the design in each stage of development. At these presentations and at the open houses that followed, people were free to ask questions and fill out comment cards – or to mail or email comments to the library, to post comments to the SPL's website, and even, as Jacobs joked, to accost her at the grocery store. Every public comment was inventoried by either the library or the project manager and forwarded to the design team. And, in her introduction to OMA/LMN's schematic design presentation, Jacobs informed the audience that changes in the design 'are in direct response to your comments and your thoughts and the thoughts and comments from the Library Board, staff, the design commission, and anybody else' who made his or her opinions known.[11] *Seattle Times* journalist David Brewster commented that 'with other projects there never seems to be time for input, but the library has a genuine rhythm of proposal-counterproposal' (Olson, 2000). But was this 'rhythm' the pulse of a public sphere, in which a genuine process of public participation reshaped the architects' initial ideas, or only the cadence of an information-retrieval system, soliciting and inventorying comments that were rarely seriously considered? At times, it seemed that the designers used public comments to construct nothing more than justifications for their designs; they collected criticism only to refute it, or explain it away, in the next public assembly.

Metaphors

Capitol Program Director Alexandra Harris said of those public presentations, 'certainly Rem [Koolhaas, principal of OMA] brought his own kind of star power to the equation that attracted a lot of people with interest in architecture. I think that created the buzz initially, and then we had to be careful to provide enough information to the press', in part to meet the public demand for information.[12] These ideas of meeting public demand and giving the press and public what they want unavoidably influenced the way the design team and the library talked about the project. Initially, metaphors of commerce crept into their discourse. In its early scope briefing before the Seattle Design Commission, the design team spoke of 'stealing back' the aura that was stolen from the library by the bookstores – and in effect 'stealing back' patrons, too. They planned to 'take cues' from retail design, and even referred to the reception area of the library as 'the retail store' and the interstitial spaces as 'trading floors'.[13]

The Design Commission was greatly troubled by the idea of a Barnes and Noble-inspired public library, and they decided to reorient the initial direction of the design by reassessing the metaphors used to describe it. Commissioner Nora Jaso encouraged the design team to think of the library as 'the last real public place that isn't trying to sell you something'.[14] Harris acknowledged that 'if you look at Rem's body of work', which includes retail outlets for Prada, the Italian clothing designer, and a book on shopping produced through his Harvard project on the city, 'it makes sense that he uses that [commercial] vocabulary'.[15] Still it is indeed important to consider the metaphors adopted and the rhetorical registers tapped throughout the discussion of the design. In the November 1994 issue of *JAE*, Coyne, Snodgrass, and Martin also address the importance of examining metaphors used in the design studio. They suggest that metaphors have the power to 'define problem regimes and to prompt action' in design practice (Coyne et al., 1994, p. 122). In this case, commercial metaphors defined a 'problem regime' that the commission found inappropriate for such a prominent public building.

Yet, only a few years before, in 1998, the SPL's search for a site for the new central library led them to consider sharing space with condominiums and retail outlets across from Pike Place Market (Byrnes, 1998). And two years prior, the city contemplated moving City Hall to Key Tower, a 64-floor skyscraper built as the AT&T Gateway Tower (Cameron, 1998). The commission had been troubled for some time by the growing commercialization of the civic realm and pressed for serious debate on what constituted an appropriate design vocabulary for the city's civic realm.

Even as the commission reviewed the schematic design for the Central Library, the SPL made plans in several neighbourhoods, including Delridge, Greenwood, Ballard, and the International District, for mixed-use development, combining libraries with low-cost housing, other public agencies, and even banks.[16] Branch libraries, it seemed, may not only 'take cues' from retail design, but actually partner with retail designers to create more vital neighbourhoods. Rainer Beach, catering to time-pressed car-dependent patrons, even integrated drive-through drop-offs. It wasn't until spring of 2002 that the Seattle Design Commission expressed its concern that branches were designed for drivers.[17] Increasingly, the rhetoric of city agencies reconceptualized citizens as customers and library patrons as consumers, giving rise to serious concerns about the intrusion of market ideologies and practices into the civic realm.

It is these metaphors – of public service or commerce, of enlightenment or efficiency – that shape the direction of the pre-design deliberation and, consequently, the form of the design itself. They establish the nature of the public relationship between a library and a city's citizens: whether these people are regarded as 'patrons' or 'consumers' makes a big difference, both experientially and ideologically. Should the library be compared to a superstore, a mom-and-pop shop, a bazaar, or an amusement park? Again, each of these metaphors dramatically influences the definition of the design problem, the direction of the schematic design solution, and shared perceptions of the institution's mission. What may seem to be semantic squabbles and over-intellectualized debates over 'concept' are actually necessary and consequential deliberations that set the agenda and tone of further communications – and ultimately influence the programme and character of the built space and the ideals and values embodied in it.

Personas and publicity

But why not have a library for consumers when even the architect is a brand name? Having an architect with star power surely drew a host of aspiring contributors – and, of course, critics – who might not otherwise have cared about building a new library in Seattle. And, from the time Koolhaas began his work in Seattle, his persona and professional reputation expanded exponentially. In April of 2000, he was named that year's recipient of the Pritzker Prize, and, in November, even though the library design

How public is the Seattle Central Library? 27

was still undergoing revision at the end of the design development stage, OMA/LMN's design was recognized with an award from the American Institute of Architects.[18] 'It's not hard to figure out why young architects flock to Rem's speeches like teenage girls to a Britney Spears concert,' wrote James Bush of the Seattle Weekly (Bush, 2000).

For some, however, the architect's and the project's celebrity bred suspicion. In an email message to the library, a Seattleite describes her unresolved impression of the architect:

> Mr Koolhaas is clearly one of the most dazzling luminaries in the architectural heavens... But it is for that same reason that I am concerned... Despite all their intentions to the contrary, their work often fails to capture the 'feel' of simple humanity, beauty, and common sense that makes great architecture liveable... But, hey, why am I worrying? He's a Pritzker Prize winner: how can he go wrong?

Despite its sarcastic tone, the email raises an important issue: the credibility and fame that come with critical acclaim can confer a sense of legitimacy that places the laureates outside the realm of debate and above criticism. The Pritzker, an institutional endorsement of the architect's work, seemed to bestow sovereignty, even invincibility, on its recipient.

According to Sheri Olson (2000), Koolhaas had become a 'phenom here in Seattle... Front-page articles and editorials regularly analyze everything from his Pritzker Prize to his Prada wardrobe'. He became the stuff of myth. A *Seattle Times* editorial from 16 December 1999 insinuated that the library would contain transparent floors, and this single piece of misinformation was propagated in subsequent newspaper articles and by word of mouth for months to come.[19] The *Seattle Times*' Susan Nielsen wrote in her 23 December 1999 column that 'To Koolhaas, glass floors represent the blurred ephemerality of the urban context, or something like that. To me, it means one thing: No skirts or dresses on library day.' Her columns were among the most venomous in all the local press. 'I have this fantasy that Rem Koolhaas will wake up one morning and realize – oops! – he designed for Seattle the ugliest library in the world' (Nielsen, 2000). Other journalists described the design as 'an example of media hype', and 'pure ugliness and stupidity cloaked in a honeycomb of elitist self-importance' (Ochsner, 2000 and Cheek, 2000, p. 23).

These press reports legitimated non-supporters' feelings of alienation, transformed their confusion into anger, and unleashed a flood of angry letters to the editor and emails and letters to the library.

Many citizens were concerned with the library's lack of 'Northwestern-ness' and attributed the design's anti-contextuality to Koolhaas's foreignness: a bit of protectionist thinking that for decades had rationalized the choice of local architects for major civic projects. Several critiqued the design's dismissal of the urbanist's mantra that new designs need to 'fit' into the existing urban fabric and historic context. Seattleite Louise Hirasawa said of Koolhaas's 'disdainful' design, 'it's as if he were thumbing his nose at Seattle'. Another imagined the library as a toned-down version of what Koolhaas really wanted to build: a 'gigantic fist thrusting out from the downtown soil, its 20-story middle digit upraised to the infinite' (Nielsen, 2000). Koolhaas's active rejection of regionalism, Harris suggested, 'has been a struggle for some of our audience because there's a lot of pride in the Northwest'.[20] I discuss these concerns later.

One critic addressed a common public perception that libraries ought to be recognizable as a type, in keeping with the coherent style that was applied to the old Carnegies. He said, 'Not only does it not look like a library; it does not look like a building'. For many, the design simply did not make sense, and they found commiseration for their confusion through the press. Several writers even encouraged Jacobs to read Nielsen's articles to find out 'what people are saying' about the library. The press thus became the voice of the people – many of whom, perhaps disarmed by Koolhaas's persona, seemed to have lost confidence in their own right and ability to critique the design.

On those occasions when negative press incited a deluge of angry correspondence, the library entered crisis management mode. In the first six months of 2000, library officials received several hundred emails, letters, and phone calls – most from infuriated patrons. Each of those messages was documented and passed along to the design team, and each message received a response. 'Clearly we were presenting a library design that was challenging to many people,' Harris said.[21] 'They assumed that the building was a dominant architectural concept at the expense of function.' Harris referred people to newspaper articles and images and documents on the library's website that explained the logical, functional derivation of the design. 'We couldn't convince people to like it,' she said, 'but we could answer their questions and provide them with information'.

Many were so surprised by the library's response that they promised to 'further educate themselves' about the project before making hasty judgements. Some one-time critics reassessed their positions after reading local journalists' rebuttals of initial misinformation and earlier criticism of the design (Stadler, 2000; Ochsner, 2000; Corr, 2000). 'I opened the Seattle Times… to an article by Matthew Stadler about [the library] and concluded that many of my fears might be totally unfounded,' admitted one letter writer. 'Now I'm thinking I may be totally incorrect and it may indeed be quite a nice library'.

Jacobs agreed with Harris that much of the public process is 'like a political campaign where you just explain things to people. My favorite thing to do is to go meet with groups and talk about the library,' she admitted.[22] Jacobs found these public appearances integral to the public process – particularly because 'the press… trust[s] us. They trust library staff… And when we told them that [the library design] works for us, that's really… all they wanted to hear. Because they worried that we're… not standing up to the architect, and letting them take over the design'.[23] Jacobs used the local press as her political ally to reassure the public that the librarians, the good guys, were still in control.

Thus, while the architectural and national presses functioned to develop Koolhaas's 'star power' and to build around him a shield of fame and a cocoon of acclaim, the local press worked on both the public's and the library's behalf, often mediating debates between the two. Functioning as a forum for the 'discursive struggles' of representation, the press shaped the public process, coloured public opinion, and framed the design agenda. The press had the power to both inflame and appease, to make claims on behalf of a public whose opinion hadn't objectively been measured, and then to turn around and shape public opinion.

Furthermore, the comments of Harris and Jacobs suggest that public criticism was regarded as a 'public relations problem', rather than taken as an indication that the architect had not adequately responded to legitimate public concerns about the design.

It could be argued that civic leaders were merely 'using' the participation process to manufacture consent rather than to design a building that incorporates grassroots concerns. Their comments raise questions about the operative definition of 'participation' in the SPL's project: to provide information to the public or to provide critical information to the architect?

Yet the architect's and project's popularity were not only public relations liabilities; Koolhaas's 'avant-garde aura', says Olson (2000), may have drawn in a 'new breed of philanthropists… [who]… embraced the library as a particularly hip cause'. A contingent from the tech community began to attend every public event, and the project attracted millions in funding from computer billionaires like Paul Allen and Bill Gates. These large contributions led the Seattle Public Library Foundation to increase its fundraising goal from $40 million to $75 million, and later to $77.5 million (Le, 2000).[24] According to Elizabeth Castleberry, Deputy Director of the Seattle Public Library Foundation, $32 million of those private funds are to go toward the library's collections, $8.5 million toward programming, and $37 million toward a 'building fund', which is then distributed to the Central Library or to branches at the discretion of the Library Board.[25] Donors may identify which libraries or which segments of the library's collection will benefit from their contributions, said Castleberry, but their authority ends there. Funders receive subscriptions to the foundation's newsletter and invitations to special programmes and events, but no special privileges in dictating how the buildings will take shape.

Jacobs also assured the design commission that these donors sought neither to influence the designs, nor to affix their names in gold letters to library facades (although Paul Allen did stipulate that $5 million of his $20 million gift would go towards the construction of the Faye G. Allen Children's Center, named after the donor's mother (Le, 2000)).[26] And, even if Allen made no attempts to reshape the library design to reflect his personal tastes or interests, his contribution was, as Sue Coliton, manager of the Paul G. Allen Charitable Foundation, put it, a 'show [of] support for innovative architecture'.[27] Funders' contributions provided tacit commendation for the library's project and Koolhaas's design attracted additional funding, and drew public attention – media coverage and public discourse that often associated the goodness of philanthropy with the goodness of libraries, and, by extension, the goodness of this library.

Rhetorical skill

As mixed as was his reception in the press, Koolhaas delivered consistently compelling performances in his public presentations. He was funny and accessible – and, as usual, a master rhetorician. Matthew Stadler, a local writer and a member of the advisory panel that endorsed OMA, noted that the architect 'outlined, step-by-step, the way consultations with library staff, and workers in associated fields, led directly to the allocation, arrangement and design of the building's 355,000 square feet of interior space' (Stadler, 2000). Belinda Luscombe of *Time* magazine commented on Koolhaas's rhetorical ability, which she attributed in part to his exceptional media savvy: 'He knows that the arcane architectural language and connect-the-dots academic ephemera that fill his books only go so far among the media, or their clients – and his – the public. So he has learned to be multilingual: he speaks to architects, to clients and to the press' (Luscombe, 2000). In public open houses, for example, the design

30   Shannon Mattern

team offered models of the building, floor plans, and computer-generated videos of the design – different representational formats to appeal to different viewers with different ways of learning.

Koolhaas's finesse and eloquence proved particularly persuasive when paired with graphics by designer Bruce Mau. 'OMA generates this metaphysical face in something that they call data,' said Stadler.[28] Their graphs and charts and diagrams imply that their research has 'objectively directed them toward some spatial organization'. Timelines, flowcharts, and bar graphs, with their precise spatial organization and their implied linearity and logic, become 'natural[ized] expressions of data', which consequently naturalize their proposed designs.[29] OMA's graphics function as scientific data sets, seemingly derived through objective study and rigorous testing. Who could refute such an elegant solution? According to Stadler, OMA 'anchors their design arguments in the graphical presentation of research data'. In the firm's hands, data visualization became yet another rhetorical device.

Photographs functioned rhetorically, too. Koolhaas began one of his public presentations with an evocative image of the World Trade Organization riots, explaining to his audience that, while Seattle was trying to decide whether or not it wanted to be a real city, the world had already made that decision for it. The visual taunt hit close to home and elicited nervous laughter. In another public forum, he flashed an image of two naked boxers eating oysters – an image drawn from his 1978 book, *Delirious New York*. The image was intended not only as a commentary on the programme and functions of architectural spaces – but also as provocation. One journalist noted that 'it seemed like a moment from… "Saturday Night Live". Was he playing with us?'[30]

Mocking or not, Koolhaas's polished presentation made the design seem unassailable. A local reporter suggested that the refinement and seeming comprehensiveness of Koolhaas's proposal enhanced his persuasiveness. The public expected to see a rough design 'scheme' that would then be revised based on the library staff's and their own comments. Koolhaas offered instead a 'whole vision very early and all at once'.[31] It seemed that the design team had a head start; they presented an ambitious, seemingly complete design and supported it with 'near lawyerly arguments'.

So, too, the complexity of translating an ambitious programme for managing twenty-first-century library services into built form left Koolhaas and OMA the experts because the general public was not sufficiently educated about technical details to enter into debates over the assumptions on which fundamental decisions were based. Thus, the graphical analysis of the problem that Koolhaas presented to the public has the combined qualities of legibility at an abstract level, and indecipherability at a concrete level. In this way, graphics were marshalled to buttress a particular solution rather than to make informed debate possible.

According to Jacobs, the staff initially 'didn't necessarily believe in the mixing chamber', an area in which all reference librarians would be concentrated for 'one-stop reference'. She said, 'I think part of it was the way Rem was talking about it… we had "stock exchanges"… and a "trading floor". I think it was only when we began to understand it in terms of how it would work – then we [still] had some trepidation, but we got it.'[32] The librarians were taught to read blueprints not so that they could scrutinize the design or propose changes; rather, they learned to read blueprints to 'get' Koolhaas's ideas, to fully appreciate the functionality and appropriateness of his proposed design solutions.

Rick Sundberg, chairman of the design commission, commented on Koolhaas's 'methodical way of presenting the design that makes it seem plausible, if not inevitable' (Olson, 2000). The reviewers and the public, then, faced with a presumably complete design, were left to question the worth and possible effect of their feedback. According to Nielsen, the public was 'too timid to do anything but ask small questions', such as 'How much Windex do you need to clean the glass walls? Can you see up a woman's dress through the translucent floors?' (Nielsen, 2000).[33] The designers' rhetorical skill seemed to disarm the public. Nielsen claimed to have a 'warehouse of input from card-carrying library users who want to speak up, but worry the Big Idea has too much momentum to slow down for good advice' (Nielsen, 2000).

Rhetorical aggrandizement

Yet the design team responded to whatever criticism the public was brave enough to voice. In a presentation the following spring, Koolhaas addressed the rumours and misinformation with his usual charm, proclaiming 'it's always a real pleasure to contribute to an urban myth' (Kaiman, 2000). In all of his presentations, Koolhaas assuaged the public's fears – often by directly addressing the concerns they voiced in the press and in their letters to the library, and by making use of rhetorical 'framing' strategies. He began several of his public presentations by issuing a challenge to the city. Seattle has a promising future, he acknowledged, but he 'wasn't convinced that it was already a city'.[34] When Koolhaas showed a picture of the December 1999 World Trade Organization uprising, he cautioned: 'Your previous ideal is coming to an end… You have to face the kind of responsibilities that come with being really urban' – one of which is to 'live with architecture'.[35]

Was Koolhaas suggesting that he, the Pritzker laureate, would give Seattle its first 'really urban' architecture? According to several journalists, Koolhaas, cosmopolitan and worldly, represented everything that Seattle aspired to be. Nielsen wrote, 'This is a city poised at the edge of the millennium, a temporal excuse to forbid the questioning of Progress'.[36] Koolhaas's paternalistic – and, in Jacobs's and Harris's estimation, oftentimes elitist approach essentially belittled opponents as uncultured hicks, which had a stultifying effect on public discourse. Could it be that celebrity, aspirational desires, and the promise of delivery from provinciality and architectural blandness stultified criticism in the context of the public process – even in this process-loving city?

In presenting himself as Seattle's redeemer, Koolhaas also rhetorically aggrandized the weight of the library project, elevating Seattle's architectural naissance to a level of global significance that only an international star could effectively realize. Koolhaas also made frequent mention of the changed social context in which the contemporary library must function. Today's library must deal with commercialization, the 'unpredictable proliferation of new technologies', 'the multiplication of [the library's] social obligations', and the 'erosion of the public realm'.[37] In this 'over stimulated world', a world 'drenched in imagery', the high-minded architecture of the Carnegie era 'doesn't convey the same image' of goodness and morality that it once did. Today, 'an earnest presence like that of the library in its pure and traditional form would simply fail to register'.[38]

This is why OMA's library cannot 'look like a library', at least not like the Carnegie libraries most had grown up with. In establishing this social context, Koolhaas set up an argument for why his library had to be unconventional. In this new world, the library was obligated to 'make a shift' in its 'mental image'.[39] This updated image might prove challenging, or seem alien, to many, but such an imagistic shift was necessitated by new social conditions – conditions beyond most people's recognition or comprehension.

Meanwhile, in Seattle's neighbourhoods, library officials sought landmark status for old, outmoded buildings; they would of course renovate the interior, but the Carnegie exterior was to remain. It seemed that these new global social conditions failed to reach the suburbs; outside of downtown, 'the library in its pure and traditional form' was still an appropriate architectural expression for the modern institution. Indeed, the strategy of pursuing more conservative contextual design in the neighbourhoods itself provided a kind of rationale and springboard for Koolhaas's more urbane downtown design. Finally, in March 2002, the design commission encouraged the library to establish as one of its goals to '"design contemporary libraries", rather than urging design teams to design libraries to appear historic'.[40]

But in his discussion of the Central Library, Koolhaas's repeated attention to contemporary social themes – global politics, commercialization, technologization, privatization – reflected his intention to link his design to a larger framework, a context that extended beyond the immediate time and place to include the 'social, political, economic and technological disruptions wrought by globalization' (Speaks, 2000). Faced with such an overwhelming obligation – to confront the forces of modernization – Seattle may need a redeemer, after all. Koolhaas would serve that role by providing Seattle with the architecture it needs to become not just urban but urbane in the process.

What is 'context', anyway?

But what is 'really urban' architecture? It is easy to see that a 'really urban' design could meet the library's demands for a 'signature building', an 'enduring and instantly recognized Seattle landmark', but could a design that is responsive to the delocalized, highly dynamic forces of modernization also embody 'Seattle's civic values', convey 'a sense of wonder, expectation and discovery', and 'engage and express the richness of Seattle's public, cultural and intellectual life'? Could a library be both 'urban', as Koolhaas defined it, and 'public', in the sense that it reflected the local public's history, values, and sense of place?

What does it mean to reflect a sense of place? Is that sense defined by local history, values, and geography, or is the 'place', the context, now defined by global social, economic, political, and technological forces? When the library selected a Dutch architect, people wondered if a local firm might be better equipped to represent the public's values in the design process and to capture the 'spirit of the city' in the design. Some Seattleites' objection to Koolhaas's appointment raised additional questions regarding the responsibilities of the architect – especially a foreign architect – in addressing issues of context. Was it the architect's duty to reflect the context – perhaps employing Scandinavian aesthetic references or Japanese architectural details, or, as Koolhaas joked, by throwing in some bearskin rugs? Or was it his duty to exploit the context by capturing as much precious daylight as possible, by celebrating Seattle's drizzle, or by providing views of the region's splendid geography? Or was it his duty to enhance the cityscape by introducing something new, visually interesting, and provocative – if out of 'context'?

Koolhaas chose the latter interpretation. He made his case for an innovative, provocative design by arguing that the library must 'make a gesture'; it must somehow distinguish itself from the characterless, 'generic' office buildings immediately surrounding the site (Rahmani, 2000). Stadler supports Koolhaas's interpretation of context, and, in fact, claims to 'find the building's intentions consummately Northwest'.[41] Seattle, he said, is a region that 'destroys its history. All we've had are 200 years of apocalypse. Why not import [new architectural] forms?' Yet, according to Koolhaas, the design 'can't be simply eccentric', nor can it be as 'boring as its context'.[42] The SPL paraphrased Koolhaas's statement: Koolhaas 'has proposed a solution that seeks to create a dynamic and attractive presence in the downtown without mimicking adjacent buildings'.[43] Innovation was appropriate for downtown, but tradition and contextuality were, for a long while, expected from the branch library architects.

There was also the possibility for differences in interpretation of the term *contextuality* or the phrase *sense of place*. The architects repeatedly attempted to explain to the public why the building looked as it did. According to the designers, the form and the surfaces that mark that form – the curtain wall – were both derived rationally. They were defined by internal function and by structural soundness and efficiency. They were derived from context, by their responsiveness to views and daylight. The designers focused their attention on the interior experiencing of views and daylight – that is, what geographic features one sees from inside, and how daylight enters the building. To the architect, 'place' was something appreciated from inside, not enhanced from the outside. To much of the public, however, it seemed that place was something reflected through the building's exterior and interior aesthetics. These differences in orientation – that is, the vantage points from which a building reflects its context – highlighted differences in the architects' and some Seattleites' 'senses of place', which may have explained their opposing interpretations of and reactions to the building's exterior.

Once again, semantic differences launched large-scale disputes over the design's ability to serve and reflect its city's history, geography, and spirit. Furthermore, this long debate over the contextuality of the design also had implications for the library's values, in terms of how this institution would serve as a representative space – and for civic architectural values, in terms of how 'sense of place' can be represented architecturally without resorting to nostalgic gestures.

The output of public input

Some detractors still undoubtedly feel as if they have been cheated of hard-earned tax dollars and still nurse wounds to their civic pride inflicted by a library that seems to disparage the city by declaring nothing 'Northwestern'. Perhaps some resent Koolhaas's paternalism and fear that they've been hoodwinked. Yet Seattleites did have a place in the process of designing this library. Of course, the Library Board had the final say in all design decisions – and the Seattle Design Commission's opinions weighed heavily, as well, because Department of Design, Construction, and Land Use permits were carried out with advice from the commission – but public and staff comments did result in revisions to the design. The staff and public were concerned about the initial location of the children's area in a subterranean space amidst the print shop, recycling area, and parking deck. Subsequent versions of the design showed that the kid's area shared a level of the library with the English as a Second Language (ESL) area and the auditorium, and was placed along the facade to allow for maximum sunlight.

34   *Shannon Mattern*

Members of the ESL public work group were concerned that patrons with language barriers would be reluctant to travel deep into the library to find assistance. So the designers moved the ESL and multilingual collections from the upper levels of the library to locations adjacent to a major entrance to allow for 'direct and easy access to these important departments... for patrons who may find it difficult to navigate a large, public building using signage potentially foreign to them'.[4445]

The book spiral, one of the more innovative features of the building, underwent rigorous testing and numerous revisions as a result of public and library staff criticism. The library's main collection was to be organized into a continuous spiral that looped through four levels of the building. This organization would allow for a 'continuous Dewey run' to facilitate book shelving and browsing and exploit adjacencies between related subject areas that, in any other library, might have been located on separate floors. The Department of Justice had been made aware of the accessibility issues related to the sloped floors, and they were investigating the design's compliance with the American with Disabilities Act standards for accessible design.

Late in the design process, the library invited Seattleites to test two versions of the book spiral and to fill out comment cards indicating their preferences and criticism of either design. According to Alexandra Harris, the library sought comments from 'older users, parents with strollers, the visually impaired and users with mobility issues – as well as Library users without disabilities'.[46] In the end, the library and design team settled on a design that met with the approval of the public and library staff and satisfied the Department of Justice. By means of participatory mock-ups of controversial elements of the design scheme, Jacobs succeeded in diffusing public overreaction to innovation. Thus, public participation was successfully mobilized to support design innovation, unlike the conservative and obstructionist tendencies that tend to arise in the course of public testimony in the design review process.

Yet some patrons and librarians were still concerned that the spiral and the mixing chamber would eliminate special subject areas and their knowledgeable subject librarians. Modified designs of the book spiral incorporated space for subject staff – initially in the spiral's core, and then pushed to the side of each floor at the librarians' request.

Later versions of the book spiral also included work spaces interspersed throughout the stacks to break up the monotonous run of books – an alteration requested by both patrons and librarians.[47] And subsequent renderings included an expanded book spiral. The provision of ample space for books had been a primary public concern, and this change helped to alleviate the public's fears that Koolhaas was phasing out the book.[48] Through a series of design revisions, programmatic elements moved between floors, floor layouts metamorphosed, additional circulation routes appeared, entrances became grander and accessible, public spaces became visible at street level, spatial characters were defined and refined – all in response to public and staff comments.

Yet throughout the two-and-a-half-year deliberation process, the major design scheme remained, for the most part, intact. Like the model presented in late 1999, the library building opening its doors in early 2004 would have five 'quaked' platforms wrapped in an aluminium skin. The preliminary design was presented, rhetorically, as a *fait accompli* – and, essentially, it was. Not much changed between 1999 and 2002. What became of those meticulously logged and categorized public comments? What happened to the public process?

Where is the public in this public library?

The public process, according to Matthew Stadler, was alive and well. Its critics, he said, have based their opinions on misconceptions of both the nature of public process and the nature of OMA's work. 'When people hear "public process", they think "my vote will count"', he said.[49] But OMA's research-based design – according to Stadler, one of the primary reasons the library found the firm so attractive – is not based on vote counting. Anyone who expects from OMA a populist approach to design is bound to be disappointed. Similarly, as *Seattle Weekly*'s James Bush wrote, 'Hiring Koolhaas and getting angry over [his] conceptual model is a bit like hiring McDonald's to cater your party and being annoyed when they serve hamburgers'. When Seattle chose Koolhaas, they also chose his approach to design – one based more on exerting leadership to realize a vision than on pandering to public taste.

Yet the public was led to believe – through Jacobs's frequent grassroots public meetings, through regular solicitation of their comments and criticism, and through repeated promises that changes in the design reflected their desires – that this library would physically manifest their every idea, that every voice would hear itself echoed in this library. And their financial support of the programme, they thought, guaranteed them significant influence in the design process. But, from the very beginning of the process, the library and design team delimited the field of imaginable ideas and framed the discourse surrounding the project. It was these decision makers who chose the metaphors, designed the imagery, framed the debates, set the agendas, and established the basic framework of the design. A public process with an unequal distribution of rhetorical power is bound to have limited effects.

What was true in Seattle is true elsewhere: the communications within and around a public design project serve not only to deliberate over the design itself but also to negotiate just how 'public' a public space will be. Architects must be made aware of the political implications of particular rhetorical strategies. They must learn to critically examine the metaphors they use in talking about design. They must recognize the effect on architecture of mass media and public opinion and the related institutions of celebrity and critical acclaim. They must realize that interpersonal communication and public relations, visual communication and media management are central to their practice – particularly in public design projects. In the public realm, much depends upon the designers' ability to monitor and responsibly manage the communication surrounding and informing their practice. In the public realm, architects are in the business of building not only buildings, but also consensus – and, in the process, values, identities, and ideologies.

Notes

1 This chapter originally appeared, in illustrated form, as Shannon Mattern, Just How Public is the Seattle Public Library? Publicity, Posturing, and Politics in Public Design, *Journal of Architectural Education* (2003, pp. 5–18). Reprinted with permission.
2 United States Census Bureau, American FactFinder, http://factfinder.census.gov.
3 Seattle Public Library, Vision for the Central Library System, in Libraries for All Proposed 1998 Capital Plan for the Seattle Public Library, 13 March 1998.
4 In This Town, We Love Our Libraries, *Seattle Times*, 11 November 1998.
5 Seattle Public Library, 'Concept Book' for New Central Library Now Available on Seattle Public Library Web Site, press release, 27 January 2000.

6 Caution on Library Plan: Go Slowly on Shift of Library Bond Money. *Seattle Times*, 5 November 1999.

7 Seattle Public Library, Seattle Library Board Endorses Legislation to Incorporate Gates' Gift into Libraries for All Budget, press release, 5 November 1999.

8 City of Seattle, Council Bill #113013, Ordinance #119778, 22 November 1999.

9 Deborah L. Jacobs and Gordon McHenry, Jr., Memo to City Council Re: Bond Reallocation Ordinance, 9 November 1999.

10 Seattle Public Library, Staff Update on Workgroups, memo, 18 January 2000.

11 Seattle Public Library, Rem Koolhaas, Seattle Library Architecture Design Presentation, videocassette recording, Seattle, 3 May 2000.

12 Alexandra Harris, personal interview, 24 August 2001.

13 Seattle Design Commission, meeting minutes, 28 October 1999, http://www.spl.org/lfa/central/sdc102899.html.

14 Seattle Design Commission, meeting minutes, 28 October 1999.

15 Harris, interview.

16 Seattle Design Commission, meeting minutes, 21 March 2002.

17 Ibid.

18 Seattle Public Library, Central Library Project Receives AIA Award, press release, 15 November 2000.

19 Seattle's Downtown Library. *Seattle Times*, 16 December 1999.

20 Harris, interview.

21 Ibid.

22 Jacobs, interview.

23 Ibid.

24 Elizabeth Castleberry, personal interview, 16 October 2002.

25 Ibid.

26 Seattle Design Commission, meeting minutes, 4 October 2000.

27 Ibid.

28 Matthew Stadler, personal interview, 17 October 2002.

29 Ibid.

30 Kool with Koolhaas. *Seattle Times*, 28 May 1999.

31 Glowing Lantern of Glass, http://www.glennweiss.com/koolhaas.htm: E1.

32 Jacobs, personal interview.

33 Glowing Lantern of Glass, http://www.glennweiss.com/koolhaas.htm: E1.

34 Seattle Public Library, Koolhaas Central Library Presentation, video-cassette recording, Seattle, 15 December 1999.

35 Seattle Public Library, Rem Koolhaas, Seattle Library Architecture Design Presentation.

36 Ibid.

37 Ibid.

38 Ibid.

39 Ibid.

40 Seattle Design Commission, meeting minutes, 21 March 2002.

41 Stadler, personal interview, 17 October 2002.

42 Seattle Public Library, Koolhaas Central Library Presentation.

43 Seattle Public Library, Q&A on the New Central Library, Seattle Public Library Libraries for All Capital Projects.

44 OMA/LMN, Seattle Public Library Schematic Design, vol. 1, May 2000.

45 Office for Metropolitan Architecture and LMN Architects, 100% Schematic Design: Seattle Public Library, architectural drawings, 1 May 2000.

46 Seattle Public Library, Public Invited to Test 'Book Spiral' Design Element Planned for Seattle's New Central Library, press release, 13 September 2000.

47 Office for Metropolitan Architecture and LMN Architects, 100% Schematic Design: Plan Level 8.

48 OMA/LMN, Seattle Public Library: 100% Design Development, architectural drawings, 6 March 2001, Drawings #A205, A206, A207, A208.

49 Stadler, interview.

References

Bender, Thomas. 2000. The New Metropolitanism and a Pluralized Public, paper presented at the International Center for Advanced Studies Project on Cities and Urban Knowledges Lecture Series, New York University, New York, October 6.

Brewster, David. 1998. Seattle Should Dare to Build a Great New Public Library. *Seattle Times*, 6 March.

Bush, James. 2000. Our Lopsided Library: Rem's Ruse? *Seattle Weekly*, 3–9 February.

Bush, James. 2000. The Art of Being Rem. *Seattle Weekly*, 20–6 July.

Byrnes, Susan. 1998. Library-Complex Idea Catching On. *Seattle Times*, 16 January.

Cameron, Mindy. 1998. Making a Good Deal Better May Be Key to Civic Spaces. *Seattle Times*, 29 March.

Cheek, Lawrence. 2000. Seattle Gives Koolhaas the Cold Shoulder. *Architecture* 89/2 (February).

Corr, Casey. 1999a. The Hiring of Rem Koolhaas and the Shock of the Shoes. *Seattle Times*, 16 June.

Corr, Casey. 1999b. Trying to Build a Library in a Climate of Distrust. *Seattle Times*, 17 November.

Corr, Casey. 2000. Looking for Rem. *Seattle Times*, 9 April.

Coyne, Richard, Adrian Snodgrass, and David Martin. 1994. Metaphors in the Design Studio. *JAE* 48/2.

Harvey, David. 1996. *Justice, Nature and the Geography of Difference*. Malden, MA: Blackwell.

Harvey, David. 1998. *The Condition of Postmodernity: An Enquiry into the Origins of Cultural Change*. Cambridge, MA: Blackwell.

Hinshaw, Mark. 1999. *Citistate Seattle*. Chicago, IL: *Planners Press*.

Kaiman, Beth. 2000. Koolhaas Fans Check Out Refined Plans for Library. *Seattle Times*, 4 May.

Kurian, George Thomas. 1994. *World Encyclopedia of Cities*, vol. 2. Santa Barbara, CA: ABC-CLIO.

Le, Phuong. 2000. Allens Give $20 Million to Seattle Libraries. *Seattle Post-Intelligencer*, 30 August.

Luscombe, Belinda. 2000. The Rem Movement: Architecture Is Changing: Its Biggest Prize, the Pritzker, Goes to a Thinker Rather than a Pure Designer. *Time Europe* 155/16, 24 April: 64.

Nielsen, Susan. 1999. Shhh, My Little Parakeets. *Seattle Times*, 23 December.

Nielsen, Susan. 2000. Library Lovers Speak Out: Rem, We Just Want to Help. *Seattle Times*, 23 January: B4.

Ochsner, Jeffrey. 2000. Fusing Form and Function: Give-and-Take on Central Library Should Segue into Civic Conversation about Remaking Downtown's Public Persona. *Seattle Post-Intelligencer*, 6 February: F1.

Olson, Sheri. 2000 How Seattle Learned to Stop Worrying and Love Rem Koolhaas' Plans for a New Central Library. *Architectural Record* 188 (August): 125.

Pastier, John. 1999. Advisory Panel to Showcase Architectural Design Finalists for $156 Million Downtown Library Project. *Seattle Times*, 9 May.

Rahmani, Ayad. 2000. Library as Carnival. *Arcade* 19 (Winter): 25.

Speaks, Michael. 2000. Rem Koolhaas and OMA Lead the Dutch onto New Turf. *Architectural Record* 188/7 (July): 92.

Stadler, Matthew. 2000. Koolhaas, Library Design Deserves Kudos. *Seattle Times*, 8 February.

3 OMA's conception of the users of Seattle Central Library

Ruth Conroy Dalton

Introduction

The impetus behind the research presented in this chapter was an initial observation that the Seattle Central Library is a building of paradoxes. It appears to occupy a Schrödinger's cat-like state of architectural superimposition: just as Schrödinger's cat may be held to be simultaneously both alive and dead, the Seattle Central Library occupies a state betwixt and between architecturally iconic and revered and, at the same time, deeply flawed and problematic. Clearly, as an architectural scholar and researcher encountering such a phenomenon, it is necessary to ask two questions. First, how can a building be both outstanding and defective? And second, and perhaps most importantly, is it possible to find the causes of this incongruity?

First let us first briefly examine the evidence for the 'how' question: how can a building be both outstanding and defective? What evidence can be found to support this statement?

Let us unpick this a little and first begin by presenting evidence that the library is a great building. Aside from the usual crop of architectural awards that the library received upon its opening in May 2004 (of greatest significance: Time Magazine's Building of the Year in 2004 and the American Institute of Architects Honor Award for Architecture in 2005), this is a building that has been positively reviewed and written about, for example, Herbet Muschamp from the New York Times wrote,

> At a dark hour, Seattle's new Central Library is a blazing chandelier to swing your dreams upon. If an American city can erect a civic project as brave as this one, the sun hasn't set on the West. In more than 30 years of writing about architecture, this is the most exciting building it has been my honor to review. I could go on piling up superlatives like cars in a multiple collision, but take my word: there's going to be a whole lot of rubbernecking going on.
>
> (Muschamp, 2004)

A locally based commentator, William Dietrich of the Seattle Times, remarked, 'Seattle's new downtown library is so striking, so revolutionary, so odd and so lovely that one struggles to find a metaphor to explain it' (Dietrich, 2004). The Chief Librarian, Jacobs, in a half-hour documentary made by the Seattle Channel to mark the opening of the library, enthuses, 'This building was absolutely, perfectly designed for this site! Everything from where the loading-dock, to where the parking is, to where the entries are, it makes use of the site... it is perfectly designed' (*A Library for All*, 2004). And what of the experience of being inside and using the library? What are the internal spaces like? Equal praise has been given to the experience of being

OMA's conception of the users of the Library   39

inside and using the building, 'Spaces are now designed especially for different modes of reading, from cozy corners with comfortable reading chairs to monumental reading rooms that elevate the act of reading by situating readers at long rows of tables within a community of intellectual engagement' (Van Slyck, quoted in Mattern, 2007) and from Mattern, '[The] reading spaces are… given the most majestic spaces. Within the [reading] room are differing conditions, from the intimate and informal to the rigorous and organized' (Mattern, 2007, p. 110). The primary impression given by the reviews above is that the architects have succeeded in creating a variety of spatial experiences intended to satisfy a diverse set of patrons. In an interview with a local architect, who worked on the building as part of the Seattle-based (LMN) team, he describes this phenomenon in more detail,

> The building affords hundreds of places that you can go find your own space, read, study or work… no one else may ever find that place in the building; so, because of its uniqueness, you can find these intimate places within the building that you can make your own.
>
> (Brown, 2011)

An anonymous volunteer suggested that people enjoy the building because its uniqueness and manifold idiosyncrasies stimulate their curiosity and hence they want to explore the building further. Returning once more, for a final statement, to Dietrich of the Seattle Times, the following striking observation is made, 'Perhaps no other Seattle building has involved so many really bright people, thinking really hard, about what architecture is supposed to accomplish' (Dietrich, quoted in Mattern 2007, p. viii). Here is clear evidence, from a wide range of commentators, from journalists and critics, to academic scholars and library employees, that this is, indeed, an exhilarating, remarkable, and innovative building.

The question raised initially concerned how the library can be both outstanding yet defective. Given that such an assertion is being made in this chapter, what evidence is there, conversely, that this is a building that is flawed in some fundamental manner? When beginning to study this building we heard, anecdotally, that this was a building that people experienced as both disorienting and confusing and furthermore that it was a building in which they frequently lost their way. The Chief Librarian, despite finding the building 'perfectly designed' (see above) also expands upon this particular aspect of the building's performance, 'The wayfinding isn't working. By the second or third day, we had to put up signs to help people' (Jacobs, 2004). This admission is sadly echoed by the signage designer, the renowned Bruce Mau, responsible for the large-scale, oversized graphics that were such a striking and integral aspect of the library's original design, when he says,

> It is not without heart-breaking irony that we acknowledge a near-total lack of legibility… While librarians themselves should be commended for their improvisational tactics, overall the patrons confront a constant meddle [the temporary signs], with one organizational layer of information Scotch-taped over another.
>
> (Mau, 2005, p. 242)

See Figure 3.1 for examples of the temporary, paper signs that were put up by the librarians in order to help the users.

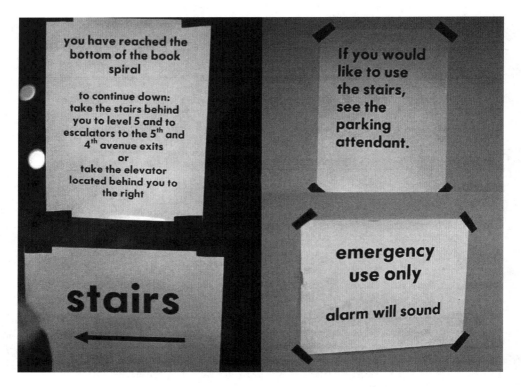

Figure 3.1 Temporary signs in the library. Photographs courtesy of Matt Haughey, 2004.

Another library employee also comments on the patron's confusion,

> It takes the average user a few times of visiting before they know how to use it... Part of their initial confusion might derive from the fact that the spiral is actually a misnomer; it is really a squared-off series of ramps. Once people understand that and know how to find the cut-through spots that [connect] them from one side of the spiral to the other, and to the stairs, escalators, and elevators, they are able to take full advantage of the spiral's easy navigability – and to appreciate its wonderful Borgesian qualities.
>
> (Jill Jean, Director of the Central Library, quoted in Mattern, 2007 p. 80; see also Figure 3.2)

It is particularly noteworthy, or at least somewhat amusing, that Jean compares the library's ease of navigation with Borges's Library, the prototypic (and surely dystopian rather than utopian) 'library-as-maze'. Dovey, in Chapter 4 of this book, describes it as 'one of the most disorienting buildings one can imagine' and points to the proliferation of navigational aids produced by the management as evidence of this statement. Zook and Bafna describe it as having a 'disconcertingly complex circulation system' in Chapter 6. Another anonymous volunteer suggested that two of the most confusing circulation elements are the book spiral (since a number of

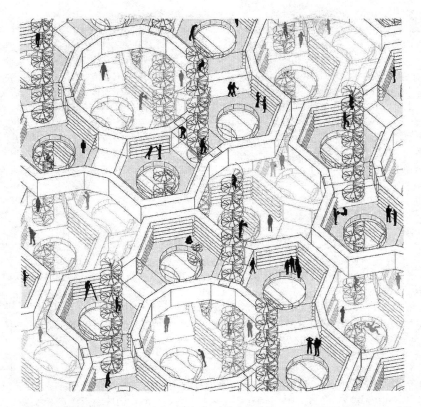

Figure 3.2 A dystopian vision of the labyrinthine qualities of Borges's Library, an analogy made by Jill Jean, Director of the Central Library. Drawings courtesy of Rice+Lipka Architects, 2013.

floors merge into a single continuum without obvious access/exit points) and the elevators that shoot past floors without stopping at the intermediate ones. Since these are both aspects of the building's circulation that are contrary to our usual experience of buildings, it is not hard to understand why they might contribute to the building's reputation for being confusing and disorientating. Finally, we present a quote from OMA's project architect, who acknowledges,

> The wayfinding wasn't done perfectly, to put it kindly… When you understand the building, it is very simple – just a series of boxes. But what we didn't understand is, to the uninitiated person, someone not an architect or library staffer, it can be complex if they don't understand that. What we thought is blatantly obvious, isn't.
>
> (Prince-Ramus, quoted in Marshall, 2008)

Having presented abundant evidence for both points of view ('great building' versus 'flawed building'), we have hopefully managed to demonstrate the fact that there are strong supporters for both views (and sometimes even the self-same person expressing both views at different times), namely that it *is* 'great architecture' whilst simultaneously being 'deeply flawed'. This is, in our opinion, the fascinating contradiction inherent in this building. If we go back to our question (how can a building be both outstanding and defective?) we can perhaps answer that it depends upon which aspect of the building is being judged: at a functional level this building is unequivocally problematic whilst still providing some quite memorable and exhilarating architectural moments. This leads us to the second question posed at the beginning of the chapter: whether it is possible to determine or uncover the causes of this incongruity. In particular, this chapter will now focus on whether an examination of OMA's design process can reveal the cause, or causes, of this contradiction. We will explore whether the clues to this puzzle lie, not in the building as an artefact or object, but in the evidence that we can gather about the architect's design process. We do not intend to search blindly such evidence; rather, we will establish a hypothesis that we wish to test and search for evidence that supports or refutes this hypothesis. Our hypothesis is, quite simply, that the reason that the Seattle Central Library is both 'great' and 'flawed' is that it arises from a failure by OMA to fully take into consideration their users' wants and needs – essentially a failure to 'put themselves into the shoes of their users' during the design process. Since the library's design process has been unusually well documented by others (i.e. Yaneva, 2009; Mattern, 2007; see also their chapters, Chapters 1 and 2, respectively, in this book), in the next section we will principally be examining secondary data sources for evidence about OMA's attention to the needs of the library's users and, where possible, we will augment these secondary sources with primary interview data.

However, before we present the results of our search for evidence in the available documentation on the design process, we want to first devote some time to presenting and discussing the concept of 'perspective taking' since this is essential to our hypothesis. The concept of perspective taking (or being able to take another person's perspective) has been around since the 1930s and was, for example, discussed by Piaget (1965 [1932]) in the context of his work on childhood developmental stages (Piaget talks about the development of 'reciprocity' and 'the desire to treat others as he himself would wish to be treated' (1965 [1932], p. 194) Such reciprocity requires a child to be able put him or herself into the place of an 'other'. This social ability is extremely useful for many tasks and situations since 'Well-developed perspective-taking abilities allow us to overcome our usual egocentrism' (Davis et al., 1996, p. 713) and, furthermore, 'Perspective-taking allows an individual to anticipate the behavior and reactions of others' (Davis, 1983, p. 115). Clearly when architects design buildings, one of the activities that they ideally need to do is to put themselves into the shoes of the person, or people, for whom they are designing and thus imagine inhabiting the building, from their perspective. And although this is rarely discussed in the context of architectural design or architectural education, this is an example of perspective taking as defined in the psychology literature. Perspective taking is also strongly aligned to the more general ability to show empathy for others (and hence, in a design context, is plainly also associated with empathic design (Rayport and Leonard-Barton, 1997), sometimes mislabelled as empathetic design). Plank and Zisch also refer to *empathy* as being essential to both the understanding and designing of architecture in the final chapter in this book.

Tenbrink et al. (2014) have discussed the fact that architects actually perform two different types of perspective taking, the first is in the psychological sense, that of

OMA's conception of the users of the Library   43

putting themselves into the shoes of their users, and the second is in a far more literal sense, by which we mean being able to look at a two-dimensional drawing or sketch of a building and immediately imagine themselves moving through and experiencing the corresponding three-dimensional space (in perspectival vision). This is directly comparable to the way in which some musicians are able to sight read sheet music and imagine the music playing in their heads, known as 'inner hearing skills'. Given the analogy to music, this ability of some architects could, perhaps, be termed 'inner spatial-experiencing skills'.

This ability, that we are proposing in this chapter be termed 'inner spatial-experiencing skills', relates to another theory proposed by the Japanese cognitive scientist, Yutaka Sayeki. Sayeki describes the following scenario:

> Let us propose that we see, understand, and reason by dispatching imaginary selves, called kobitos (which means 'imaginary little people' in Japanese), into things: Kobitos are offshoots of the Self, extensions of the body of the Self, thrown into another person or another thing. A single person dispatches (or throws into) a number of kobitos to form a 'society' of kobitos, each of which assumes a different role.
>
> (Sayeki, 1989, based on an earlier work, Sayeki, 1978)

Sayeki describes three ways in which we might throw ourselves (via our kobitos) into an object. The first is the 'Throwing-in' or imagining yourself inside, or as an imaginary object, the second is 'Acting-out' or simulating behaviours of, or in, that object, 'You may explore or move around, either within the existing world in the environment (strictly following the constraints in the reality) or in a possible world generated by modifying some of the existing constraints' (Sayeki, 1989) and the final stage is 'Feeling-about' or exploring the imagined object or space via your projected senses, 'You may see, touch, and feel, with your transformed body, the environmental constraints that are significant and relevant to the current activity, and the object you have been thrown into' (Sayeki, 1989). It is clear that what we are terming an architect's 'inner spatial-experiencing skills' could easily be seen as an example of Sayeki's anthropomorphic exploration and understanding of the world, and would encompass all these stages, the 'Throwing-in', the 'Acting-out', as well as the 'Feeling-about' (see Figure 3.3).

Tenbrink et al. (2014) suggest that highly skilled and experienced architects are able to employ both excellent 'perspective taking' as well as outstanding 'inner spatial-experiencing skills', but that the hardest task of all is to simultaneously combine the two mental activities: to imagine yourself, *as someone else*, inhabiting an imaginary space. The reason why this is difficult for an expert architect is that it requires, to an extent, being able to offload or disregard their expert knowledge in order to imagine experiencing a building as a layperson. Also, since an architect who designs a building has an almost 'godlike' (at least omniscient if not omnipotent) knowledge of the project, how do they try to 'get in the shoes' of a naive user, visiting a building for the first time, without such complete knowledge of it or even simply knowing what is around the next corner? So do the failures of the Seattle Central Library stem from a failure of either perspective taking (the architects putting themselves into the shoes of their users) or, indeed, of this trickier, combined activity of putting themselves into the shoes of the library users, whilst simultaneously imagining inhabiting the as yet

Figure 3.3 An example of a Sayeki-like anthropomorphic exploration of the world, 'Paradise' by the artist Slinkachu from his recent Miniaturesque show. Photograph courtesy of Slinkachu and Andipa Gallery, 2014.

unrealized library? Perhaps we could call this empathic or reciprocal 'inner spatial-experiencing skills' or even 'third person-' as opposed to 'first person-inner spatial-experiencing skills'.

In the next section, we examine three pieces of evidence which demonstrate the ways in which the architects attempted to consider the user's perspective. Via available secondary data, we were keen to try and determine whether, and how, the architects conceptualized their user. In Mattern's chapter on the Seattle Central Library in her book on *The New Downtown Library* (2007) she describes one way in which OMA refer to two primary types of library user that they are imagining will come to the library. 'They made a distinction between the groups that they nicknamed the "knowledge acquirers" or those seeking a holistic understanding… a deeper and wider body of knowledge and the "information gatherers", those prioritising an ease of access, efficiency and speed' (Kubo, 2005). Furthermore, they imagine the different behaviours that these different groups might engage in, the different parts of the library that they would visit and the different ways in which they might move around the building.

Information gatherers will take the elevator directly to their pre-selected materials, while knowledge acquirers will wander through the book spiral, hoping to serendipitously discover resources within a general subject area. Browsers can simply climb the ramp... and elevator stops throughout the spiral are labelled with the Dewey Decimal numbers.

(Mattern, 2007, p. 119)

The information gatherer is a user with limited time and a pre-determined goal of finding the exact book that they are seeking. This is in direct contrast to the knowledge acquirer who is imagined as spending far more time browsing through the library collection and exploring more of the spaces, and book collection, in their quest to seek knowledge. In an interview we conducted with one of the Seattle-based architects, a third category of user is suggested,

> The third one I would add... is people coming to hang out and read without feeling like they have to buy a book or buy a coffee. If you go to a book store you feel you should purchase something if you're there. There was a huge discussion about [the] quality of space for that.

(Brown, 2011)

We might call this third group the 'hang-outers'. Although these three groups (the information gatherers, knowledge acquirers, and hang-outers) represent a somewhat romanticized notion of the user (and it is not clear whether these descriptions are based upon any user-profile data provided by the Seattle Public Library system or the Library Board) it is clear that the architects thought hard about the fact that the library patrons were not simply a homogenous set of users. Furthermore they recognized that by beginning to classify users into different groups, they were able to begin to think about how certain groups might use the building in different ways. It could be argued that this is the first step necessary for architectural 'perspective taking'.

This process can be seen to have been taken to the next level in a set of diagrams produced by OMA, which they term 'Reference Strategy Scenarios' (Connection, 2004). Each diagram represents a different type of patron of the library, indicated by a black question mark (?) and their questions or queries are expressed as speech bubbles. Each archetypal user has a need that can only be met by successfully navigating through the library and a dotted red line indicates their resultant trajectory or path. In one of these reference strategy scenarios, for example, the user (or black question mark) is characterized as a research student in conversation with a roving librarian. They provide the following scenario, 'My professor claims that OMA is a postmodern practice, and I'd like to prove her wrong.' Further up the library (and further into their search) they encounter a second librarian, of whom they ask, 'Maybe I should refer to Mies van der Rohe... do you have any publication of his works?' This is an example of the type of user that OMA characterizes as a 'knowledge acquirer' (see above). The alternative user type, the 'information gatherer', is exemplified in a different diagram/ scenario, with the accompanying speech bubble query, 'Which way to the latest Tom Wolfe Book?' Other reference strategy scenarios show yet another user wanting to buy tickets to a concert in the auditorium and another, asking in Spanish, '¿Dónde están los libros de inglés como segundo idioma?' (Where are the English as a Second Language books?)

What is particularly interesting about this set of reference strategy scenarios is that they share some strong characteristics with a tool used by software designers to understand,

and design for, their users, namely *personas* (Cooper, 1999; Cooper and Reimann, 2003). A persona, as Cooper writes, is a characterization of a user or groups/types of user that exhibits the most prominent attributes of the whole group: in other words, it is an archetype presented in the guise of a fictional character (Cooper, 1999). There can be as many descriptions of archetypal users, or personas, as it makes sense (to the designer) to differentiate, but in general they should remain concrete and distinct from each other. The most powerful personas are frequently based on focus groups and user interviews and, as such, they can also protect the researcher from forming false assumptions.

Through first-hand accounts of OMA's design practices (Yaneva, 2009), we are relatively confident that OMA architects were not consciously employing personas in order to create these reference strategy scenarios (insomuch as these diagrams were not explicitly described as personas). Rather, we suspect, it was the architects' own intuitive response to how to 'get inside the head' of what otherwise would have been an amorphous and intractable multiple-user group. So, although these are not fully developed personas in the way that is typically used in software and product design, we would argue in this chapter that this does represent an innovation in terms of architectural practice and clearly was an attempt by the architect to try to consider the different perspectives (and wants and needs) of very different user types.

The final, main piece of evidence, that we would like to highlight, with respect to how OMA thought about their users, concerns their use of full-scale mock-ups of part of the library. It was clear from our interviews with the local architect that the use of models was particularly key to the design and development of this building.

> [We built] hundreds and hundreds of models... We built a significant number of mock-ups to ensure what we were doing was actually going to work... We built a mock-up of [the ramp system], had people walk around on it, had the disabled community try it, and give us feedback.
>
> (Brown, 2011)

It is interesting that the use of models or 1:1 mock-ups would also be key to how they directly engaged with their users. In Yaneva's book describing her first-hand, ethnographic experience of spending time in OMA's office, she also reports on a number of interviews that she conducted with OMA staff in 2002. In these interviews, the architects describe the use of these full size mock-ups.

> We also [built a mock-up of] the book ramp. We basically did one bay of it and we went from ground level, maybe 6 feet high, just to check two different ways of rafting. And even the public was invited to examine it, including disabled people who could test whether they could actually use the wheelchairs.
>
> (Yaneva, 2009, citing from interviews in 2002)

A description of the mock-ups and subsequent public participation in testing them is also described briefly in Mattern's chapter in this book. The fact that OMA invited members of the public, particularly those representing groups with mobility challenges such as older users, parents with pushchairs, and wheelchair users, to come and test a mock-up of the book spiral ramp cannot be underestimated: this is not typical architectural practice and is certainly not indicative of a practice that is neglecting or disregarding the needs of its end users.

Results of evidence

If we consider the evidence presented above, it is clear that there is a strong case to be made that OMA *did* think deeply about the library's user, the different types of users that might use the library and, to some extent, even about how different groups might find their way around the building. As Dietrich of the *Seattle Times* stated, and as we already quoted at the beginning of this chapter, 'Perhaps no other Seattle building has involved so many really bright people, thinking really hard, about what architecture is supposed to accomplish'. And this also seems, to some extent, true of the architects with respect to their consideration of the library's users. The evidence can be summed as follows:

1. They thought deeply about the different types of user: making a distinction between '*knowledge acquirers*' (seeking a holistic understanding... a deeper and wider body of knowledge), '*information gatherers*' (needing ease of access, efficiency, and speed), and even the '*hang-outers*' (simply relaxing in the spaces).
2. The use of personas or different strategy scenarios, which is quite unusual, and arguably innovative, in architectural practice.
3. The construction of a public mock-up of a section of book spiral and subsequent test/s with different people including wheelchair users.

The original hypothesis at the beginning of this chapter was that the problems or issues inherent in the building can be attributed to a failure in perspective taking and that OMA simply failed to get inside the heads, or step into the shoes, of their users. The first conclusion that can be drawn from the above exercise is that there is insufficient evidence to suggest that the architects failed in their perspective takings (or at least in their attempts to do so) and, indeed, it can be considered that they went over and beyond what most architects currently do (or would expect to do). Most large firms of architects do not make full-size mock-ups and engage in public participation events, they do not research, write about, and give labels to different user groups, and they do not use personas (either implicitly or explicitly). We clearly need to reject or revise our hypothesis.

If we therefore revise, rather than fully reject, our hypothesis (which was that OMA failed to put themselves into the shoes of their users) we might do so by making a further differentiation between some of the different ways in which an architect can do this. This becomes possible if we borrow a distinction from human–computer interaction: namely between 'building usability' and 'building user experience'. In a recent text by Krukar, Dalton, and Hölscher, the following definitions are proposed: 'A building is usable when it allows the user to execute his/her tasks effectively, efficiently and with satisfaction in the specified context of use' (Krukar et al., 2016), whilst, in contrast, many users will wish to go beyond mere 'usability' and will wish to 'seek, positive and memorable experiences while interacting with [a building]' (Krukar et al., 2016), i.e. will want, and even actively seek, a satisfying (building user) experience. (Interestingly, in Chapter 8, Kuliga also discusses the concept of building-user experience, so for an environmental psychologist's view on experiencing architecture please also refer to this chapter.) If we relate these two ideas back to the theories of perspective taking and empathy presented at the beginning of the chapter, it should be clear that both concepts require forms of architectural perspective taking, i.e. the ability of

48   *Ruth Conroy Dalton*

the architect to put themselves into the shoes of their user. Our revised hypothesis can therefore be refined: OMA's attempts to put themselves into the shoes of their users disproportionately focused more on the 'user experience' aspect of perspective taking and less on the, arguably more fundamental, 'usability' aspect. This has resulted in a building that certainly provides a variety of stimulating experiences whilst, at the same time, containing seemingly paradoxical flaws in basic functionality.

So, if, as we suggest, the architects were more preoccupied with 'user experience', what kind of 'user experience' were the architects attempting to create? Again we can return to primary and secondary evidence from the design process itself to examine this. One of the most revealing sources for this is the interview that we conducted with the local, Seattle-based architect. The first clue occurs when he touches upon some of the quirks inherent in the vertical circulation of the building,

> There was an interest in... having people experience... more of the building by not having [the circulation work in] such a simple way. There... is a path which people can take to experience the building in a way that was new to them or different from how they experience other buildings.
>
> (Brown, 2011)

This comment is important as the architect is essentially stating that parts of the circulation system were conceived of as being less about moving around the building for functional reasons (the 'building usability' aspect) but rather intended to create a sequence of highly choreographed, spatial experiences. This is clearly an unusual stance to take with respect to what is normally a very functional aspect of a building's performance (namely how to get around). As Mattern suggests in Chapter 2, 'The designers [rather] focused their attention on the interior experiencing of views and daylight', or as Zook and Bafna propose more controversially in Chapter 6, the circulation in the building is primarily used 'to create unexpected and ironical juxtapositions'.

There is certainly evidence that the architects were attempting to create a variety of different spatial experiences from the spectacular reading room '[the] space at the top of the building that's beautifully lighted [with] natural light' through to the, potentially rather disturbing, mezzanine level meeting rooms, '[Koolhaas] got intrigued with this idea of [the meeting room level] being an organ or internal body part, that it was completely rounded and red and all of those things' (Brown, 2011). We would suggest that the desire to create a dazzling panoply of visually stimulating spatial experiences, as expressed above, was met.

Another portion of the interview with the local architect, which was particularly revealing, concerned the orientation of the main bank of lifts (were they originally intended to face Fourth Avenue, as they currently do, or to face Fifth Avenue?) In Chapter 11, by Plank and Zisch, they suggest 'The concept of engendering moments of surprise through unpredictability is used frequently by Rem Koolhaas'. The local architect has this to say on the matter,

> There was a lot of debate [about the lift orientation] for the design team... I think, for an organisational and visual orientation, it probably would have been the better side. I think that's almost why it wasn't done. In Rem's mind, [it] was that because it seemed so logical and it seemed so like what anybody would do, we

OMA's conception of the users of the Library 49

should probably put it on the other side... There are certain parts of his design process that are looking for ways to not just do the things that seem obvious, so it ended up on the back side.

Notice here the phrase, 'looking for ways to not just do the... obvious'; there is clearly an idea that part of what this building was about was overturning expectations, not only about libraries but even about our previous experience of how a building works: to surprise, astonish, to be cutting edge, and perhaps even controversial. This is clearly an outcome of the user experience that they wanted to create.

And so it can be summarized that the intended user experience was about achieving three things: overturning expectations, creating a variety of spatial experiences, and, finally, having movement through the building serving to choreograph these different views or experiences. Furthermore, it can be suggested that this focus on building-user experience was frequently at the expense of basic building usability. If we return to the two initial questions raised at the beginning of this chapter, we are now in a position to suggest answers. The first question asked how a building could be simultaneously outstanding yet defective. The answer to this is the architects achieved their goal of creating a number of outstanding spatial experiences but that the problems inherent in the building are to be found in the more operational aspects of the building. The second question, which sought to find the cause of this mismatch, can equally be answered by saying that OMA's desire for 'usability' (as demonstrated through their efforts to consider the user perspective, for example, through making a mock-up of part of the book spiral) often came into conflict with the desire to overturn expectations (to be contrary) and in some cases the desire to be 'edgy' won out. Furthermore, although efforts were made to 'get into the shoes of the user', this attempt at perspective taking focused on 'user experience' rather than basic 'usability'. To conclude, this is precisely how you can design a building that is 'dysfunctionally award-winning'.

References

A Library for All: Seattle's Central Library (2004). USA: Seattle Channel, http://www.seattlechannel.org/misc-video?videoid=x30961.

Cooper, A. (1999). *The Inmates Are Running the Asylum*. Indianapolis, IN: SAMS.

Cooper, A. and Reimann, R. M. (2003). *About Face 2.0: The Essentials of Interaction Design*. New York: Wiley.

Davis, M. H. (1983). Measuring Individual Differences in Empathy: Evidence for a Multidimensional Approach. *Journal of Personality and Social Psychology* 44(1): 113.

Davis, M. H., Conklin, L., Smith, A., and Luce, C. (1996). Effect of Perspective Taking on the Cognitive Representation of Persons: A Merging of Self and Other. *Journal of Personality and Social Psychology* 70(4): 713.

Dietrich, W. (2004). Meet Your New Central Library: It's Both a Testament to and a Test of Civic Chutzpah. *Seattle Times*, 23 April, http://community.seattletimes.nwsource.com/archive/?date=20040423&slug=pacific-plibrary25.

Ferré, A. (2004). *Connection: The Changing Status of the City, of Architecture of Urbanism*. Barcelona: ACTAR.

Jacobs, D. (2004). Quoted in Pogrebin, R., Inside the Year's Best-Reviewed Buildings. *New York Times*, 26 December, http://www.nytimes.com/2004/12/26/arts/design/26pogr.html?_r=0, accessed February 2012.

50 *Ruth Conroy Dalton*

Krukar, J., Dalton, R., and Hölscher, C. (2016). Human-Environment-Interaction: Taking HCI to Architectural Design. In: Dalton, N., Schnädelbach, H., Wiberg, M., and Varoudis, T. (Eds), *Architecture and Interaction: Human Computer Interaction in Space and Place* (pp. 17–35). New York: Springer.

Kubo, M. (2005). *Office of Metropolitan Architecture: Seattle Public Library*. Barcelona: Actar.

Marshall, J. (2008). A moment with... Joshua Prince-Ramus/Architect. Seattlepi website, http://www.seattlepi.com/ae/article/A-moment-with-Joshua-Prince-Ramus-Architect-1284976.php, accessed February 2013.

Mattern, S. C. (2007). *The New Downtown Library: Designing with Communities*. Minneapolis: University of Minnesota Press.

Mau, B. (2005). *Lifestyle*. London: Phaidon Press.

Muschamp, H. (2004). Architecture: The Library that Puts on Fishnets and Hits the Disco. *New York Times*, 16 May, http://www.nytimes.com/2004/05/16/arts/architecture-the-library-that-puts-on-fishnets-and-hits-the-disco.html.

Piaget, J. (1965 [1932]). *The Moral Judgment of the Child*. New York: Free Press.

Rayport, J. F. and Leonard-Barton, D. (1997). Spark Innovation through Empathic Design. *Harvard Business Review* 1 November: 107–19.

Sayeki, Y. (1978). *Knowing and Learning by Imagination*. Tokyo: Toyo-kan (in Japanese).

Sayeki, Y. (1989). Anthropomorphic Epistemology. Unpublished paper. Laboratory of Comparative Human Cognition, University of California, San Diego.

Tenbrink, T., Hölscher, C., Tsigaridi, D., and Dalton, R. C. (2014). 13 Cognition and Communication in Architectural Design. *Space in Mind: Concepts for Spatial Learning and Education*: 263.

Yaneva, A. (2009). *Made by the Office for Metropolitan Architecture: An Ethnography of Design*. Rotterdam: 010 Publishers.

Part II
The building as artefact

4 One-way street

Kim Dovey

> Koolhaas' designs are blatantly straightforward... one and only one cultural aim drives the work... to discover what real, instrumental collaboration can be effected between architecture and freedom.
>
> (Kipnis, 1998, p. 27)

The success of the work of Rem Koolhaas and his firm OMA rests strongly on the implicit or explicit claim to be an architecture of emancipation.[1] Koolhaas can be interpreted as resuscitating the early modernist imperative to develop an architecture of social relevance through a mix of programmatic and formal change. He seeks to challenge practices of social reproduction as they are embedded in architectural ideologies and spatial programmes. Programmatic innovations include the production of fields of social encounter, new functional juxtapositions, and forms of spatial segmentation designed to resist social reproduction and enable certain 'freedoms' (Zaera and Koolhaas, 1992). In this chapter I want to examine such claims as they play out in the design and use of the Seattle Central Library. The primary method of analysis for this critique is an adaptation of space syntax analysis filtered through a framework of assemblage theory (Deleuze and Guattari, 1987) and Bourdieu's (1977) concept of habitus.

Space syntax as developed by Hillier and Hanson (Hillier and Vaughan, 2007; Hillier and Hanson, 1984) is a largely structuralist form of spatial analysis that would surely be anathema to Koolhaas for its positivist and reductionist tendencies. Yet space syntax involves an interrogation of the 'genotypes' or 'diagrams' embodied in buildings as forms of social reproduction and represents a research-based parallel to Koolhaas's design approach. It is at least an interesting congruence that both Hillier and Koolhaas deploy the 'machine' as a primary metaphor in their approach to architecture and space. In both cases this is a critical response to the Corbusian notion of architecture as a 'machine for living'. Hillier's major book is entitled *Space Is the Machine* and Koolhaas's work often deploys machines both literally and metaphorically. Both approaches privilege the idea of buildings being produced systemically through generic (in the case of Koolhaas) or genetic (Hillier and Hanson) codes or structures; both treat buildings as forms of infrastructure that variously accommodate or constrain flows of life. The loose adaptation of space syntax methods here may not be acceptable to either Koolhaas or Hillier and Hanson; the goal is to bring a more rigorous critique to some of the claims for programmatic innovation in Koolhaas's

54   Kim Dovey

designs. To do this I will first set aside the formalist aesthetic critique of Koolhaas's work except as it informs this task. This does not suggest that form and programme can be easily separated – such a presumed separation is one of the deepest complicities of architecture with power. It is also not because the aesthetic dimension of his work is less interesting or innovative; Koolhaas is a master form maker and major producer of symbolic capital. The problem is that architectural critique is so skewed towards the formal that it is all that many critics see of his work, and formal innovation can camouflage programmatic issues.

Fields

The works of Koolhaas/OMA have been termed the 'social condensers of our time' (Graafland, 1998). This reflects a return to the early modernist imperative toward an architecture that would remake the habitat of everyday life. This is not, however, a return to the social engineering reflected in ideas like the 'social condenser' of the Soviet constructivists. Rather it is a vision of an internalized 'culture of congestion' inspired by the formal and social multiplicities of urban life (Koolhaas, 1978). This vision is reflected in the name of Koolhaas's firm – Office for Metropolitan Architecture – which can be read as both an 'architecture of the metropolis' and an insertion of the 'metropolis into the architecture'. Koolhaas's work is strongly ordered by trajectories of movement through the building. The role of vertical movement via escalators, stairs, ramps, and elevators is a key to the order which is set up, as they become the modes of access to fields of event and encounter. Koolhaas is inspired by the notion of an architecture of liberation in terms of the multiple 'freedoms' for new forms of action which architecture is seen to make possible (Zaera and Koolhaas, 1992). Space is programmed for indefinite function and chance encounter. Koolhaas seeks an architecture that can resist the imperative to become a diagram of social and institutional structure. For Kipnis, Koolhaas's version of freedom is not an overt resistance to authority but rather a form of programmatic sabotage:

> More like a sadist than a surgeon, he has begun to knife the brief, hacking away its fat, even its flesh, until he has exposed its nerve... the focus on these reductions is always on disestablishment, that is, always on excising the residues in the project of unwarranted authority, unnecessary governance and tired convention. Reductive disestablishment provides the crucial stratagem in each of Koolhaas' recent projects, the intellectual modus operandi by which the architect begins to transform the design into an instrument of freedom.
>
> (Kipnis, 1998, pp. 29–30)

Koolhaas seeks an architecture that encourages an eruption of events, social encounters, and opportunities for action. Rather than designing with a particular hierarchy of spaces and narratives of spatial movement in mind, he generally works towards a spatial structure that allows a multiplicity of choices for pedestrian flow and encounter. Koolhaas wants to 'liquefy rigid programming into non-specific flows and events... to weave together exterior, interior, vestigial and primary spaces into a frank differential matrix that rids the building of the hackneyed bourgeois niceties of cosmetic hierarchies' (Kipnis, 1998, p. 30).

Koolhaas often designs interiors as if they were exteriors, importing the randomness of social encounter from urban space into public interiors. These interiors are often designed as 'fields of play' or 'artificial landscapes' which dissolve boundaries between inside and outside, between architecture and metropolis. Such spaces are often functionally open and visually transparent to maximize social encounter. Jameson situates Koolhaas's work in the context of the prevailing social dialectics of publicity/privacy and freedom/control in what he terms the 'post-civil' society. He suggests that Koolhaas's work enables patterns of free play within a rigid spatial order:

> the originality of Koolhaas is that his work does not simply glorify differentiation in the conventional pluralist ideological way: rather he insists on the relationship between this randomness and freedom and the presence of some rigid, inhuman, non-differentiated form that enables the differentiation of what goes on around it.
> (Jameson and Speaks, 1992, p. 33)

There is an interesting connection here with what Allen (1997) suggests is a shift in architectural thinking from a focus on the architectural object to a focus on field relations paralleling the development of field theory in mathematics. A field consists of contingent relations, forces, trajectories, and patterns of movement such as those which govern a 'flock' of birds. Field conditions are described as: 'any formal or spatial matrix capable of unifying diverse elements while respecting the identity of each… Field conditions are bottom-up phenomena: defined not by overarching geometrical schema but by intricate local connections' (Allen, 1997, p. 24).

The field is a material condition rather than a discursive practice. Allen draws analogies between field theory and architectural attempts to encourage a spontaneity of action. He suggests that systems with 'permeable boundaries, flexible internal relationships, multiple pathways and fluid hierarchies' are capable of responding to emerging complexities of new urban contexts (Allen, 1997, p. 31). A major innovation in Koolhaas's work lies in the extent to which he has utilized such strategies in the interiors of buildings where they contribute towards the emergence of new kinds of social space. The promise here is that the field-like nature of Koolhaas's work opens up the work to multiplicities of experience and action. This idea of the building as a field rather than an architectural object entails a shift in critique from form to spatial analysis. We must then ask, to what extent do these designs restructure social space or reproduce familiar spatial structures?

Space syntax

Methods of space syntax analysis, first developed by Hillier and Hanson, represent an attempt to reveal a deep social structuring of architectural and urban space (Hillier, 1996; Hillier and Hanson, 1984). This work has developed in a number of distinct directions including the axial analysis of urban space and the mapping of integration and connectivity values (Hillier and Vaughan, 2007; Zook and Bafna in Chapter 6 of this volume). My primary interest here lies in the syntactic relations between different building components and their relative depth from the street – generally known as gamma analysis (Hillier and Hanson, 1984). From this view buildings reflect social organizations as congealed socio-spatial structures; architecture mediates social reproduction through spatial 'genotypes'. These are not formal 'types' or 'archetypes' but clusters of spatial entities structured in certain formations with syntactic rules of sequence and adjacency. Genotypes are seen as institutionally and epistemologically embedded – schools, offices, factories, libraries, and houses are reproduced from a limited number of spatial genotypes. Each of these is linked to specific social institutions with forms of knowledge, production, and reproduction. Markus (1993) has written about the nineteenth-century library as a genotype that deploys a large domed central space as a metaphor for universal knowledge, modelled on the pantheon. This was also a panoptic form of disciplinary technology with readers visible from a central desk, designed to construct and reproduce a particular kind of subjectivity as part of a knowledge/power regime (Foucault, 1977).

While the gamma analysis developed by Hillier and Hanson can be very revealing it also works best for more traditional buildings where spaces are more clearly segmented – such measures become less clear in open-plan buildings such as the one in focus here. However, Koolhaas's programmatic innovations demand critique in terms of the link between spatial structure and institutional authority and the space syntax approach is the most sophisticated available. The analysis deployed here is a loose adaptation of gamma analysis that translates the building plan into a diagram of how life and social encounter is framed within it. The upper part of Figure 4.1 shows how similar plans with different access points yield quite different syntactic structures and illustrates three primary cluster relations – the fan, net, and line. Each displays a differing level of spatial control and freedom: the line (or enfilade) controls the choice of pathway; the fan (or branching) structure controls access to a number of segments from a single space; and the net is a ringy or permeable network with multiple choices

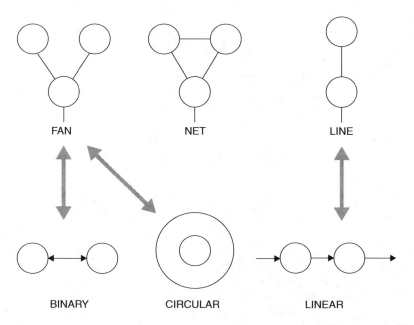

Figure 4.1 Syntax and segmentarity. Adapted from Hillier and Hanson, 1984, in Deleuze and Guattari, 1987. Source: Author.

of pathway. The three may seem a limited set, but all spatial structures can be understood in terms of combinations and additions of them. These are abstract diagrams; they are at once immanent or embodied in particular buildings and are also deployed across a wide variety of place types. A key characteristic is the 'depth' or 'shallowness' of any segment from the nearest external entry points and the overall depth of the structure. A deep building requires the traversing of many segments with many boundaries and points of control. The diagrammatic method shows the spatial segments of the building layered into levels of depth so that the level of a space indicates the least number of segments from the exterior. Depth is an important mediator of social relations both between inhabitants (kinship relations or organizational hierarchies) and between inhabitants and visitors.

All architecture involves combinations of the fan, net, and line, including a range of decisions regarding how spatial assemblages are interconnected and linked to external space. The fan is characteristic of bureaucratic and hierarchic organizations with large numbers of cells controlled by a hallway. The network syntax is defined by a ringy spatial structure and a choice of pathways; it is common in places designed to maximize exchange such as markets and department stores. The linear assemblage is an enfilade of spaces with controlled movement – it may or may not be a cul-de-sac. It is common in traditional centres of power (such as Versailles) and in some modern retail buildings (like Ikea) and blockbuster art exhibitions with an entry at one end and an exit at the other.

There are important links between these diagrams and Bourdieu's (1977) concept of the habitus. Part habit, part habitat, the habitus is an embodied structuration of both material world and lifeworld, a socio-spatial set of divisions between people, things, and practices as well as a 'sense of one's place' within this world. Such analysis maps the ways in which buildings operate as fields of socio-spatial encounter – what kinds of agency are enabled and constrained by the particular building genotype within which it is structured and whose interests are served? How is everyday life bracketed and punctuated into socio-spatially framed situations (Goffman, 1963)? How does architecture frame the social gaze through structured realms of visibility? What regimes of normalization are enforced and in whose interest? What prospects or freedoms are enabled, and again, in whose interests? Hillier and Hanson (1984) have argued that the key difference between internal and external space relates to localized degrees of ideological control – interiors are generally more strictly controlled into lines and fans while streets are more networked.

Segmentarity

The works and writings of Koolhaas show many influences including modernism, psychoanalysis, Marxism, and deconstruction; assemblage thinking derived from the work of Deleuze and Guattari (1987) is clearly among them (Rajchman and Koolhaas, 1994, p. 99; Kwinter, 1996; Speaks, 1994). Such an approach involves a focus on flows and rhizomic connectivity rather than tree-like hierarchies and stabilized identities (DeLanda, 2006; Dovey, 2010, chapter 2). Assemblage thinking incorporates a critique of socio-spatial segmentarity of which there are three main types – the binary, circular, and linear – also diagrammed in Figure 4.1 (Deleuze and Guattari, 1987, p. 195). For Deleuze and Guattari segmentarity is primarily social rather than spatial. Binary segmentation is generally a division of binary social categories such as upper/

58 Kim Dovey

lower social class, male/female, young/old, black/white, and major/minor. Everyday spatial examples might include airline seating (class), children's libraries (age), and toilets (gender). Circular segmentation involves nested scales as when a room is encircled in turn by a building, neighbourhood, city, and nation. Linear segmentation involves a progression over time through different segments which may or may not be spatially contiguous: pre-school > primary > secondary > university. Architectural examples include the choreographed sequence of the blockbuster art exhibit (entry > gallery > gallery > gallery > shop > exit) and airport (check-in > security > shops > lounge > aircraft). Each of these segmentation types is geared to micro-practices of power. Binary segments not only divide according to race, class, age, and gender but also ensure there is little space for hybridity. Concentric segments can operate to ensure a resonance between places at different scales and rungs in a hierarchy: as the bank branch resonates with the corporate tree. Linear segments stabilize sequences of identity formation. These three diagrams of segmentarity are interconnected and overlapped since segments may be lodged in binary, nested, and sequential relations simultaneously.

This discussion of segmentarity begs comparison with space syntax analysis, as juxtaposed in Figure 4.1. Only the linear type of segmentarity maps easily against the linear syntax. The binary type can be linked to the fan as a diagram that effects divisions of class, gender, age, rank, etc. through a spatial division of pathways off a common entry. The fan is also linked to the concentric type in the sense that it is based on a hierarchic connection between a control space and sub-spaces accessed through it. The network syntax does not appear in Deleuze and Guattari's scheme largely because segmentarity is a critique of control and constraint while the network is identified with choice and with freedom; the rhizomic flows of networks are opposed to the tree-like hierarchies and strict sequences of segmentarity.

A permeable network of spaces and the open plan have long been linked to practices of social freedom, yet any conflation of physical enclosure with social constraint, or of open space with liberty, is a dangerous one. Buildings are increasingly called upon to produce an illusion of freedom coupled with the reality of control and surveillance. A spatial assemblage that mixes people of different social identities is in general less likely to reproduce those identities and more likely to promote new identity formation. Such spaces are much more characteristic of the urban public realm than the private interior. Interior space is more rigidly segmented and deterministic with primary functions of social reproduction. Thus two kinds of spatial assemblage are counterposed: the more open and smooth networks of public space, the more closed and striated private spaces; this distinction between the ideological control of segmented interiors and the spaces of open encounter of the street is also drawn by Hillier and Hanson (1984, p. 19) – there is a different social logic of space of interior and exterior space. Public and private realms have a symbiotic relationship, and it is the ambiguous zone between them that is often the most interesting and vital part of a city. In general terms the random encounter and open access of the public realm is a threat to the social reproductive function of private space and the determinism of interior structures is a threat to urban diversity. The programmatic innovations of Koolhaas involve an experimentation with this tension between inside and outside, using the encounter structures of urban space to effect innovations in interior space.

Mapping the library

The Seattle Central Library, completed in 2004 is perhaps Koolhaas's most developed attempt to create an internal culture of congestion through architecture. The programmatic innovations here have a genesis that goes back to earlier library competition designs that were not built, but which incorporated both new understandings about knowledge exchange and a spatial organization around a spiral flow. The building is an 11-storey volume occupying an entire city block of the downtown Seattle grid with main entries on two different street levels. While the external form of the building is not of particular concern here it has been described as a fishnet stocking that has been crammed with children's building blocks; it has also been described as a stack of books. The complex interior geography of this building has rendered plans close to useless in navigating the building; Figure 4.2 shows a figurative section through the building.

The spatial structure of the building is its key innovation. The lower street entry contains children and foreign language sections while the upper street enters directly into a vast 'living room'. Connecting the two are both an escalator and public auditorium. Further escalators rise to an information hub ('mixing chamber') housing catalogue and internet connections. Sandwiched between is a mezzanine floor of meeting rooms. This cluster of spaces is an extremely smart design that assembles five storeys of programme within two spatial segments deep from the street. The 'living room' is effectively one vast floor space extending across the city block with good light and outlook (Figure 4.3); the sense of public accessibility works in both programmatic and representational terms and makes it one of the finest public interiors of its era. This space is effectively the main reading room of the library with generous light and seating. It is open to the auditorium, is overlooked from the mezzanine levels of meeting

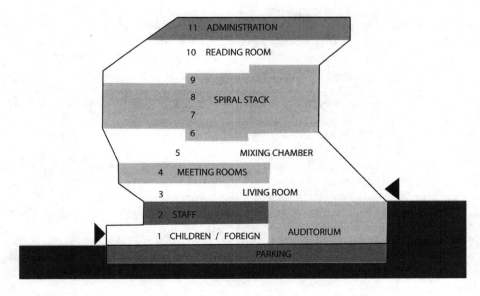

Figure 4.2 Seattle Central Library, figurative section. Source: Author.

Figure 4.3 Living room, auditorium, and street entry. Source: Author.

rooms and mixing chamber, and houses a café and small fold-up shop. It incorporates a highly urbanized mix of functions and is integrated with a series of permanent public artworks. This is perhaps the most successful of Koolhaas/OMA's attempts at an urbanized interior. It brings the auditorium, café, shop, checkout counter, books, artworks, and reading areas into one mixed space that is also the foyer of the building. Beyond the mixing chamber the main pathway continues up an escalator to the spiral ramp housing the main collection. From floors six to ten the building floorplate becomes a continuous ramp that winds up around the escalator. Books are organized according to the rationalist Dewey system from 0 to 999 with numbers marked on the floor (Figure 4.4). At the top of the ramped spiral is a grand reading room with a reorientation to the city.

Figure 4.5 shows how traffic flows through the building with three modes of vertical transport: escalators, elevators, and stairs. The sequence of escalators is designed as the primary flow connecting the two street entry levels to the information area (mixing chamber) and then up to the stacks and reading room. There are two sets of stairs, one for access between levels within the spiral and an enclosed fire escape. The elevators service every level but are less accessible.

This is one of the most disorienting buildings one can imagine. Library management has produced several sectional diagrams to be used as navigational aids by unfamiliar users, one of which appears in Figure 4.6. The spiral is particularly confusing because while it is very clear where you are within the Dewey system, it is difficult to figure out

Figure 4.4 Spiral stack. Source: Author.

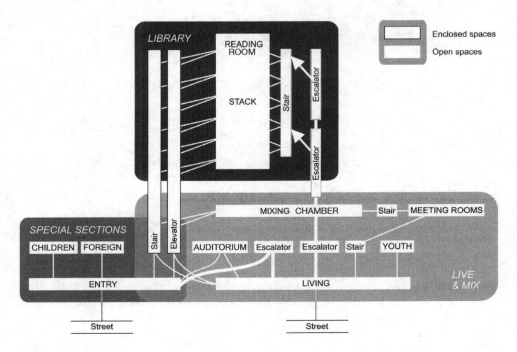

Figure 4.5 Spatial structure. Source: Author.

62 Kim Dovey

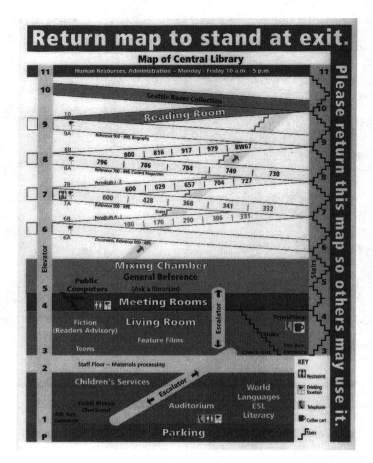

Figure 4.6 Diagram produced by Seattle Central Library management. Source: The Seattle Public Library.

which floor you are on because there are no boundaries between floors (Figure 4.6). Floors 6–10 comprise one continuous pathway from 0–999. In a rather literal sense here one becomes disoriented within the building and reoriented towards the books – lost in a world of knowledge. However, there is a problem created by the fact that the escalator going up to the spiral is one way and there is no similar egress (Figures 4.5 and 4.6). Since this is clearly the dominant traffic route, the escalator becomes an effective one-way street for first-time users who can see no way out. There are some fire escape stairs and the elevators but these egress points are well removed from the access elevators. With no easy way back to the mixing and living rooms this is a structure not unlike the way the shopping mall or department store generate one-way portals to a world of consumption; where disorientation and reorientation takes place and modes of egress are camouflaged. Without a more detailed evaluation it is difficult to judge the effects of this on local readers, however, conversations with the librarians confirm that many people have to ask to find a way out and makeshift notices direct them to the fire stairs.

One-way street

So what does it mean that one of the world's great architects should create a public building, indeed a library, as a one-way street in this manner? While the history of architecture is replete with beautiful designs that malfunction in crucial ways – the disorientation that is produced here appears to me to be deliberate. Koolhaas is an architect who has always engaged with programme and ignorance is not credible; this is a deliberate design of a place that is easy to enter but a challenge to exit. I suggest this is a deconstructive strategy.

The building is based on the idea of the spiral stack – the diagram that Koolhaas invented for an earlier library. One is powered up by the escalators into a world from which there is no easy exit. This world of one-way portals is also the diagram that was largely invented for the shopping mall and is now applied to many other urban building types. Yet the strategy here is not one of entrapment; the disorientation is not a means but an end, the goal is architectural. If the sense of place gives us an existential foothold, as Norberg-Schulz (1980) suggests, stabilizing who we are and where we are, then the library embodies the deconstructive desire to pull the rug from such preconceptions. Yet in architectural terms it misses the mark, lacking either the shock value of deconstruction or the joy of getting delightfully lost in the labyrinth. One enters the world of knowledge but lacks the knowledge needed to get out. This sense of disorientation creates a phenomenological distinction between insiders and outsiders (Relph, 1976), between those who are familiar with the strange circulation and the first-time users who are not – on a second visit you will know how to get out. I suspect that the disorientation is designed primarily for the architectural cognoscenti – in other words, us. In that sense it has clearly worked because here we are devoting an entire book to just one building.

One-way building

This is in many ways a very fine public building that reinvents the library as a building type and opens it to the street but it also seems to divide its public. Some patrons prefer the branch libraries because they find this one too 'industrial' and not 'homely'. While there are regulars who seem very comfortable there is very little sense of enclosure. The shop, café, sitting areas, and shelves of the meeting room are all treated as parts of a large open space; one is always and everywhere exposed to a public gaze. There are no edges to provide the psychological comfort of prospect and refuge. The sitting spaces along the spiral are placed right on the main pathway and some are exposed on three sides (Figure 4.4). There is a sense that the machinic approach has become an aesthetic ideology embodying a denial of comfort. What is at stake here is an issue of designing for difference – some people want the psychological protection of a nook or alcove and some don't; some people find it difficult to concentrate with strangers looking over their shoulder. The level 10 reading room offers a rather different setting but it is essentially a cul-de-sac and appears to be underused. Beyond his desire to undermine ideologies embodied in architecture, to unsettle the habitus, Koolhaas has a somewhat cavalier approach to questions of inhabitation: 'People can inhabit anything. And they can be miserable in anything and ecstatic in anything. More and more I think that architecture has nothing to do with it' (Koolhaas, in Heron, 1996, p. 1). This is a building largely designed for a particular kind of cosmopolitan subject: confidently

64   Kim Dovey

engaged in information exchange rather than quiet reflection. It is hard to avoid the conclusion that this is both a one-way street and a one-way building.

Freedom?

So what can be made of Koolhaas's desire to unhinge architecture from its role in social reproduction? Koolhaas's goals are generally laudable, especially when he treats interior space as a field of play which resists any simple mimetic relationship with social structure. A permeable spatial network is a primary design tactic. He wants to defy the social logic of space, to free up the programmatic imperatives which lock architecture into the service of a highly choreographed and ritualistic reproduction of social life. The larger project here can be seen as an urbanization of architecture. Urbanity can be defined as an assemblage that produces a high intensity of encounter with difference; for Sennett (1973, 1996) this random encounter is what grants public space its key role in identity formation. Good cities are paradigmatic places of becoming. Yet interior spaces generally serve a very different role than that of the street – much more closely aligned with a strictly striated habitus and functions of social reproduction. Graafland (1998) has suggested that Koolhaas's work is a somewhat Faustian practice which embodies a dialectic between the freedoms he seeks and the tree-like institutional structures in which such practices are embedded; I have argued something similar in relation to his other projects (Dovey, 2008, chapter 11; Dovey and Dickson, 2002). This reflects an acceptance of prevailing social and economic forces, a realpolitik wherein the desire for the new is harnessed to make what one can in a difficult world. One of Koolhaas's metaphors for architectural practice is that of 'surfing' the waves of capital and power politics, a commitment to taking the opportunities of architectural practice without the illusion of control or autonomy. The claim to produce certain freedoms is distinct from any claim to produce real social change.

Kipnis (1998, p. 27) suggests that: 'For Koolhaas, architecture is able… to engender provisional freedoms in a definite situation, freedoms as the experiences, as the sensations, as the effects – pleasurable, threatening, and otherwise – of undermining select patterns of regulation and authority'. While such claims are relatively untestable they need to be considered in the context of everyday experience and social practice, enmeshed in the micro-practices of power and liberation that infuse everyday life. Yet such critique of place experience is one that Koolhaas explicitly eschews. One slightly bitter retort to his critics was entitled 'No Grounds against a Non-Place' (Koolhaas, 1996) and elsewhere he derides the very idea of local place identity as an obsession with stabilized identity and essentialized meanings (Koolhaas, 1995). His idealized 'Generic City' floats free of any roots, liberated from character and identity. It also often floats free of logic or veracity; in 1995 he wrote: 'In five to ten years we will all work at home' and that 'the street is dead' (Koolhaas, 1995, pp. 1252, 1260).

Magic

Colomina suggests that he operates in the mode of a magician, distracting the eye with one hand, concealing what he is up to with the other (Colomina and Lleó, 1998). This is also affirmed by Koolhaas: 'a public accus(es) a trickster of deceiving them. But don't blame the magician for having fooled them, for having given them these sublime moments of illusion' (Koolhaas, 1996, p. 190). Koolhaas's formal inventiveness distracts critical attention from the programmatic surgery that at times constructs illusions of freedom that can conceal both conservatism and dysfunction. Programmatic innovation can be reduced to significations of practice. One of the axes of assemblage theory is the opposition and tension between the poles of materiality and symbolic expression (Deleuze and Guattari, 1987, p. 89); Koolhaas uses the expressive pole of the assemblage to conceal materialistic interventions; formal expression distracts attention from critique of material outcomes. There is no suggestion here that the 'magic' does not work in certain ways. What is missing, however, is an understanding of 'freedom' as a form of practice – something people do rather than images they consume. Koolhaas does indeed challenge the primary genotypes of socio-spatial reproduction, yet at the same time he generates illusions that can be a cover for new practices of power or for more of the same.

Note

1 This chapter is substantially based on parts of chapter 7, 'Urbanizing Architecture', from Dovey, K. (2010) Framing Places. London: Routledge, pp. 103–23. All figures and photos are by Kim Dovey except Figure 4.6.

References

Allen, S. (1997) 'From Object to Field', *Architectural Design* 127: 24–31.
Bourdieu, P. (1977) *Outline of a Theory of Practice*, London: Cambridge University Press.
Colomina, B. and Lleó, B. (1998) '"A Machine Was Its Heart": House in Floirac', *Assemblage* 37: 36–45.
DeLanda, M. (2006) *A New Philosophy of Society*, London: Continuum.
Deleuze, G. and Guattari, F. (1987) *A Thousand Plateaus*, London: Athlone.
Dovey, K. (2008) *Framing Places*, 2nd Ed, London: Routledge.
Dovey, K. (2010) *Becoming Places*, London: Routledge.
Dovey, K. and Dickson, S. (2002) 'Architecture and Freedom: Programmatic Innovation in the Work of Rem Koolhaas', *Journal of Architectural Education* 55 (4): 268–77.
Foucault, M. (1977) *Discipline and Punish*, New York: Vintage.
Goffman, E. (1963) *Behavior in Public Places*, New York: Free Press.
Graafland, A. (1998) 'Of Rhizomes, Trees and the IJ-Oevers, Amsterdam', *Assemblage* 38: 28–41.
Heron, K. (1996) 'From Bauhaus to Koolhaas', *Wired* July: 1–3.
Hillier, B. (1996) *Space Is the Machine*, Cambridge: Cambridge University Press.
Hillier, B. and Hanson, J. (1984) *The Social Logic of Space*, Cambridge: Cambridge University Press.
Hillier, B. and Vaughan, S. (2007) 'The City as One Thing', *Progress in Planning* 67: 205–94.
Jameson, F. and Speaks, M. (1992) 'Envelopes and Enclaves: The Space of Post-Civil Society', *Assemblage* 17: 30–7.
Kipnis, J. (1998) 'Recent Koolhaas', *El Croquis* 79: 26–31.
Koolhaas, R. (1978) *Delirious New York*, New York: Oxford University Press.
Koolhaas, R. (1995) 'Generic City' in Koolhaas, R. and Mau, B. (eds) *Small, Medium, Large, Extra-Large*, New York: Monacelli Press.
Koolhaas, R. (1996) 'No Grounds against a Non-Place' in *Euralille*, Basel: Birkhauser: 51–71.
Kwinter, S. (1996) 'Flying the Bullet, or When Did the Future Begin?' in Kwinter, S. (ed.) *Rem Koolhaas: Conversations with Students*, Houston: Rice University, School of Architecture: 68–94.
Markus, T. (1993) *Buildings and Power*, London: Routledge.

66 *Kim Dovey*

Norberg-Schulz, C. (1980) *Genius Loci: Towards a Phenomenology of Architecture*, New York: Rizzoli.

Rajchman, J. and Koolhaas, R. (1994) 'Thinking Big', *Artforum*, 33 (4), December.

Relph, E. (1976) *Place and Placelessness*, London: Pion.

Sennett, R. (1973) *The Uses of Disorder*, Harmondsworth: Penguin.

Sennett, R. (1996) *Flesh and Stone*, New York: W. W. Norton.

Speaks, M. (1994) 'Bigness', *Any*, 9: 60–2.

Zaera, A. and Koolhaas, R. (1992) 'Finding Freedoms: Conversations with Rem Koolhaas', *El Croquis* 53: 6–31.

5 A phenomenological and hermeneutic reading of Rem Koolhaas's Seattle Central Library

Buildings as lifeworlds and architectural texts

David Seamon

There is a wide range of conceptual and methodological approaches for researchers to study buildings and other architectural works (Gifford, 2016; Groat and Wang, 2013; Seamon and Gill, 2016; Zeisel, 2006). In this chapter, I suggest ways whereby the related philosophical traditions of phenomenology and hermeneutics might examine Rem Koolhaas's Seattle Central Library. On the one hand, phenomenology works to understand phenomena – i.e., any experience, thing, action, event, or situation that a human being can experience.[1] On the other hand, hermeneutics works to understand texts – i.e., artefactual expressions like novels, poems, art works, photographs, buildings, historical documents, and so forth.[2] For phenomenology, the aim is a more accurate, comprehensive knowledge of human experience; for hermeneutics, the aim is a more accurate, comprehensive knowledge of human meaning.

One methodological difference between these two approaches is that phenomenology uses some form of experiential accounts (e.g., in-depth interviews, careful observation of places, or critical reflection on one's own first-hand experience) as its source of real-world evidence whereas, for hermeneutics, that source of evidence is the researcher's continuing, intensive encounter with the text that he or she hopes to understand (e.g., immersive reading and rereading of a novel or poem, in-depth study of historic photographs, or thorough first-hand engagement with a building or critical accounts written about it). What the two approaches share in common is, first, an emphasis on qualitative description and interpretation; and, second, a recognition that knowledge of experience and meaning is inexhaustible. In this sense, description, interpretation, and understanding are always tentative, in process, and open to new insights and points of view (Bortoft, 2012; Mugerauer, 1994). Tables 5.1 and 5.2 identify some key commonalities and differences between phenomenological and hermeneutic research.

In relation to architectural research, one can study any building both phenomenologically and hermeneutically. From a phenomenological perspective, a building is a constellation of experiences, actions, situations, and events, all generated by and related to the individuals and groups that make use of that building, whether for living, working, recreating, or something else. In this sense, architecture helps sustain lifeworlds – i.e., the ordinary, everyday, taken-for-granted experiences, events, and worlds within the building or associated with the building (e.g., the world of sidewalks, streets, and neighborhoods surrounding the building). Phenomenologists study buildings as lifeworlds and ask, for example, whether a building's design supports or undermines the building's function, or whether a building's users make use of the building in the ways the architect envisioned.

68   David Seamon

Table 5.1 Phenomenology and hermeneutics: some thematic and methodological commonalities

1. Both approaches work to be open to the thing studied; the aim is an empathetic awareness and engagement that allow the thing studied to be as fully present, describable, and understandable as possible.
2. Both approaches draw on qualitative evidence as a descriptive and interpretive basis for substantive discoveries and conclusions; examples of qualitative evidence include reports from in-depth interviewing; first-person descriptions of one's own experience or understanding of a text; careful, prolonged observation of a place; careful, prolonged study of a text and other commentators' interpretations of that text.
3. Both approaches recognize that the thing studied can be explored and understood in a wide range of ways; the thing studied is inexhaustible in its potential aspects, expressions, significances, and underlying lived or interpretive structures. The researcher's specific interests, sensibilities, and investigative skills play a major role in establishing which specific dimensions of the thing are studied. The researcher's dedication, insight, and persistence (rather than any specific research instruments) are largely responsible for the comprehensiveness, accuracy, and quality of the research results.
4. Both approaches emphasize the crucial importance of finding "fitting language" to present the experience and meaning; a major aim is precise, well-crafted writing.
5. Both approaches aim for accurate, trustworthy accounts of the phenomenon or text; phenomenological and hermeneutic criteria for descriptive and interpretive validity include:

- Comprehensiveness, whereby the account offers an understanding of the experience or text that seems to be thorough and well integrated.
- Semantic depth, whereby the account is accepted as reasonable by a wide audience and holds its meaning over time.
- Inclusivity, whereby the account offers an appropriate range of understanding and an encompassing frame of reference that provides thematic context for other phenomenological and hermeneutic studies.
- Architectonic structure, whereby the account structures the experience or meaning into a broader intelligible pattern that "makes sense" in terms of the original phenomenon or text (Wachterhauser, 1996).

From a hermeneutic perspective, a building is a material text that evokes some set of meanings for users and other individuals associated with that building (Jones, 2000). Depending on the researcher's study focus, these meanings might be visceral, bodily, emotional, intellectual, aesthetic, and so forth. For instance, a hermeneutic study might focus on a specific building's visceral sense – does the building seem heavy or light, for example? Does it evoke a sense of motion or seem to remain in place? Does it welcome its outside surroundings in or does it remain steadfastly apart from the outside? Yet again, the hermeneutic researcher might give attention to shifting intellectual understandings of a specific building type – for example, how has the high-rise building been understood by the lay public over time and how and why have those understandings changed? Most broadly, the hermeneutic emphasis is on understanding the range of meanings and significances of a building, whereas the phenomenological emphasis is examining experiences and lifeworlds associated with that building. Since human meanings and experiences always interrelate and overlap in human life, the conceptual and methodological approaches of phenomenology and hermeneutics share much in common. As this chapter demonstrates, one often finds that researchers specializing in phenomenology also conduct hermeneutic research as well (Finlay, 2011, chapter 7; Mugerauer, 1994, 1995; Palmer, 1969, pp. 3–11; Seamon, 2000, pp. 167–9).

Table 5.2 Phenomenology and hermeneutics: some thematic and methodological differences

Phenomenology	*Hermeneutics*
1. Studies phenomena – i.e., things or experiences as human beings experience those things or experiences; examples include the experience of color, of being-at-home, of feeling out of place, or of encountering a specific building or a specific architectural style.	1. Studies texts – i.e., any more or less coherent human creations that evoke meaning, whether intellectual, emotional, aesthetic, visceral, or otherwise; examples of texts include novels, photographs, films, songs, dances, rituals, landscapes, or buildings.
2. Works to describe and understand aspects of the lifeworld – the world of everyday, taken-for-granted experience of which people are typically unaware; one aim is to identify and understand tacit, unnoticed aspects of the lifeworld so that they can be accounted for theoretically and practically.	2. Works to understand how and in what ways a text might be interpreted, and how and in what ways interpreters of the text might clarify their interpretation and broaden their engagement with the text; asks what it means to understand and why the understandings of a text can vary by individual, group, or historical era.
3. To describe and understand the phenomenon, phenomenologists use some form of experiential accounts – e.g., intensive participant observation, evidence from in-depth interviews, thoughtful explication of first-hand experience, careful observation of environments or places; experiential accounts from art, film, literature, photographs, historical documents, or other descriptive sources.	3. To interpret and find meaning in the text, hermeneutic researchers engage in intensive, immersive involvement with the text as well as critical engagement with other researchers' interpretations of the text; hermeneutic researchers recognize that how a text is interpreted can be different from what the original creator intended and can vary because of differences among interpreters.
4. Assumes that, by gathering and probing real-world lived descriptions, researchers can facilitate a more comprehensive understanding of the phenomenon, including unnoticed patterns and structures (e.g., place defined via modes of lived insideness and outsideness (Relph 1976).	4. Assumes the interpretive value of the "hermeneutic circle" – that the whole of the text can only be understood through its parts, but those parts can only be understood by knowing the whole; the aim is an interpretive interplay between parts and whole whereby the researcher gains a fullness of meaning for the text (Palmer 1969).

In relation to Rem Koolhaas's Seattle Central Library, one phenomenological aim is to identify, describe, and integrate the building's spectrum of experiences for the designers, builders, users, staff, professional critics, and other individuals and groups associated with the library. The phenomenological question might be broad (e.g., what is a successful library experience and in what ways is that experience sustained or undermined by Rem Koolhaas's design?) or narrow (e.g., what is the work experience of the window washers who clean the building's complex, sloping glass walls and how does it compare with cleaning situations for other large-scale structures?). One can identify a similar topical range for hermeneutic studies of the library (e.g., how can the building be understood as an aesthetic object? Or what do reviews of the building in the professional architectural press presuppose in terms of which current architectural styles are considered successful and which are not?).

70   *David Seamon*

To illustrate what phenomenology and hermeneutics offer architectural research, I examine the Seattle Central Library from four different perspectives for which I procure real-world evidence via a range of research methods. I begin with a phenomenology of naïve architectural encounters in which I draw on visceral, visual reactions to the building on the part of laypersons who have never before seen the building. Second, I ask how the Seattle Central Library might be interpreted and better understood via Norwegian architect Thomas Thiis-Evensen's phenomenology of architectural experience, of which a central premise is that architecture is the making of an inside in the midst of an outside (Thiis-Evensen, 1989). Third, drawing on over 200 social-media "reviews" of the building by voluntary contributors, I delineate possibilities for a phenomenology of place as these accounts provide one kind of interpretive evidence. Last, I examine three reviews of the building written by Seattle architectural critic Lawrence Cheek. Using these reviews as an illustration, I suggest that our experience and understanding of a building may shift over time and that a comprehensive phenomenological and hermeneutic interpretation of architecture must incorporate the lived history of any building, including its design origins and its uses and users over time.

First impressions of the Seattle Central Library

Phenomenological study is sometimes described as the "pristine innocence of first seeing" (Spiegelberg, 1982, p. 680). How, in other words, might we look at and understand the phenomenon if our taken-for-granted assumptions, values, and points of view could be set aside and the phenomenon encountered afresh as if it might be "a thing in itself"? One important phenomenological question is how such moments of naïve, originary encounter are to be evoked, described, and recorded. In teaching a large undergraduate lecture course in Appreciation of Architecture to non-design majors, I work during the first few weeks of class to get students to look at buildings more carefully and comprehensively. Most of these students have minimal background or interest in architecture and take the class because it helps to meet a university "general-education" requirement.

One aim I have for the class is to develop students' visual and aesthetic sensibilities through looking at architecture. A device I use toward this end is showing images of recent buildings with which most students are unfamiliar. As they look at an image, I first ask them to guess the building's use. Next, as a means to make contact with their immediate, visceral reactions to the building, I ask them to write down at least three single words or short phrases to describe what they see. I show the images quickly and emphasize that there are no right or wrong responses. Rather, the central point of the exercise is to get students to become more aware of their spontaneous, in-the-moment response to the building. I emphasize that they are not to think about the image but simply "to see and record what you see." The pedagogical assumption is that, with practice, making the effort to say what one sees intensifies one's seeing, which in turn deepens one's ability to articulate what one sees (Bortoft, 2012).

Tables 5.3 and 5.4 summarize the 138 student responses received in my fall 2014 class when I presented an image of the Seattle Central Library (Figure 5.1). My aim here is to provide an incipient phenomenological interpretation of these responses. When asked to guess the building's function (Table 5.3), over half the students (77, or 56 per cent) supposed that it housed offices or businesses. Fourteen students remarked that it might be an arena or stadium, and seven students labelled it a museum. Five

A phenomenological and hermeneutic reading 71

Table 5.3 Student responses when asked to guess what kind of building is the Seattle Central Library

Student responses: "What would you guess this building is used for?" (N=138)

Offices or businesses	77	Movie theater	1
Arena or stadium	14	World trade center	1
Museum	7	Showroom	1
Theater	5	Casino	1
Hotel	5	Nightclub	1
Events center	5	Gallery	1
Bank	3	Library	1
Convention center	3	Performing arts center	1
Concert hall	2	Parking garage	1
Shopping mall	2	No response	5
Stock market	1		

Table 5.4 Descriptors of the Seattle Central Library provided by at least two students

Student descriptors given at least twice: "Provide at least three words or short phrases to describe what you see" (asterisks indicate evaluative descriptors)

Glass	56	Awesome*	3	Pattern	2
Reflective	39	Cool*	3	Top heavy*	2
Modern	17	Busy*	3	Important*	2
Windows	13	Odd*	3	Bold*	2
Shiny	10	Gleaming	2	Impressive*	2
Angles/angular	9	Glossy	2	Grand*	2
Unique*	7	Illumination	2	Majestic*	2
Transparent	5	Tall	2	Innovative*	2
Mirrors	5	Blocky	2	Complex*	2
Hourglass	5	Huge	2	Energetic*	2
Sharp	5	Rectangular	2	Intense*	2
Geometric	5	Tesseract	2	Strong*	2
Shapes	4	Trapezoid	2	Fancy*	2
Expensive*	4	Edged	2	Flashy*	2
Large	3	Anvil/anvil-shaped	2	Interesting*	2
Bright	3	Fish scales	2	Flamboyant*	2
Futuristic	3	Spider web	2	Odd shaped*	2
Fragile*	3	Light	2	Weird*	2
Beautiful*	3	Open	2		

students each suggested that the building might be a theater, hotel, or events center. Other guesses included a bank, shopping mall, nightclub, and casino. Only one student identified the building correctly as a library.

The fact that many students associated the building with a commercial rather than a civic function is revealing because, in his original vision of the library, Rem Koolhaas drew on metaphors of commerce: "the design team spoke of 'stealing back' the aura that was stolen from the library by the [big-chain] bookstores – and in effect 'stealing back' patrons, too" (Mattern, 2003, p. 25, Chapter 2 in this book). Using cues from retail design, Rem Koolhaas's design team referred to the library's reception area as "the retail store" and service spaces as "trading floors" (Mattern, 2003, p. 25).

72 David Seamon

Figure 5.1 Seattle Central Library, 2008. Photography by Mary Ann Sullivan and used with permission.

The Seattle Design Commission opposed these commercial metaphors, which Rem Koolhaas eventually replaced with the image of "tailored flexibility" whereby the library was envisioned as "spatial compartments" relating to specific institutional services – for example, reference assistance or book accessibility (Kubo and Prat, 2005, p. 11). Although the architect claimed a shift in the building's guiding metaphor, it is telling that, at least as an exterior, the non-design students "read" the building most often as a place of business and much less often as a place of public service. On the other hand, one could argue that the wide range of ways in which the students labeled the building's function illustrates the conventional modernist supposition that form should follow function and that there is, therefore, no essential building type for a particular building function. Since only one student saw the building as a library, student responses vindicate this modernist assumption, though there remains the question as to whether ordinary users do or do not prefer buildings that clearly express their function, visually, aesthetically, and contextually (Groat, 1982, 1988).

Visceral descriptions of the Seattle Central Library

I now turn to single-word and short-phrase descriptions of the Seattle Central Library. The 138 students made use of 214 unique descriptors to provide a total of 465 words or short phrases to depict the building. In other words, many students used the same words and phrases in their descriptions. The average number of student descriptors was 3.4, though this number ranged from no descriptors (one student) to six descriptors (provided by six students and the maximum number for which the recording form provided space). Nine students provided five descriptors; 24 students, four; 28 students, two; and six students, one. By far the most number of descriptors provided (by 64 students) was three, which obviously would be the case, since students were asked "to try to provide at least three descriptors."

Table 5.4 summarizes the 56 descriptors provided by at least two students. A first feature noticeable in this list is the prominence of words associated with materiality, specifically the building's glass sheathing. The most frequently provided word is "glass" (56 times), followed by "reflective" (39), "windows" (13), "shiny" (10), "transparent" (5) "mirrors" (5), and "bright" (3). Related words, all indicated by two students each, include "gleaming," "glossy," and "illumination." Though much less frequently mentioned, the descriptors of "fish scales" (2) and "spider web" (2) point toward another aspect of the building's materiality – its web-like surfaces generated by the steel latticework holding the glass skin. The students also provided a considerable number of words relating to the unusual physical form of the building, including "angles" or "angular" (9), "hourglass" (5), "sharp" (5), "geometric" (5), "shapes" (4), "large" (3), "tall" (2), "blocky" (2), "huge" (2), "rectangular" (2), "tesseract" (2), "trapezoid" (2), "edged," and "anvil" or "anvil-shaped" (2). Perhaps the most significant aspect of Table 5.4 is that the largest number of descriptors (25 or 45 per cent) are evaluative in a positive or negative way: for example, "beautiful," "awesome," "cool," "bold," "majestic," and "energetic," versus "top heavy," "flamboyant," "weird," and "odd" or "odd shaped." Only two of the descriptors used at least twice relate to architectural style: "modern" (17) and "futuristic" (3).

In examining students' descriptor clusters and words and phrases provided only once, one notes that the interpretive picture of the building widens considerably. Examples of striking words and phrases used by only one student include "anti-gravity-like," "attention getter," "disco ball," "feels unsafe," "funnel-shaped," "how is this a thing?" "illusion," "Las Vegas," "textile," "woven," "metallic," "overbearing," "power," and "resolute." Many of the descriptive clusters are particularly insightful, for example:

- "sleek, shiny, cool";
- "transparent, suit and tie";
- "reflective, hourglass, fancy";
- "strong, teetering, transparent";
- "loud, flamboyant, impractical";
- "business, money, growth, greed";
- "hard, unforgiving, cage-like, prison";
- "flashy, reflective, top heavy, pointed";
- "amazing, awesome, erupting from the ground";
- "Tron, geometric circuit, cubical, spaceship station."

Though these clusters evoke a wide range of meanings and images, they all specify reasonable interpretive descriptions. Some clusters suggest a strong liking for the building (e.g., "sleek, shiny, cool") whereas others seem to criticize or even condemn the building, whether for its aesthetics, its size and structure, or its possible functions (e.g., "loud, flamboyant, impractical" or "business, money, growth, greed"). The major point that these student descriptions illustrate is that any building can be described and interpreted visually and aesthetically in a wide range of ways that no doubt vary according to each perceiver's individual, social, and cultural background. One could examine, for example, whether male and female students' descriptions of the building varied or whether students in different professional and academic programs saw the building differently. These perceived differences are important, but the primary phenomenological aim here is to gain a more comprehensive understanding of how the building is first engaged visually. Although the architectural encounter presented here involved only one visual image and no actual first-hand experience of the building, the explication offers some preliminary evidence for how newcomers first see and respond to the Seattle Central Library as architecture.

I next turn to the work of Thiis-Evensen, who has developed a phenomenological language to clarify the visceral, sensuous, embodied dimension of architectural experience. My aim is to suggest how Thiis-Evensen's descriptive language offers one useful means for clarifying one's encounter with, and understanding of, Rem Koolhaas's building.

Thiis-Evensen's architectural archetypes and the Seattle Central Library

In *Archetypes in Architecture*, Thomas Thiis-Evensen's aim is to understand "the universality of architectural expression" (Thiis-Evensen, 1989, p. 8). His interpretive means is what he calls architectural archetypes – "the most basic elements of architecture," which he identifies as floor, wall, and roof (Thiis-Evensen, 1989, p. 8). Thiis-Evensen proposes that the lived dimensions of a building can be clarified phenomenologically through what he calls the three existential expressions of architecture: motion, weight, and substance (Thiis-Evensen, 1989, p. 21). By motion, he means the architectural element's expression of dynamism or inertia – i.e., whether the element seems to expand, to contract, or to rest in balance. In turn, weight refers to the element's expression of heaviness or lightness, and substance involves the element's material expression – whether it seems soft or hard, coarse or fine, warm or cold, and so forth. How, asks Thiis-Evensen, does a building's floor, wall, and roof express "insideness" and "outsideness" through motion, weight, and substance?

At the start, it is important to understand that Thiis-Evensen's architectural phenomenology applies only to the experience of being outside a building. The interpretive context is encountering the building's exterior expression as a whole and then moving toward its main entrance and partaking in the entry experience right up to the experiencer's entering the building. Other than in his discussion of the roof, Thiis-Evensen says little about interior architectural experiences or the experience of being in a building and exiting. He infers that interior architectural experience points to a complementary phenomenological project that might be inspired by his work on exterior architectural experience (Thiis-Evensen, 1989, pp. 17–18). Here, then, I give attention only to the Seattle Central Library as one is outside and preparing to go in. I examine the two pedestrian-entry facades of the building – the west and east walls (or Fourth and Fifth Avenue elevations) – and ask how they might be interpreted via Thiis-Evensen's phenomenological language (Figures 5.2 and 5.3). My aim is not to provide an exhaustive explication but to use lived aspects of the west and east walls to illustrate what Thiis-Evensen's phenomenological approach entails. I hope

Figures 5.2 Seattle Central Library, 2008. West entry wall. Photograph by Mary Ann Sullivan and used with permission.

to demonstrate its considerable value for understanding the visceral, pre-conscious dimensions of architectural experience of which we are normally unaware and mostly take for granted.

In interpreting any exterior wall, Thiis-Evensen is primarily concerned with its expression of the inside–outside relationship. Does the wall seem open and welcoming, closed and withholding, or neutral? Do material and structural qualities of the wall draw the outside in or the inside out? How is the relative degree of connectedness, separation, or neutrality between inside and outside evoked through motion, weight, and substance? To answer questions like these, Thiis-Evensen examines the wall in three ways: first, its horizontal expression, or breadth theme; second, its vertical expression, or height theme; and, third, its expression of approaching and entering – the wall's depth theme (Figure 5.4). Since via depth, we encounter buildings most directly by passing into their interiors, depth is the wall's most complex dimension, which Thiis-Evensen explores in terms of three aspects: first, main form (e.g., flat versus curved or degree of slant inward or outward); second, building system (e.g., massive, skeletal, infilled, or layered); and, third, openings (for the most part, doors and windows). Here, I examine the west and east entry walls of the Seattle Central Library, first, in terms of breadth and height themes. I then consider depth qualities and ask how the resulting insights help to clarify one's architectural experience of the building.

76 *David Seamon*

Figure 5.3 Seattle Central Library, 2008. East entry wall. Photograph by Mary Ann Sullivan and used with permission.

The west entry wall: breadth and height

In interpreting a wall's horizontal and vertical expressions of breadth and height, Thiis-Evensen envisions every wall as a surface with three vertical fields (right, middle, and left) and three horizontal fields (upper, middle, and lower) (Figure 5.4, breadth and height). Using as evidence building examples throughout architectural history, he contends that there are four major ways each that the breadth and height themes have typically been expressed in building form. As summarized in Figures 5.5 and 5.6, each of these eight motifs, as he calls them, involves contrasting lived expressions of motion, weight, and substance and the building's inside–outside relationship.

In explicating the Seattle Central Library's west entry wall (Figure 5.2) in terms of the horizontal expression of breadth, one realizes that, breaking the wall into three clear vertical fields is not possible or appropriate. In its overall horizontal expression, the wall is one continuous field with shifting planar surfaces offering no indication of divisible side and middle fields. One could argue that the folding back of surface planes on the wall's southwest corner conveys a weak right motif that often incorporated, traditionally, an important building entrance intimating a sense of inside–outside separation and privacy (Thiis-Evensen, 1989, p. 125). Here, however, the library entry has minimal visual or experiential connection in relation to the canopy's shifting roof

A phenomenological and hermeneutic reading 77

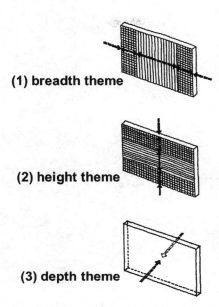

Figure 5.4 According to Thiis-Evensen, the wall expresses insideness-outsideness and motion, weight, and substance in three ways: first, horizontally, in terms of *breadth*; second, vertically in terms of *height*; and, third, directly, through *depth* – i.e., approaching and moving through the wall. To better identify qualities of breadth and height, Thiis-Evensen envisions the wall as three vertical and horizontal fields of energy; see Figures 5.5 and 5.6. Figure based on Thiis-Evensen, 1989, p. 117.

line. As a result, the frequent architectural association between entry and right motif is not present.

The west wall does have a clear height theme: a sinking motif, marked by the wall's overall vertical sense of downward movement, in spite of the gridded glass transparency (Figure 5.7). An upper field is marked by the entire multi-planar surface running from the top of the building to the deep, overhanging cantilever running the full extent of the west wall. The building's middle horizontal field is the vertically grilled glass wall below the cantilevered canopy and accommodating the west entrance. As in many buildings with sinking motifs, the dominant downward thrust of the upper field – in this case, intensified by the overhanging "weight" of the entry canopy – is so powerful that the building's bottom field is pushed vertically into the earth and thus is not visible (Thiis-Evensen, 1989, p. 135). Thiis-Evensen contends that a sinking motif can be so expressive of downward motion and overwhelming weight that the building evokes a sense of potential collapse and, therefore, bodily threat (Thiis-Evensen, 1989, p. 135). This situation seems true for the west wall, which suggests a ponderous mass pushing down and closing shut the wall's middle field that includes the Fourth Avenue entry. In terms of the inside–outside relationship, this heavy, downward thrust evokes a sense of separation and even severance between the building's interior and exterior.

Although this division and disconnection are partly blunted by the transparency and seeming lightness of the entry wall's glass surfaces (a feature of depth), the cantilevered overhang at the base of the upper field neutralizes and even overcomes this transparent

78 *David Seamon*

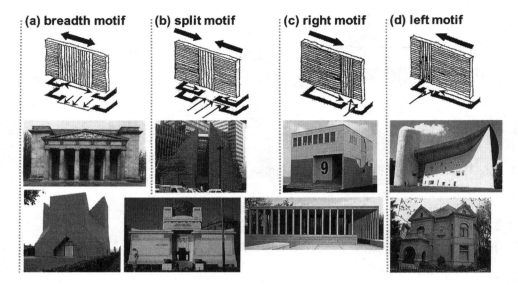

Figure 5.5 Thiis-Evensen's four breadth themes and two building examples of each. In the *breadth* motif (a), the center field dominates, and the connectedness between inside and outside is strengthened (Soldiers' Memorial, Berlin, 1817–18, Karl Friedrich Schinkel; Church and Pastoral Center, Seriate, Italy, 2004, Studio Architetto Mario Botta); in the *split* motif (b), the side fields dominate with the result that the inside is protected and outside excluded (St. Peter's Church, New York City, 1977, Emergy Roth and Sons; Modernist Succession Building, Vienna, 1899, Josef Olbrich); in the *right* and *left* motifs (c and d), one side field or the other dominates, a situation that shelters the inside and invokes a more private character (Lieb House, Barnegat Light, New Jersey, 1969, Venturi and Rauch Architects; Museum of Modern Literature, Marbach am Neckar, Germany, 2006, David Chipperfield Architects; Chapel of Notre Dame du Haut, Ronchamp, France, 1954, Le Corbusier; Reed O. Smoot House, Provo, Utah, 1892, R. K. A. Kletting). Figure based on Thiis-Evensen, 1989, pp. 118–27; photographs from author's collection.

lightness with the curious result that a civic building's interior seems cut off from the urban world outside. At the visceral, pre-reflective level of awareness that Thiis-Evensen's language attempts to locate, one can argue that the Seattle Central Library's west entry wall intimates a "keep out" rather than a welcome – seemingly, a contradictory architectural expression for a public building meant to serve Seattle citizens.

The west entry wall: depth

In turning to depth, Thiis-Evensen examines how architectural qualities contribute to the experience of directly approaching and entering a building. As explained earlier, he delineates three key aspects – the wall's main form, construction system, and openings. The Seattle Central Library's west entry wall is a complex set of depth features that both enhance and inhibit the building's entrance approach and entry. In terms of main form, the entry wall (the glazed, rectangularly gridded stretch of wall beneath the cantilevered canopy) runs the full length of the Fourth Avenue block and illustrates a horizontal wall, associated with a movement impulse "to follow along beside it in either direction" (Thiis-Evensen, 1989, p. 143). This visceral tendency to

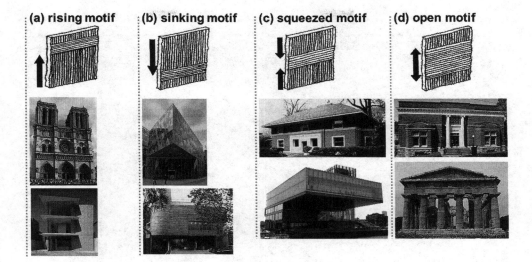

Figure 5.6 Thiis-Evensen's four height motifs and two building examples of each. In the *rising* motif (a), the middle field is pushed upward in relation to the wall's center, and the wall seems well anchored and heavy yet upright and free (Notre Dame Cathedral, Paris, 1163–1250; M-Clinic, Hiroshima, Japan, 2005, Kubota Architect Atelier); in the *sinking* motif (b), the middle field is pushed below the wall's center by the upper field, a situation that may evoke either a sense of shelter and protection or a sense of collapse and threat (Emporio Armani store, Manchester, UK, 2010, Sheppard Robson Architects; Glucksman Gallery, Cork, Ireland, 2004, O'Donnell and Tuomey Architects); in the *squeezed* motif (c), the lower field seems to rise, while the upper field seems to sink with the result that the inside seems closed off from the outside (Winslow House, River Forest, Illinois, 1893, Frank Lloyd Wright; Institute of Contemporary Art, Boston, 2006, Diller Scofidio and Renfro); in the *open* motif (d), the middle field expands by pushing the two other fields up and down with the result that there is an openness between inside and outside (Carnegie Library, Catskill, New York, 1893, George W. Halcott); second temple of Hera, Paestum, Italy, c. 460–450 BC; note that the classical temple façade expresses both open and breadth motifs). Figure based on Thiis-Evensen, 1989, pp. 128–39; photographs from author's collection.

move along the west wall rather than to enter is attenuated by the fact that the wall's construction system is a skeletal grid of framed glazing whereby experiencers outside can readily see the building's inside and, thus, feel invited to enter. This framed glazing is somewhat unsettling, however, because its vertical dimensions are irregular – door-height rectangular framing at ground level but, above, framing units of varying vertical lengths that make the framing grid seem arbitrary and slapdash.

In looking at the openings of the library's west wall, one finds some difficulty in applying Thiis-Evensen's language to Rem Koolhaas's building. Thiis-Evensen relates the window to the architectural penetration of inside out. The window, he says, involves "the 'struggle' between interior space and exterior space" and "a question of whether the interior seems to be drawn outwards or whether it remains protected within the dividing wall" (Thiis-Evensen, 1989, p. 251). Particularly significant here is the placement of a window's face because it is the "boundary relating to the interior," whereas the wall face itself is "the boundary towards the exterior and… perceived as the outer shell of [the building]" (Thiis-Evensen, 1989, p. 265). As with much modernist architecture,

Figure 5.7 Seattle Central Library's west wall vertical expression as a sinking motif contributing to a sense of separation between inside and outside; note that the "heaviness" of the wall's upper field "pushes" the bottom field into the earth.

the "windows" of the library are mostly broad sheathes of glazed wall whereby "the interior space appears to extend right out to the wall face" with the result that the building envelop and windows seem "one and the same" and walls thus seem thin or even invisible (Thiis-Evensen, 1989, p. 269). The power of the library's glass walls to "dissolve" and bring the inside out is particularly dramatic at night when interiors are illuminated and the building appears as a block-sized lantern. During the day, however, the varying transparencies of the various glazed wall surfaces generate a range of visual connectedness between inside and outside – along the west wall below the cantilevered canopy, an appropriate amount of transparency and "seeing in," though in other parts of the west wall (e.g., the walls of floors 4–11), reflections or opacity. Also relevant here is the way that much of the glass skin is held within the diamond-patterned steel latticework, which works, in relation to all the building's walls, as a kind of retaining net that holds the inside in and projects a sense of confinement and stasis.

The west wall: entry

If the window, according to Thiis-Evensen, refers to the architectural penetration of the inside out, the door expresses the architectural penetration of the outside in (Thiis-Evensen, 1989, p. 251). In entering a building, one forsakes the outside and succumbs to the inside, "'occupying' the building with all its fundamental meanings"

A phenomenological and hermeneutic reading 81

Figure 5.8 The splayed entry frame of the Seattle Central Library's west wall. Photograph by Mary Ann Sullivan and used with permission.

(Thiis-Evensen, 1989, p. 283). The door entry of the library's west wall incorporates what Thiis-Evensen terms the frame motif – in this case, a splayed concrete casing sized to fit the rectangular framing of the west wall's entry-level glazing. Thiis-Evensen points out that a frame motif typically "conveys the feeling of entering through something" and therefore prepares us for a particular mode of entry, "a process that that may begin long before one reaches the entrance itself" (Thiis-Evensen, 1989, p. 289). He illustrates how many doors with framed motifs "accentuate the person about to enter" – he gives, as examples, the Roman triumphal arch and the elaborate portals of Baroque churches.

Because Rem Koolhaas's building is an important public place for Seattleites, one would expect its entrances to invoke a significant amount of architectural force and symbolism, but this is not the case for either entrance of the Seattle Central Library. The west wall entry is a puzzling form of frame because its sides and top are splayed (Figure 5.8). A splayed frame, Thiis-Evensen contends, is typically an inappropriate entry expression because the sense of entry motion is deflected back toward the entrant because of the jam and lintel diagonals "that 'resist' motion from outside" (Thiis-Evensen, 1989, p. 259). Rather than intimating a smooth, alluring movement in, the splayed frame of the west wall entrance evokes a sense of "stay out" hesitation. Viscerally, experiencers approaching the entry are "thrown back" on themselves. Once experiencers approach the entry more closely, however, the considerable expanse of the entry's splayed sides contributes to an opposite visceral response whereby the entrant feels "sucked" into an interior of which little is now visible because of the bulk of the splayed frame. The west wall entry is doubly odd because, on one hand, it ricochets entry movement back outward, yet on the other hand, evokes an inside pull of forcible suction. Mostly, the west wall works viscerally and unselfconsciously to keep the outside out, rather than to welcome the outside in.

The east entry wall: breadth and height

As with the west wall, the east wall encompasses a sweeping, multi-planed surface not readily placed in terms of Thiis-Evensen's four breadth motifs (Figure 5.3). There is the east wall's awkwardly positioned, cage-like entry that suggests a weak left motif only indicated by the hole-like entrance opening but not extending upward into the rest of the wall above or to the sides. As already explained, the west wall's vertical expression is readily associated with a sinking motif, but the east wall is not so easily identified. The first question to ask is how the east wall might be most accurately broken into three horizontal fields. As I view the wall, I note a lower field marked by the diamond-grilled entry wall that slants inward to meet a second field, marked by the vertical wall of the library's four-story spiral book stacks. This middle field, in turn, continues upward to meet the jutting-out walls of the reading room and administrative level (tenth and eleventh floors) that mark the west wall's upper field. If the building's three vertical fields are identified in this way, what is this wall's vertical expression in terms of motion and weight? On the one hand, the façade seems to evoke lift, a gesture sustained by the recessed central field and the slanting-outward upper field that projects a sense of ascension and lightness – a situation that marks a rising motif (Figure 5.9). On the other hand, there is a certain amount of upward and downward pressure on the east wall's middle field – a situation that marks a squeezed motif (Figure 5.10). This constricting expression is conveyed by the pushing-upward thrust of the lower field's slanting inward and the upper field's slanting inward and downward. This upper field does evoke a certain amount of skyward lift (suggesting, as already said, the rising motif), but its inward-slanting surface can also be read as pushing in and down on the middle field (suggesting the squeezed motif). In short, this east wall seems ambivalent in that it conveys aspects of both rising and squeezed motifs. In this sense, the vertical expression of the south wall is uncertain and contributes to the odd sense that the east wall "moves" both "earthwardly" and "skywardly."

The east entry wall: depth and entry

One unusual feature of the Seattle Central Library's east facade is two slanting walls, to which Thiis-Evensen devotes considerable attention when discussing the wall's main form, especially how different types of main forms (convex, concave, horizontal, vertical, sloping, and so forth) evoke different approach and entry sensibilities. An entrance wall that slants outward, says Thiis-Evensen, "threatens the space where we stand" (Thiis-Evensen, 1989, p. 151). It leans over us and, like the sinking motif, suggests potential collapse. In contrast, an entry wall that tilts inward "no longer concerns us but threatens whatever is within the space on the other side" (Thiis-Evensen, 1989, p. 152). If the sloping-inward wall is a planar surface, then the wall seems to "turn its back" on the exterior space and evoke, in the approach experience,

Figure 5.9 Seattle Central Library's east wall vertical expression as a rising motif in which the middle field is pushed upward in relation to the wall's center with the result that the wall seems to lighten and lift. Source: Author.

a sense of separation and architectural difference between outside and inside (Thiis-Evensen, 1989, p. 152).

Thiis-Evensen's explication of entry walls slanting inward seems correct for the Seattle Central Library's east facade. Although the diamond grid of the inward-sloping arcade structure is unglazed and open at street level, the slant of this wall still projects a buffer-like quality that, reminiscent of a train engine's "cow catcher," seems to project an invisible "push away" energy that, coupled with the east wall's ambiguous expression of the squeezed motif, contributes to a visceral hesitation for the approaching entrant (Figure 5.11; also see Figure 5.3). In turn, this repellent quality contributes to the building's lived sense of being hermetically sealed and its interior being a world apart from the city outside.

Once one passes through the east façade's inwardly slanting entry wall, one immediately encounters the outward-slanting, glazed wall of the building interior proper – a wall type that, as already explained, Thiis-Evensen associates with potential collapse and personal threat (Figure 5.12). This visceral discomfort is partly ameliorated by a perpendicular, rectangular doorframe. This frame, however, is minimal, warehouse-like, and offers no lived sense of entering an important public building. In several different ways, the visceral qualities of the east wall weaken the connectedness between

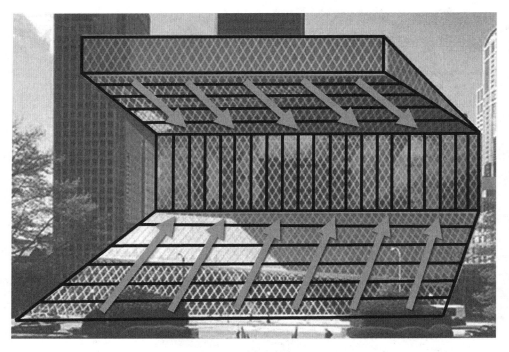

Figure 5.10 Seattle Central Library's east wall vertical expression as a squeezed motif in which the lower field seems to rise and the upper field seems to push downward with the result that the middle field's inside seems apart from the outside.

Figure 5.11 The east wall's inward-sloping arcade structure and entry. Photograph by Mary Ann Sullivan and used with permission.

Figure 5.12 The east wall's arcade entry. Note the outwardly slanting wall surrounding doors through which one enters the library. Photograph by Mary Ann Sullivan and used with permission.

inside and outside. In its ambivalent expressions of motion and weight, the east wall works to undermine the wish to enter, at least at the pre-reflective, unself-conscious level. As with the east wall entry, the west entrance viscerally sabotages the entry experience and calls into question the public function one would expect it to sustain.

Toward a phenomenology of the Seattle Central Library as a place

I next indicate some ways that a phenomenological approach might consider the relative success of Seattle Central Library as a place, which I define as "any environmental locus through which individual or group actions, experiences, intentions, and meanings are drawn together spatially" (Seamon, 2014b, p. 11). Has this library become an important place for its various user groups? How do users describe their experiences of the library, and in what ways, experientially and behaviourally, does the library sustain or undermine its central purpose – to be a repository of information conveniently accessible to patrons?

In asking these questions, we move toward a phenomenology of the Seattle Central Library experience. To illustrate how this phenomenology might unfold, I draw on two sources. First, I examine a collection of social media descriptions of the library

86 *David Seamon*

provided voluntarily by contributors to Yelp, a digital site publishing crowd-sourced reviews of businesses, public institutions, and other visitor sites. Second, I draw on a set of three reviews of the Seattle Central Library written by Lawrence Cheek, the Seattle Post-Intelligencer architectural critic (Cheek, 2004, 2005, 2007). Though there are many ways phenomenologically and hermeneutically to interpret these social media and journalistic "texts," I argue that they collectively depict the wide range of ways in which a building can be experienced and understood. Drawing on Cheek's shifting, first-hand encounters with the building, I suggest that architectural experiences and understandings often change over time. I emphasize that a building can only be fully evaluated as a place via long-term experience with the building's central purpose – in this case, being a library.

Yelp contributors' understandings of Seattle Central Library as a place

Thanks to the professional generosity of this volume's editors, I was provided access to 249 Yelp reviews of the Seattle Central Library that they and colleagues had already analysed as part of a broader social media study related to methods for post-occupancy evaluations (Conroy Dalton et al., 2013, reprinted as Chapter 10 in this book). The first Yelp review of the library appeared on 10 July 2005, and the last on 8 July 2012, the date the editors and colleagues gathered the Yelp reviews from the web for analysis. Here, I identify some of the key thematic patterns discernible in these 249 Yelp reviews. My way of working was hermeneutic in that I considered the reviews as a "text" that, with careful study, might point to broader themes and connections relating to library experiences and meanings. Procedurally, I read each of the Yelp reviews several times with the aim of locating underlying commonalities and differences that might coalesce in broader interpretive themes helping one to better understand the Seattle Central Library as a place.

In studying the reports, I was first struck by differences between library users and visitors. Of the 249 reports, I inferred that there were likely 126 user reports (50 per cent) and 104 visitor reports (42 per cent); the other 19 reports (8 per cent) weren't readily identifiable as users or visitors. I also considered each report in terms of whether, overall, it evaluated the library positively or negatively. Ninety-two visitor reports praised the library (88 per cent), five wrote negative comments, and seven offered a mixed review highlighting both strengths and weaknesses. In contrast, 94 user reports praised the library (75 per cent), but 22 (17 per cent) emphasized weaknesses and another ten (8 per cent) described both strengths and weaknesses. This evaluative difference between visitors and users is important because it indicates that time spent with a place extends users' understanding of that place, including faults and disappointments of which visitors would less likely be aware because of a more time-limited encounter.

Table 5.5 provides 12 representative Yelp user and visitor reviews, including two supportive, two critical, and two incorporating both supportive and critical aspects. One notes that, broadly, the user reviews cover a wider range of library features and qualities than visitor reviews, which mostly speak to the building's architectural design and emotional ambience. The user reviews highlight architectural design, but they also refer to wayfinding, staff support, collections, and less tangible aspects like aesthetic encounter and environmental character. One phenomenological project is to examine a greater number of Yelp and similar social media reports to identify a more

Table 5.5 Examples of Yelp reports on the Seattle Central Library: users and visitors (entries are edited to improve flow of text)

User reports	Visitor reports
Positive: My absolute favorite library. It's eleven stories of amazing architecture, fantastic book selection, and tons of nooks and crannies for you to grab a book, read, study, or do work on your laptop (free WiFi). Even if you don't need to do work there, you must stop in and go to the tenth floor to get a great view of the city and take some fun photos. The escalators and elevators are a super-fun-bright yellow, and the fourth floor is really awesome – all red. It's a Seattle gem.	Positive: The building is huge, beautiful, and full of books. The children's room on the first floor was inviting and hundreds of titles were prominently displayed. The reading room on the tenth floor was very peaceful with lots of natural light. The coolest part of the library was the book spiral. The floors slope down, and every half floor goes in a different direction. It's difficult to describe but definitely worth visiting. There is a unique digital-art display on the fourth floor showing what titles and genres people have checked out in the last two hours.
Positive: I have fallen completely in love with this library. Yes, the architecture is slightly bizarre, but it grows on you in the best way possible. Once you spend time there, the craziness of the layout starts to make more sense. The collection is vast and varied, although there can be long wait lists for popular items. The staff is generally helpful and knowledgeable. The programming they put on is top-notch. In short, this is everything a public library should be.	Positive: The architecture and ambience of this library are all I remember. The design is very modern and edgy. The library is filled with color, whether it is a red tunnel of rooms or bright yellow escalators. You have to go to the top and check out the glass windows. No words.
Negative: I believe this building fails as a library. There is a huge amount of wasted space. Some floors are metal, and you make a lot of noise when walking around. This library is noisy in general and un-library-like. The interior is chaotic and not conducive to reading and studying. Who wants to sit reading in a huge open area with a black wall? I found the ever-narrowing, floating escalators to be frightening. The building would make a good airport terminal where a captive audience sits waiting for their flights. As an airport terminal, it succeeds. As a library, it does not.	Negative: Yes, it has stunning architecture but so much unused space. I can only wonder that, if they hadn't been so concerned with doing something stunning and unconventional, they could have built something with more space to put things. Cool concept but questionable in practice. Great library for people who don't go to libraries.
Negative: This library needs to be viewed with a critical eye. I say this because it is so deceiving. Yes, it's an architectural marvel. Yes, it's sublime. Yes, it stands out. But it lacks a gut. This library has no soul. I liken it to a laser show – all chimera and no substance. Yes, the place has lots of technology, architectural mysteries, and expensive accessories, but what's the point if the book selection is limited, the audio-visual department is paltry, the chairs and common areas are sterile and uncomfortable, and the staff is less than accommodating?	Negative: I don't like this building. Inside it confuses me and reminds me of [the] Clockwork Orange.

(*continued*)

88 *David Seamon*

Table 5.5 (*cont.*)

User reports	Visitor reports
Both positive and negative: This library is always interesting to visit. I always come to this branch for my research papers, and I can always find many helpful books to check out. This library is very organized with specific floors for non-fiction, a floor for teens, a floor for meetings, etc. The staff people are very helpful, though never that friendly. The only downside for me is that the library doesn't give off a typical homely feel like other libraries do. I guess this is just a more high-tech library than those old-fashioned ones I'm used to.	Both positive and negative: Looks like it landed from outer space. And what's with all the escalators that go up but none that go down? Confusing. But you've got to love this library. On a recent Friday afternoon, the library was packed with Seattleites reading, exploring learning, occasionally napping. If you want to check email or surf the web, ask the friendly tech folks for a temporary username and password, then help yourself to the massive bank of public computers. I found the internet speed pokey and my keyboard had a sticky "e." Don't miss the dizzying suicide-leap elevator landing on the top floor. Peek over the rail for a terrifying view.
Both positive and negative: The building itself is amazing – beautiful. The colors are bright and clean. There are many books and many floors. Just watch out for panhandlers – they can't read "no soliciting." The library is right on bus lines. It is a great location.	Both positive and negative: I sure as hell wouldn't want to try to find a book here, but it looks cool.

complete range of architectural, environmental, and human qualities that sustain or undermine Seattle Central Library as a place.[3] This task is beyond the range of the present chapter; rather, I use the contrasting user and visitor reports to illustrate a basic phenomenological point: that the same place is encountered and understood differently, partly because, in relation to any building, there is a range of lived modes in terms of experiencing, understanding, and acting in that building. I end this chapter by considering potential ways in which this range of lived modes of building experience might be envisioned phenomenologically.

Conceptualizing building experiences and meanings

As far as I know, there have been few research efforts to conceptualize the various lived possibilities for who uses and encounters a building and how they do it. Some 30 years ago, Hillier and Hanson (1984, pp. 146–7) identified three groups of building users: inhabitants, those users who control the building (e.g., residents at home or sales staff in a store); visitors, users who also "occupy" the building but are in a subordinate position to inhabitants (e.g., hospital patients, hotel guests, or prisoners); and strangers, "guests" in that building (e.g., friends visiting residents at home, or store shoppers). Though somewhat confusing label-wise, these user designations are significant phenomenologically because they point to three different lived modes of encountering, understanding, and taking responsibility for a building. In this regard, the Yelp reports and similar social media descriptions are incomplete in that they

A *phenomenological and hermeneutic reading* 89

provide interpretive accounts of only "strangers" – in other words, patrons and visitors, many of them tourists. Clearly, the user base of Seattle Central Library is much broader and includes administrative staff and librarians ("inhabitants"); and maintenance and cleaning staff ("visitors"). Particularly significant in terms of user experiences is the wide range of library "strangers" – not only visitors and patrons but also homeless persons, students on class field trips, outside repair people, and no doubt others. In turn, each of these user groups incorporates varying subgroups – for example, teen, elderly, and less abled patrons. A central phenomenological question is how a particular user's lived situation leads to different modes of experiencing and understanding that building.

In this regard, one important conceptual outline is phenomenological geographer Edward Relph's explication of different modes of place experience, grounded in the phenomenological assumption that an environment becomes a place when the person or group feels a sense of lived insideness in relation to that environment – in other words, they feel comfortable, at ease, at home, and in place (Relph, 1976, pp. 49–55). The opposite lived relationship with place is what Relph terms outsideness – feeling a sense of separation, difference, and even alienation from place. Relph uses this outsideness–insideness continuum to identify several modes of place experience. These modes do not relate to one's "role" or "social status" associated with the building. Rather, they describe the kind and intensity of experience that one encounters via the building as a place. For example, incidental outsideness refers to an experience in which place is largely a background or contingent setting. This is the way the library is probably experienced by many tourists who visit the library because it is on their list of "sights to see" in Seattle. In encountering the library briefly, these "users" would typically leave with a limited sense of the building probably focused on its more unusual and dramatic aspects – a pattern indicated in many of the Yelp visitor reports described above. This mode of incidental outsideness contrasts considerably with what Relph calls existential insideness – feeling completely at home and immersed in place, to such a degree that experiencers do not usually notice its overriding significance in their lives unless that place dramatically changes in some way. One might imagine that many of the library staff and perhaps many of its users feel a sense of existential insideness in relation to the Seattle Central Library, though it is also possible that a disgruntled user or staff member might experience what Relph calls existential outsideness – feeling alienated or separate from place, which may seem oppressive, hostile, or unreal. One wonders if this mode of place might be experienced by many of the homeless individuals who frequent the library out of necessity because they have no other place in downtown Seattle to go during the day, especially in the winter cold (Denn, 2004, p. F10).

In working to understand a particular place more fully, Relph suggests that the most useful mode of place experience is empathetic insideness – being as responsive to the place as possible and allowing the place to show itself as it most thoroughly is. From a hermeneutic-phenomenological perspective, an attitude of empathetic insideness is the most revealing way to understand the Seattle Central Library as a place. To suggest how this mode of understanding might unfold, I end by examining a provocative trio of reviews written by Seattle architectural critic Lawrence Cheek in 2004, 2005, and 2007. What is striking about these reviews is that they illustrate a progressive deepening of relationship with the building. One can argue that Cheek shifts from the celebratory phase of a new building's opening toward a more sober, realistic understanding focused on how the library actually works as a place for the people who use

90 David Seamon

it. In deepening his awareness and understanding of the building, Cheek's experience illustrates Relph's empathetic insideness.

A progressive understanding

Cheek's first review of the Seattle Central Library appeared in the July 2004 issue of the American Institute of Architects' journal, *Architecture*, shortly after the library officially opened on May 23, 2004 (Cheek, 2004). As the architectural critic for the Seattle Post Intelligencer, Cheek was well versed in Seattle architecture and the selection, design, and construction process whereby Rem Koolhaas's building came into being (see Chapter 2 for a good account of this period). Like so many of the library's first journalistic reviews (e.g., Goldberger, 2004; Muschamp, 2004), Cheek's is largely laudatory: the architects have done "nothing less than reinvent the public library on at least three fronts – form, function, and spirit. And it's the last quality, spirit, that is the most resounding achievement" (Cheek, 2004, p. 41). Pointing out the uncertainties for libraries brought on by continually advancing information technologies, Cheek compliments the architects for generating a flexible design that integrates traditional library functions with new digital media. In discussing the library's relationship to Seattle's downtown, he contends that the building will work as a "big, loud generator of urban life" (Cheek, 2004, p. 39). In spite of his overall enthusiasm for the building, Cheek does have some reservations: it is "stunning" but not "pretty"; its form does not reveal the building's functional order and therefore "looks arbitrary"; and many of the interior color schemes are unsettling, including the chartreuse escalators and green restrooms (Cheek, 2004, p. 45).

About a year later, Cheek updates his impressions of the library in a review for the Seattle Post Intelligencer (Cheek, 2005). He reports on the frequently mentioned problems with wayfinding in the building. He expects that a staff effort to develop better signage might partly help user disorientation. He points out, however, that additional elevators and escalators would be the much more effective solution, which is not possible "at least not at an affordable price" (Cheek, 2005). He emphasizes that book circulation is up by 50 per cent, and that the library has become a major downtown tourist attraction. He speaks of the building's third-floor atrium, or "living room," as Seattle's "downtown city park, the focal gathering place that Seattle has otherwise failed to build" (Cheek, 2005). He reiterates his argument that downtown Seattle has needed "a prism that would gather and refract" the energy and diversity of the city, which is "what the library accomplishes both in spirit and in practice" (Cheek, 2005). Overall, he holds to his original claim that the library succeeds admirably, not only because it celebrates and stimulates the larger city but because it works well in handling the "not-so-incidental function of storing, organizing, and handing out knowledge, free to everyone" (Cheek, 2005).

Three years after the 2004 opening, Cheek's understanding of the library as a place has shifted, mostly because of his personal experience in using the building (Cheek, 2007). He wonders why, when he needs to do library research, he goes to a suburban branch library rather than to the downtown building. He realizes that, having given several tours of the library to guests, "I'm becoming less enthusiastic about Seattle's crystal palace." It is time for a re-evaluation, he explains, by considering how the building works "for people in everyday use" (Cheek 2007: C1).

He still believes that the building has contributed strongly to energize downtown Seattle. It is both "beautiful" and "bizarre" – qualities felt at gut level "when we walk around the building or wander through as sightseers" (Cheek, 2007, C1). He realizes, however, that in terms of everyday use, the building houses a wide range of problems. The third-floor atrium may work as a place of sociability but is not conducive for sustained attention to reading: "It harvests and energizes routine noise… The vast overhead space, a thrill to library visitors, works against readers – most of us instinctively crave small, private spaces when curling up with a book" (Cheek, 2007, C1). The tenth-floor reading room may offer views that connect with Seattle's downtown energy, but "once the exhilaration subsides, the truth emerges: the room is badly designed and cheesily detailed" (Cheek, 2007, C1). He recognizes that the spiral book stacks have been lauded as one of the most innovative features of the library. He has come to realize, however, that "in practice the organic ribbon is no easier for the user to negotiate than discrete floors, and in some cases it may be harder. It's relentlessly monotonous and there are few attractive study niches" (Cheek, 2007, C1). Though he appreciates the building's wide range of emotional ambiences, he concludes that the library's central problem is that it lacks joy. He writes:

> This [building] feels, in varying places, raw, confusing, impersonal, uncomfortable, oppressive, theatrical, and exhilarating. Ponder any spot in this vast building, and two, three, or more of those adjectives inevitably swirl together. That's the first indicator of trouble. If this building were fulfilling the showers of acclaim heaped onto it, all we'd be talking about is joy.
>
> (Cheek, 2007, C1)

From a phenomenological and hermeneutic perspective, Cheek's three reviews are exemplary because they detail one perceptive person's shifting encounters with the library as a place. Though he retains appreciation for some qualities of the building, especially as it has energized Seattle's downtown, Cheek has deepened his understanding of the library and brought attention to less successful design elements originally out of sight. Through spending time with the building and becoming familiar with its less visible, more atmospheric qualities, Cheek experiences a transformative understanding that provides one architecturally related example of Relph's empathetic insideness – in other words, "a willingness to be open to significances of place, to feel it, to know and respect its symbols… This involves not merely looking at a place, but seeing into and appreciating the essential elements of its identity" (Relph, 1976, p. 54). Cheek's three reviews illustrate well this "seeing into" and serve as a partial model for building evaluations grounded in a deeper, more comprehensive, lived architectural encounter.

Toward a hermeneutic phenomenology of architecture

In concluding this chapter, I emphasize that the phenomenological and hermeneutic interpretations offered here are preliminary and incomplete. They should be seen as illustrative research sketches rather than comprehensive examinations of phenomena and texts. My aim has been to provide some heuristic examples whereby students new to architectural research methods might gain an introductory sense of what

92 David Seamon

phenomenology and hermeneutics can offer architectural research. As mentioned earlier, experience and meaning often overlap and intermingle experientially and interpretively. In that sense, this chapter can be said to illustrate directions toward a hermeneutic phenomenology of architecture rather than only an architectural phenomenology, on one hand, or only an architectural hermeneutics, on the other.

The confounding relationship between experience and meaning is sometimes called the double hermeneutic (Finlay, 2011, p. 141; Smith and Osborn, 2003, p. 51) because the original experiencers (for example, the Yelp reviewers) understand the phenomenon directly via lived experience, whereas the researcher understands the phenomenon via the "text" those experiencers provide of their experiences (the Yelp reviews). In working with these texts, the researcher first attempts to distil broader themes and patterns from the original experiences or meanings – for example, my considering the Yelp reviewers in terms of users versus visitors. The researcher then uses these refined themes and patterns to bring forward more general claims and possibilities. For example, I used the findings from the Yelp reviews to argue that, ultimately, a comprehensive evaluation of any building must take into account its full range of lived encounters. I illustrated how Relph's modes of place experience offer one conceptual language for identifying and categorizing that range of lived encounters. Finally, I used one architectural critic's shifting understanding of the Seattle Central Library as an example of Relph's empathetic insideness – i.e., an engaged, progressive discovery of the library as a place for people via everyday use.

In turning to Thiis-Evensen's architectural archetypes, one realizes that his experiential language of architecture points to a somewhat different phenomenological and hermeneutic relationship among experience, text, and researcher. In examining a building from Thiis-Evensen's perspective, researchers draw on an interpretive scheme already devised via Thiis-Evensen's own architectural experience and understanding. There are no experiencers providing accounts of their architectural experiences; instead, there is Thiis-Evensen's perceptive architectural language grounded in floor, wall, and roof; motion, weight, and substance; and insideness and outsideness. In my Thiis-Evensen interpretation above, I assumed his language is one accurate rendition of architectural experience and could provide valuable insights on lived aspects of the Seattle Central Library as it is an architectural work. I hope my interpretation demonstrates that Thiis-Evensen's perspective offers a helpful way for better understanding the building in terms of its visceral, pre-reflective architectural expression.

In relation to architectural research, a central phenomenological and hermeneutic recognition is that any building has a "time-body" that begins with the architect's design vision and ends on the day the building is demolished or destroyed.[4] During the building's life, a range of human experiences takes place and a range of architectural meanings unfolds. A comprehensive phenomenological and hermeneutic rendering offers a multi-dimensional portrait of the building's lifeworlds and meanings as an architectural work and as a site of human life.

Notes

1 Introductions to phenomenology include Finlay, 2011; Moran, 2000; Seamon, 2000, 2014b; Seamon and Gill, 2016; van Manen, 2014. Discussions of the value of phenomenology for architecture include Janson and Tigges, 2013; Pallasmaa, 1996; Seamon, 2000, 2013, 2014a; Shirazi, 2014.

A phenomenological and hermeneutic reading   93

2 Introductions to hermeneutics include Bortoft, 2012; Finlay, 2011; Palmer, 1969; van Manen, 2014. Discussions of the value of hermeneutics for architecture include Jones, 2000; Mugerauer, 1994, 1995. The hermeneutic understanding of 'text' is considerably different from the post-structural and social-constructionist understanding that assumes that the text's meaning is culturally determinant and therefore shifting, relativist, and contingent. Hermeneutic researchers recognize that the meaning of a text may vary in a wide range of ways, but they also assume that this meaning instantiates a certain amount of consistency and 'self-presence' that researchers can discover via persistent, empathetic engagement with the text. In short, the hermeneutic assumption is that meaning is not solely manufactured socially and culturally but appears via resolute encounter with the text.

3 In their analysis of social media reviews, Conroy Dalton et al. (2013) identify five evaluative categories: functionality; orientation and navigation; social aspects; aesthetics and emotion; and architecture and design.

4 There are occasions when the significance of buildings continues after their physical demise, as with New York City's Twin Towers, destroyed in the terrorist attack of September 11, 2001. Another variation involves destroyed buildings that, for historical or symbolic reasons, are reconstructed – e.g., Warsaw's Old Town, largely annihilated in World War II, but rebuilt identically as the original immediately after the war. Buildings that become ruins are another temporal variant. These different ways in which the life of a building can survive point toward a "phenomenology of architectural time-bodies," an important topic beyond the range of the current chapter; one starting point is Brand, 1994.

References

Bortoft, H. (2012) *Taking Appearance Seriously*. Edinburgh: Floris Books.

Brand, S. (1994) *How Buildings Learn*. New York: Viking.

Cheek, L. W. (2004) Reading Rem: Seattle's new library by Rem Koolhaas is a tribute to the human spirit – and technological obsolescence. *Architecture* 93, 7 (July): 39–47.

Cheek, L. W. (2005) On architecture: New library is defining Seattle's urban vitality. *Seattle Post-Intelligencer*, June 27.

Cheek, L. W. (2007) On architecture: How the new central library really stacks up. *Seattle Post-Intelligencer*, March 26, p. C1.

Conroy Dalton, R., Kuliga, S. F., and Hölscher, C. (2013) POE 2.0: Exploring the potential of social media for capturing unsolicited post-occupancy evaluations. *Intelligent Buildings International* 5 (3): 162–80.

Denn, R. (2004) Library was designed with homeless issues in mind. *Seattle Post-Intelligencer*, May 20, p. F10.

Finlay, L. (2011) *Phenomenology for Therapists: Researching the Lived World*. Oxford: Wiley-Blackwell.

Gifford R. (2016) (ed.) *Research Methods in Environmental Psychology*. London: Wiley-Blackwell.

Goldberger, P. (2004) High-tech bibliophilia: Rem Koolhaas's new library in Seattle is an ennobling public space. *New Yorker*, May 24.

Groat, L. N. (1982) Meaning in post-modern architecture: An examination using multiple sorting tool. *Journal of Environmental Psychology* 2: 3–22.

Groat, L. N. (1988) Contextual compatibility in architecture: An issue of personal taste? in J. L. Nasar (ed.) *Environmental Aesthetics* (pp. 228–53). Cambridge: Cambridge University Press.

Groat, L. N. and Wang, D. (2013) *Architectural Research Methods* (2nd edn). New York: Wiley.

Hillier, B. and Hanson, J. (1984) *The Social Logic of Space*. Cambridge: Cambridge University Press.

Janson, A. and Tigges, F. (2013) *Fundamental Concepts of Architecture: The Vocabulary of Spatial Situations*. Basel: Birkhäuser.

Jones, L. (2000) *The Hermeneutics of Sacred Architecture*, 2 vols. Cambridge, MA: Harvard University Press.

Kubo, M. and Prat, R. (eds) (2005) *Seattle Public Library: OMA/LMN*. Barcelona: Actar.

Mattern, S. (2003) Just how public is the Seattle Public Library? Publicity, posturing, and politics in public design. *Journal of Architectural Education* 57 (1): 5–18.

Moran, D. (2000) *Introduction to Phenomenology*. London: Routledge.

Muschamp, H. (2004) The library that puts on fishnets and hits the disco. *New York Times*, May 16.

Mugerauer, R. (1994) *Interpretations on Behalf of Place*. Albany, NY: State University Press of New York.

Mugerauer, R. (1995) *Interpreting Environments*. Austin: University of Texas Press.

Pallasmaa, J. (1996) *The Eyes of the Skin*. London: Wiley.

Palmer, R. E. (1969) *Hermeneutics*. Evanston, IL: Northwestern University Press.

Relph, E. (1976) *Place and Placelessness*. London: Pion.

Seamon, D. (2000) Phenomenology in environment-behavior research. In S. Wapner, J. Demick, T. Yamamoto, and Minami (eds) *Theoretical Perspectives in Environment-Behavior Research* (pp. 157–78). New York: Plenum.

Seamon, D. (2013) Lived bodies, place, and phenomenology: Implications for human rights and environmental justice. *Journal of Human Rights and the Environment* 4 (2): 143–66.

Seamon, D. (2014a) Physical and virtual environments: Meaning of place and space, in B. Schell and M. Scaffa (eds) *Willard and Spackman's Occupational Therapy* (12th edn) (pp. 202–14). Philadelphia, PA: Wippincott, Williams and Wilkens.

Seamon, D. (2014b) Place attachment and phenomenology, in L. Manzo and P. Devine-Wright (eds) *Place Attachment* (pp. 11–22). New York: Routledge.

Seamon, D. and Gill, H. (2016) Qualitative approaches to environment-behavior research: Understanding environmental and place experiences, meanings, and actions, in R. Gifford (ed.) *Research Methods for Environmental Psychology* (pp. 115–35). Wiley-Blackwell.

Shirazi, M. R. (2014) *Towards an Articulated Phenomenological Interpretation of Architecture*. London: Routledge.

Smith, J. A. and Osborn, M. (2003) Interpretative phenomenological analysis, in J. A. Smith (ed.) *Qualitative Psychology*. London: Sage.

Spiegelberg, H. (1982) *The Phenomenological Movement*. Dordrecht: Martinus Nijhoff.

Thiis-Evensen, T. (1989) *Archetypes in Architecture*. Oxford: Oxford University Press.

van Manen, M. (2014) *The Phenomenology of Practice*. Walnut Creek, CA: Left Coast Books.

Wachterhauser, B. R. (1996) Must we be what we say? Gadamer on truth in the human sciences, in B. R. Wachterhauser (ed.) *Hermeneutics and Modern Philosophy* (pp. 219–40). Albany, NY: State University of New York Press.

Zeisel, J. (2006) *Inquiry by Design* (rev. edn). New York: Norton.

6 The feel of space
Social and phenomenal staging in the Seattle Central Library

Julie Zook and Sonit Bafna

Introduction

This chapter is an attempt to study how the individual experience and the cognitive understanding of the Seattle Central Library are shaped by the way users are staged within distinct phenomenal and social settings. It does so by juxtaposing standard analytical descriptions of the structure of access and vision in the building with descriptive accounts of what is noticed by the visitors under different conditions. The differential staging of visitors is shown to be an aspect of the imaginative functioning of the building, not merely an accidentally emergent quality.

Over the last few decades, several techniques have been developed that capture the geometrical aspects of what is available to vision, and these techniques have allowed researchers to generate quantitative data that can help explain individual comprehension of an environment and aspects of behaviour within it. Our study takes the position that simply quantifying what is available to vision is not enough to account for experience. Instead, we propose that it is necessary to understand what a person is primed to see within this overall field. Seeing is not simply the passive reception of information; it is an active process of filtering and sorting from what is available. In principle, any influence of the visual structure of an environment on behaviour is mediated by what is actively perceived there. At the same time, buildings also present intelligible social settings that stage users within a rich cultural environment, cuing individuals to take on the role of a specific social self with an attendant set of behavioural norms and protocols.

In buildings designed to make cultural statements, like Seattle Central Library, the reading of the environment on which the staging depends, at least to some degree, on deliberate design choices. From this perspective, architectural design must manage several tasks; it must stage the social situation, it must prime visitors to attend selectively to some parts of the visual environment and it must structure these two things in such a way as to trigger imaginative engagement.

The present chapter attempts to develop a method for understanding how a given building – here, the library – fulfils the aim of engaging the imagination, given that the building already does acceptably well on such basics as housing its programme and presenting a navigable setting. We will show that there are two aspects to the staging of users in the building – a social aspect and a phenomenal one. We will describe how existing quantitative methods mentioned above do a fairly good job of collecting data that allows one to infer social staging in buildings, but inferring phenomenal staging is a more difficult problem because much of it is subjective and depends upon the state of mind of the subject. Before we discuss that, however, we introduce our specific interest in the Seattle Central Library.

The Seattle Central Library

The Seattle Library was selected as an illustrative case study for two reasons. First, libraries are a well-established institutional type in the United States, and this implies that there already exist fairly well-known expectations about form and programme. Second, the staging of experience seems to be part of the design intention when we consider both OMA precedents and the conceptual form of library the building.

That staging users aligns with OMA's general critical intent is apparent if we take, for example, the description of the Kunsthal[1] in *S M L XL* as an indication. In this presentation of the museum building, dialogue between Vladimir and Estragon, protagonists of the absurdist play *Waiting for Godot*, appears in large print over a sequenced series of photographs, keyed to floor plans, that reconstruct a path through the building. Fine print below the dialogue instructs the reader what to see and where to move next. The time-killing chatter from *Godot* unfolds over a serial installation of architectural incidents organized along a contrived path. The present study takes a building from a practice that has tipped its hand as to its dramaturgical intentions – its intent to dramatize the experience of the seemingly mundane – to show how the phenomenal and the social both contribute how buildings construct experience and sense of self. The library's vertical circulation, for example, creates spaces of high and low incidental in-movement, which amounts to a way of managing social staging.

Although it might be argued that OMA has an aesthetic commitment to creating a particular scenography, it is programme that is central to generating form in a number of buildings and projects in the OMA oeuvre, and the disposition of programme is essential to a preliminary description of the library. Some programme-to-form strategies in earlier works in the OMA oeuvre laid out programme sequentially in neat geometries between long walls, quilted patterned layers of programme in plan, and stacked themed floors in the pursuit of strong, arbitrary-seeming programmatic difference.[2] These early strategies are diverse; one observer notes, in more recent projects a settling-in to two common design strategies for OMA and a number of firms that have spun off from OMA. There is a 'stacking diagram design strategy', in which programmatic elements are assigned to geometric diagrams that are then manipulated to create the basis of the form, and there is a wrapping skin that unifies these elements under a membrane that constitutes, and sometimes conflates, wall and roof.[3] Both strategies appear at the Seattle Central Library. The programmatic diagram disposes the building function into floors that, rather than stacking neatly along the vertical z axis, slide along the x and y axes to form a figure of irregularly stacked boxes and interstitial open floors. The whole is wrapped in a diamond-grid cladding that forms an irregular, folded exterior. From the outside, a prismatic tendency is tentatively suggested by the applied sheets of cladding, but is, then again, cancelled out by the general boxy-ness and incidental-seeming angles of the form. On the inside, an atrium is anchored by a concrete elevator core. The main and upper tented reading rooms fall under the assembled, tilted expanses of cladding, and the interior is generally interjected with abstractly shaped masses and surface treatments.

Within the programmatic chunk of the book stacks, floor plans are roughly identical. On all other floors, not only the plan itself, but the location of the floorplate over the ground, varies. From the point of view of legibility, it is significant that the elevator core appears at different points of the floor for each of the programmatic chunks. Where nothing repeats from one floor to the next, one cannot develop – in the casual, provisional way that such things typically happen – the kinds of working navigational procedure that studies in spatial cognition have identified (Moeser, 1988), and one therefore is thrown on the mercy of the local and immediate, of what is along the path, to guide choices about how to move through the building. In the library, for the most part, the immediate and local features suffice, guiding the library goer toward socially active, functionally useful spaces. The programme is portioned out into stable, closed functions, such as staff spaces, that alternate in sections with open-ended, more socially oriented functions, such as reading rooms and reference areas (El Croquis, 2004). The building enhances incidental movement into the open, socially oriented spaces by having escalators start and end in them, while limiting such ingress to the closed functions, which the escalators bypass. There are additional, if less consistent, formal differences between closed and open functions, with attractions more often opening to the atrium, and having more frequent associations with the tilted expanses of cladding. There is also a basic plan typological distinction between closed functions, which are mainly corridor plans, and the socially oriented one, which are often open plans.

For all of these formal and programmatic manipulations, the disposition of the programme in the library keeps with certain exigencies of the library building type. Areas requiring distinct public access, such as the auditorium, are kept near the entrances, stacks are located deeper in the building, the children's area is sequestered away from the quieter areas, and the backstage and office activities are kept discreetly out of sight. Apart from the disconcertingly complex circulation system, there is little that is unexpected in the overall organization of the programme itself, considered apart from the visual form of the building.

However, the Seattle Central Library adheres less to the norms of the library building type in terms of visual form and the sense of self, elicited by visual form. American libraries in the nineteenth century accommodated an urban, professional, genteel class, and their belief in the classical tradition found a compatible architecture in the Beaux Arts style which subsumed programmatic and formal elements into a symmetrical, unified composition that, in libraries, tended to include spacious promenades and large, gracious reading rooms (Chanchani, 2002). Such a library building would seem to stage in its users a sense of self – conservative and genteel; practical, but high-minded – that is distinct from the sense of self staged in Seattle, which remains, for now, an open question. We know that the OMA oeuvre shows a standing interest in social and phenomenal staging, that there are the deliberate complexities in circulation and programme, and, of course, that the aesthetics of the place are distinctive. What we intend to evaluate is how such an interest helps explain certain formal features of the building and the quality of experience within it that a straightforward concern with function and accommodation of activity cannot.

Phenomenal staging and social staging

We have talked about staging so far as if it were a self-evident term. As the reader may well be aware, the term *staging* directly reflects Erwin Goffman's description of the dramaturgical perspective in social life (Goffman, 1959). From the perspective of a method, the first issue is how to infer staging from what we know of the building. Staging is essentially the sense that a user has of being placed in a specific location relative to a given social and phenomenal setting. The methodological problem associated with staging boils down to two tasks. The first is to *describe* the landscape of the building space from specific points of view within the building, and the second is to *gauge* what is available from of this landscape and what of it is variously attended to – in other words, how it appears to a specific user.

There already exist techniques for inferring the social landscape in the sense we refer to. We will use methods based on the two-dimensional isovist, or visibility polygon, assuming that the social landscape in a building is constituted of specific morphologies of visibility and access created by the spatial organization within buildings. For any point on a floor plan, the isovist is the area that is visible, taking into account all visually obstructing or occluding elements, such as walls or fixed furniture (Benedikt, 1979). It bears emphasizing that the isovist directly conveys certain perceptual qualities of a location, such as its relative visual exposure and various qualities of the shape and edge condition of what is visible. Patterns of visual exposure, in particular, are related to the perceived 'publicness' of locations (also see Chapter 8 on emotional responses to locations in the library); they can directly influence the social self that is adopted by the user in ways well described in sociological literature (e.g., Goffman, 1959). Generally, the greater the degree of visual exposure, the less private the activities undertaken in a space will be (following Vialard and Bafna, 2009).

The space that is immediately visible to us, however, is not the only spatial entity to stage experience; the way in which spaces interlock and form connections at multiple scales is also expected to influence social staging. One can generalize the isovist to the larger building by assessing, for a systematically sampled set of locations on the floor plan, how much area the isovist covers and how many additional isovists must be traversed to cover the entire floor. Typically referred to as *high integration areas* in the space syntax literature, the parts of the floor plan that require relatively few isovist traversals to reach the whole building have been associated in the empirical research literature with greater unplanned encounters amongst occupants (Grajewski, 1993; Penn et al., 1999).[4] We will refer to these high integration areas as implicitly public. Encountering others is a hallmark of public space, and highly integrates spaces often retain a public "feel", even when unoccupied.

To sum up, we can think of a perceived sense of publicness as arising from two situations that commonly occur in buildings and are well captured by isovist-based methods: the sense of being visually exposed in a space and the tendency to run into others frequently in that location. Where values for visual exposure and implicit publicness conform to one another (e.g., you are co-present with others in large, visually exposed spaces and more isolated in smaller, more enclosed spaces), the sense of institutionalism and conformation to the library building type is enhanced. When values for visual exposure and implicit publicness mismatch, it may trigger some sense in the user of being an outsider or an observer, prompting reflective engagement with the architectural work.

Some technical notes about the measures merit discussion here. We will assess both sense of exposure and implied publicness using UCL's Depthmap software, developed by Alasdair Turner (Turner et al., 2001; Turner et al., 2005) and currently the preeminent tool used in space syntax. Visual exposure is assessed by the size of the visual field; implied publicness is assessed as mean isovist turns; this is calculated by subtracting '1' from the *mean depth* value generated in Depthmap analysis.[5] All analyses were run only for areas of the floor that are accessible to library patrons; floors for

The feel of space 99

book processing or administration-only floors as well as other 'backstage' spaces were excluded.

Phenomenal staging – a term we introduce here – reflects the visual presentation of the building to the user. The term *phenomenal* is meant to highlight the apparent forms that buildings present, rather than the actual ones – the kind of reading that Paul Frankl (1986) characterized as 'visual form'. Phenomenal reading is what makes it possible for Vincent Scully (1991), for example, to compare the piers at Chartres with 'giant, living bodies' (p.173) or Colin Rowe (1976) to describe the chapel at La Tourette as 'a tunnel compressed between vertical planes' (p.197).

In contrast to the isovist-based descriptive technique used for inferring social staging, no ready-made technique exists for inferring phenomenal staging. Literature from the space syntax research programme provides a number of examples of attempts to infer phenomenal staging through isovist-based measures. In such studies, the formal qualities that make the building distinct are identified through patterns in the geometrical qualities of isovists or changes in the relative location or orientation of surrounding surfaces that arise from paths through a building (Peponis et al., 1998; Psarra and Grajewski, 2001). However, we opted for the present approach for two reasons. First, because the phenomenal apprehension of a building necessarily involves reading experiential qualities such as light, colour, and surface texture – qualities that the exclusively geometrical isovist-based descriptions leave out entirely. More consequentially, the phenomenal reading of a building carries an inherently subjective component, and accounting for subjectivity is basically antagonistic to syntax methods that assume all potential information contained in the field of view is equally important to or equally noticed by the situated observer.

An observer traversing a building notices it selectively, and the building as it appears – not as it is actually, but as it is phenomenally – depends upon the observer's attention. There is therefore no single phenomenal description of a building. However, phenomenal reading is also not boundlessly subjective and idiosyncratic, because once attention is directed to a specific area of the scene, its resolution into contours, subjects, and specific objects – in other words, what is phenomenally read – follows explicit rules of inference (Bafna et al., 2009; Bafna, 2012; Marr, 1982; Hoffman, 1998). Furthermore, the form of attention – its locus and content – is itself predictable to a reasonable extent as well, as it is typically guided by the task at hand.

A brief recap of some basic ideas in the psychology of attention will help here. We can begin with the basic point that attention is fundamental to the phenomenal apprehension of the building. The strong form of this assertion is that without attention to something, it is impossible to have a conscious perception of it; in this formulation, attention is a necessary condition of seeing, and a series of illuminating experiments in visual perception support this view (Mack and Rock, 2000). Attention is often described as having the character of a searchlight that provides focus on a select area in the field of view and can be narrowed or widened in keeping with the interests of the observer. However, it is also true that some seeing has to happen before focal attention is brought to bear on a particular part of the field of view; without such a capacity, the viewer would not know where to direct his or her focal attention. Some researchers describe this overall general sense of what is in the field of view as a form of pre-attentive seeing (Palmer and Rock, 1994), in which the viewer is not aware of what is in the field of view even as visual information from unnoticed parts of the field of view is filtered into later attentive processes. However, there are also strong arguments for thinking of the overall general visual sense as another form of attentive perception, as a background visual consciousness (Iwasaki, 1993).[6] The presence of this always-active background consciousness is central to the descriptions we develop below; as we will see, even a habitual user completely engrossed in his or her task will be constantly aware of his or her background, even if he or she may not be able to recall what was there with any degree of specificity. This awareness includes the ability to discern the layout of broad surfaces in the background, as well as to track a general sense of light or dark and changes in relative orientation and location, but it does not support recognition of visual details, such as shapes or specific colours. The apprehension of gross and not fine details occurs because the field of view employed by this background consciousness is much larger than that utilized by the processes of focal attention. Focal attention requires the resources of foveal and para-foveal vision, but the background consciousness uses entire retinal field of view, including peripheral vision.[7]

With these things in mind, we based our investigation into the nature of staging in the Seattle Central Library on hypothetically generated vignettes of three library users pursuing specific trajectories through the building: to attend a meeting, retrieve a book, or view the building. Giving each viewer a specific task, a path to traverse, and a specific level of familiarity with (and related interest in) the building, is a way to arm our subjects with a distinct kind of attention and a specific perspective in relation to the building. This step is designed, in other words, to overcome some of the inherent subjective aspects of a phenomenal reading. The problem of subjectivity is further ameliorated if we keep in mind the point that this is a designed environment – the interior space of the building was shaped intentionally to draw attention to it and to help the viewer organize what he or she sees in specific ways.

Our methodology relies on contrived accounts of user experiences of the library; as a method, this is admittedly provisional. It is speculated that information pertinent to background consciousness is stored for a few microseconds in iconic memory store, but that it is not sent to the short-term memory registers (Iwasaki, 1993); therefore, one cannot use post-experience interviews with subjects to assess the content of background consciousness. In the face of this issue, our approach in reconstructing the quality and nature of such background awareness was to rely largely on introspection. The introspective procedure was to let one of us assume the identity of each of the viewers and try to see the building with his or her perspective, interest, and level of distraction. The description derived from the exercise, however, is analytical, and includes more observations than our subjects would report – the point is to make explicit what is noticed by each viewer, what may be examined with focal attention, what is subject to peripheral attention registering only as impressions, and how background consciousness operates within it. Such a technique, naturally, brings with it attendant problems of bias, but this should not render the accounts below entirely worthless – taken with appropriate caution, even at the very least, they help us understand the kind of information that could be retrieved from user experience and the kind of interpretive use to which it could be put.

User trajectories

Attending a meeting

The first-time visitor en route to a meeting comes in by the third floor entry and finds herself in the 'living room' (see Figure 6.1). The immediate impression is of a visually distracting, slightly chaotic environment; a bit of focused visual scanning is required to locate the escalator that will take her to the meeting rooms level, the red façade of which is visible from the living room floor. As she crosses the reading room floor, the visitor may be briefly distracted from the wayfinding task at hand by the open pit of the auditorium, the zipping elevators, the complicated, tenting geometry of the façade as viewed from the interior, and the shooting atrium. More likely, though, these will be registered within her background consciousness: that is, registered enough that later recall is possible, but not so prominently that her attention to the navigational task at hand is noticeably disturbed.

An illuminated chartreuse escalator protrudes from below the mezzanine façade. Only after the visitor has embarked can she see that it is too long and surmise that it skips a level, bringing her to the reference floor. If she knows the floor on which the meeting rooms are located, the oddity of the path must be striking – why should the prescribed path necessitate going up two levels and then finding the way back down one? The reference floor brings a rapid switch in the visual environment, abruptly introducing metallic floor tiles, black paint, and a more geometically regulated layout and appearance. Once again, the next navigational step, a stairway down to the meeting rooms floor, is not readily apparent. It is likely that the visitor would seek directions from a librarian who is prominently visible behind the reference desk. Titles of books being checked out flash behind the librarian's head on a large display screen, and the setting may well be reminiscent, in that moment, of a chaotic commercial setting, like an airport ticketing counter.

The stair is nearby and reaching it, the visitor experiences yet another rapid switch in the character of her visual environment as the smooth, baroque red plastic curves of the floor below are unceremoniously cropped where they meet the regulated geometries and frank material expression of the reference floor. The curved staircase descends gradually into a ring-shaped corridor, which is by now quite stridently red and enclosed. The visitor's motion here is continuous, leading her past the successive doors of the meeting rooms. The visitor has experienced serial rapid shifts in her perceptual environment and the forced march of the path. She may find her way into the room paying attention mainly to the numbers on the door, possibly noticing, but not actively enjoying, the panoramic window offering views onto the living room or the subtly different colours between two adjoining wall panels, one deep red, the other an intensely saturated pink.

At various points in this experience, the architecture of the building intrudes into the foreground of the visitor's consciousness, which was otherwise occupied in the task of navigating an unknown environment. The architecture does so in at least three different ways. The most subtle is in the sharp changes of the visual environment as the visitor navigates from floor to floor; these shifts are subtle in the sense that they do not play an active role in the visitor's navigational activities. They are likely registered in background consciousness. Slightly more conspicuous in its effects is the dominant visual note of the entire experience: bright colours, glossy and translucent surfaces, a

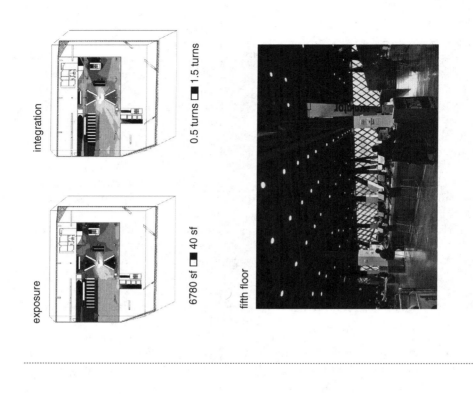

Figure 6.1 Attending a meeting. Source: Alyssa Henderson.

The feel of space 103

contrast of metals and plastics, and volumes formed from a mix of geometries. The visitor cannot relegate all of this to background consciousness because part of her activity requires sorting through visual details to find the next step toward her destination. Finally, and most intrusive of all, is the forced complexity of the route: namely, the visual and spatial disconnect between the sequence of escalators, corridors, and staircases through which the visitor needs to move and what appears to be an entirely gratuitous doubling-back of the path.

For this trajectory, the building is obtrusive in its phenomenal staging, but very normative in its social staging. For social staging, considered through visual exposure and implied publicness, the values for the floors of this trajectory generally coincide, which can be inferred by looking at similarities in the colour spectrum for the exposure values and the mean depth values. For social staging, the building behaves more normatively insofar as where one is highly visible, one is also at spatially central and potentially highly animated points of the floor, and where one is less exposed, one is in more spatially peripheral and somewhat more isolated locations.

How the library appears to a habitual user, rather than an incidental visitor, is explored through the next vignette, of a user engaged in the very typical task of retrieving a book.

Retrieving a book

The user, a regular visitor to the library, approaches the first-floor entry that opens off of Fourth Avenue, intending to duck in for a book, the call number and floor plan for the title of interest already pulled up on the screen of her phone (Figure 6.2). As she moves through the tall storefront entry, she may passively note the deep fold of façade that projects horizontally overhead. Even if she does not note it consciously, she will likely have registered a sense of going through a spacious room, composed of a diverse set of elements: a landscaped embankment on her left, geometric planting areas with low, blunt edging on her right, and the looming bulk of the building directly in front. The experience of the building, in other words, begins even before she has fully entered it. Note that these elements are all volumetrically large and simple in detail; background attention, which is characterized by scanning and surveillance and relies almost entirely on peripheral vision, is well-suited to apprehending this 'room'. It may even be argued that attending to any of these elements individually by deploying focal attention would destroy the reading of the space as a room.

As she enters the main doors, her next moves are likely to be quite automatic, and the building helps reinforce this immediacy. The doors open head-on to her intermediate destination, a bank of elevators encased in concrete. The arc of movement through the doors to the waiting area in front of the elevator is so short and abrupt that the interior of the building may barely register. But there is normally a wait for the elevators, and so her attention may be brought to bear on her surroundings. She may become aware of other users trickling into the door behind her and heading off to other parts of the building or queuing up beside her, or she may begin to passively take in the complexities of the shape of her environment, like the deep views to the circulation desk at right, the street angling uphill next to it.

The arrival at her floor (say, the seventh) brings about a sudden shift in the visual environment of the kind that we saw earlier and that is characteristic of the building. Facing the elevator is a narrow passage, and our user, as a practised visitor, knows to follow it to the right to reach her destination in the stacks. The building remains quite

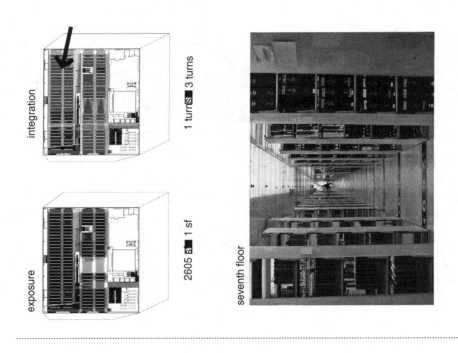

Figure 6.2 Retrieving a book. Source: Alyssa Henderson.

The feel of space   105

naturally in background consciousness here, as the user focuses on incidental details that are useful in navigating any space. Approaching the stacks, she turns right again, this time onto a corridor through the shelves. The space is long, windowless, and quite ordinary in its general ambience. The building, in other words, is unlikely to intrude into the foreground of her consciousness, allowing her to be fully engrossed in the immediate task.

A remarkable point to observe here is that the stacks are functionally and spatially one of the most innovative spaces within the building because they are organized as a continuous spiral. A first-time user might pause to reflect on this or simply test out the feel of this intriguingly, unconventional space; but, because the floor here is nearly horizontal, the fact of being on a ramp registers more intellectually than experientially.

The habitual user is more likely to register points of secondary detail, such as the periodic clearings into which small study areas have been inserted. If our visitor's search were to develop into an extended one, she might encounter another of the book spiral's spatial qualities – its relentless continuity, which progressively disorients as one naturally loses a sense of location as multiple levels are traversed and multiple turns are undertaken (Moeser, 1988; O'Neill, 1991). There are few breaks from the continuity of shelves, including a black floor-to-ceiling cube (which encloses a fire stair) and views into the central, glazed strip that houses the stairs, the long chartreuse escalators, and study areas, and these lurk peripherally in unexpected adjacencies relative to the stacks. Once again, these incidents are less likely to be actively noted by our book-engrossed user than, registered in her background consciousness; incidents like the odd visual exposure to the edges of the stairs are particularly effective because their unexpected presence and position are registered even in peripheral vision.

As for social staging, in terms of visual exposure and implied public space, the values for the floors of this trajectory diverge. On the Third Avenue entry level, where visual exposure is high, implied publicness is low and vice versa. On the floors of the stacks, visual exposure is high where there are clearings in the stacks, which tend to be remote locations, while areas of implied public space more or less occur at path crossings. This indicates that, in the stacks, the encounters and exchanges that mark public space are reduced to a function of circulation. One enters the stacks from a peripheral position, both in terms of visual exposure and spatial centrality. In a more extrapolated sense, the entire trajectory of retrieving a book takes place from marginal locations in the building. The route itself is remarkably straightforward – through the entrance, directly to the elevator, and immediately into the stacks. This is a simpler, more direct sequence of spaces than in many other contemporary libraries, which typically have more intervening spaces that act as gatekeepers.

That said, even for a completely engrossed and habitual user, the building still has the ability to leave an impression of itself and even the sparse and attenuated attention of the habitual user is sufficient for particular features of the building to make their mark on her or his consciousness. There is still the abruptness of transitions accompanied by a sudden change in the visual atmosphere, still the lurking presence of (unexpectedly inclined planes, oddly visible diagonal, building elements and momentarily unfathomable reflections). For a practised, habitual user, the building may well settle into the role of a useable entity that retains some experiential richness and liveliness of mood, but only felt as a kind of background ambience.

106 *Julie Zook and Sonit Bafna*

Then again, this inference seems to be both too forgiving and too dismissive relative to architectural intention. If all that the architects had wanted was to enrich background experience, providing what amount to moments of entertainment that break up the banality of day-to-day life in an institutional building type, then the delight of sudden changes in visual ambience, the relaxed comfort of background visual clutter, and the distracting pleasure of unexpected forms all seem to be too forced and too contrived: too much effort for too frivolous a result.

So there seems reason to posit a more consequential intent on behalf of the architects, an intent that better approximates the point of the radical approach to the library. One place to look for this is in the experience of a different kind of visitor. The library is designed not just for the everyday casual user, but also for a more architecturally oriented and thus better-prepared visitor. We continue our experiment of recreating the perceptions and experiences of hypothetical observers, focusing now on a flaneur-like, but informed sightseer, whose main purpose is a critical interest in the design of the building itself.

Sightseeing

Given the interests of the sightseer, a first-time visitor in our conception, incidental aspects of the building are likely to figure more strongly in his experience than those giving basic navigational cues (Figure 6.3). Imagine him crossing the reference floor, heading inexorably to the top of the building. The very long escalator will be what catches his eye – not just because of his navigational goal but because of the visually obtrusive way in which the escalator is present in his field of view. The strangest thing about the escalator may take a moment to register – it is just one escalator; one going up, no other coming down – and this adds to the building's sense of strangeness, of not quite knowing what to expect. Once on the escalator, the visitor momentarily releases his attention from navigational tasks and lets impressions of the building sink in. As this happens, the background awareness of the building is likely to be brought forcefully into the foreground. The phenomenal staging of the building is at its most dramatic here, as the sightseer's visual experiences merge with visceral ones. There is the sensation of rising into an illuminated puncture in the ceiling and emerging glassed-in on the other side. Floor slabs move rhythmically from the upper front to the lower rear of his visual field; similarly, the book shelves, perpendicular to the moving sightseer, rise and fall behind, one by one, and the escalator ride takes on the order of a procession that the sightseer may conceive of as rendered ironic by the revelation of the fireproofed beams, floor slab edges, and sprinklers in the near view and the harsh lighting and squat height of the book spiral floors beyond.

Not only does the visual and visceral experience combine on the escalator, the phenomenal staging it produces is further modulated by moments of unexpected social staging. Occasionally on the elevator, a person or two emerge into view on the adjacent floors. With the building already in relative motion, the appearance of people is startling. This form of staging pushes those co-present into abrupt and unexpectedly close visual contact, while they remain in their own glass-encapsulated spaces. These experiences – the odd mixture of ceremonious and utilitarian elements and the close presence of estranged others – allude passingly to experiences of urban settings or public settings like malls or airports, but the simultaneous sense of being deliberately arranged creates a sense de-familiarization.

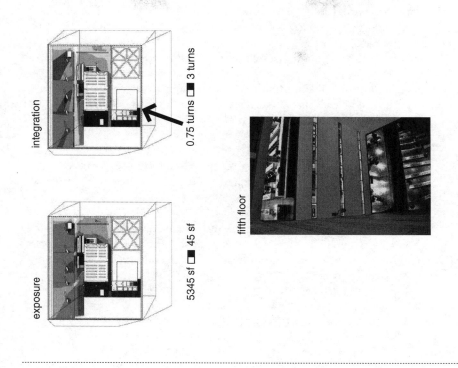

Figure 6.3 Sightseeing. Source: Alyssa Henderson.

108   *Julie Zook and Sonit Bafna*

At the top of the escalator, the sightseer registers a sudden change of visual ambience, in the way that we know to be characteristic of the building. The dark ceiling with pinpoints of light on the reference floor is here replaced by a white, cushion-tiled surface, discernible as the bottom of a suspended rectilinear block partly obscures views of the sky through a gridded glass cladding. Seeking special incidents of architectural experience, our protagonist here is very likely to traverse via ramping path to the highest, accessible point of the building, a small nub of the aisle projecting over the atrium. *Here*, he might well think, *is a view*, as he takes in the long expanse of the atrium interrupted by horizontal strips of greenish windows, the railing and metallic floor of the open mezzanine and the red band of the closed one, and the furniture and large, foliage-printed rugs of the living room floor. There may be, accompanying this appreciation, a creeping awareness of some anticlimatic sense, together with the spectacle of the view . That would be the sightseer's sense of a mismatch in the social staging; the view is grand, but it is taken alone. The extent of the view is counteracted by its isolation.

As far as social staging is concerned, the isovist measures are not well-suited to pick up important moments in the trajectory that, arise from views that occur across multiple floors. However, we can directly observe that the sightseer comes to a large overview from a spatially peripheral location that does not imply public space. The view poignantly overlooks a floor the user has likely traversed, unaware that he was visible from above.

This strategy, of presenting places one has already traversed from a distance, also occurs at the window that overlooks the living room floor from the meeting rooms floor, another large view taken from a spatially isolated position of low encounter potential. The presence of others, as well as the trace of one's prior position in the building is visible, but remote. Such staging positions the user as an outsider within the building, and this tendency is repeated in at least three other strategies within the building. First, programmatic elements are visually organized so that they are seen from the outside, but, significantly, their appearance (as a red strip façade, a black volume set in the free plan, or an atrium that is blank-faced save a few strips of windows) does not give visual clues regarding their function (as a corridor, a fire stair, and the stacks, respectively). Circulatory paths are partially occluded in dramatic ways that introduce an element of spectacle to accessing the programme. Some examples of occluded circulation paths are, stairs that ascend into a red mass and escalators that slip behind mezzanine facades or into holes in the ceiling . As a complement to this strategy, the building often frames users so that they are seen in incomplete arcs of action. If visitors are alert to all of this, they may find themselves staged socially in a distinctively fluctuating mode, sometimes as participants, sometimes as spectators, and such roles may be accompanied by secondary qualities of experience, like de-centredness or restlessness.

The library as an intensified urban setting

Buildings are designed for various purposes, not just to accommodate or facilitate certain activities, or to give a public presence to an institution. Buildings can also aim to advance thought, to present a position in the world of ideas, much as a poem or a novel might do. In the different ways that the building appeared to differently engaged visitors, we see how these different purposes have shape the form of the building presented to its various users. What appear to be liberties taken with function,

The feel of space   109

complicated navigation for the unfamiliar visitor and created abrupt changes in the visual ambience of the habitual user. These same attributes turned out to be strategies for deliberate and careful visual presentations intended to prompt thought and reflection in the more attentive visitor.

But the three vignettes above do more than bring home this essential point, a point often overlooked by those who simply criticize functional failures of buildings as failures of design; they also help reveal what is distinctive about the way the building functions. What is revealed to be truly distinctive in this building is not that it offers itself differently to differently engaged visitors, or that while catering to the reflective, imaginative attention of the interested sightseer, it also manages to lurk semi-obtrusively in the background consciousness of the distracted or inattentive visitors in a potentially enriching way; it is that the building form sustains a productive tension between the social staging and the phenomenal staging. More precisely, phenomenal staging is used in the building to create unexpected and ironic juxtapositions in social staging. Phenomenally, the library may appear as a whimsical, irreverent environment, but socially the presentation of the space may be more akin to the intensification of certain qualities of the contemporary city, characterized by close proximity and awkward encounters with strangers that never turn into events of the community-constructing variety. Such a view would seem to be in line with Koolhaas's long-standing interests in the contemporary city, interests that were articulated as early as 1978 in his *Delirious New York*. Here, we wish to point out that Koolhaas's vision of New York takes on its poignancy, at least in part, from his attention to the gap between social staging (e.g. the often-conventional links from street-to-building and from elevator-to-floor), and phenomenal staging (e.g., the intensity and variety of what was there to be experienced inside). The other thing of which we need to remind our readers is that Koolhaas's interest is not in the city per se, but in its capacity to guide a design approach based on chance and randomness rather than careful contrivance to serve instrumental ends.

The interpretive treatment of the library as an intensified urban setting, especially as an environment of accidents and possibilities, also makes the case for how the building works imaginatively. The sightseer, who is really the ready stand-in for the student or critic of architecture, explores the building, and as he does so, he becomes imaginatively involved with the building and how it presents itself socially and phenomenally. Imaginative engagement here less resembles free-form reverie than situated, perception-driven exploration, impelled as much by critical questions that the sightseer has of the design as by the simple desire to experience more phenomena.

But is the depth of such thinking available only to the architecturally alert and imaginative sightseer? Our account above would seem to suggest that the architectural experience of our habitual user, for instance, is relatively less rich. The visitor or the patron might maintain a sense of the environmental qualities and a few indistinct images of the library, but would not otherwise be a witness to the imaginative content that is potentially available in the building. In practice, even a user completely engrossed in navigation, reading, or searching would experience moments of distraction – moments in which aspects of the building would surge into the foreground and to which he or she might give some reflective attention. It is here that the semi-obtrusive visual quality of the building comes into play – even for the habitual user, the building offers a lightly nagging kind of invitation to reflect on issues of social staging.

To say that the building is able to prompt and support a focused, reflective, and imaginative engagement in its visitors, is not to declare the building a critical success; it is merely to show that it is the kind of building to which critical attention may be fruitfully given. To assess the building critically, further steps would have to have been taken, including questions such as how consistent and how original is its conception of the library as an intensified urban setting, or how profoundly and seriously does it investigate the consequences of the idea of design as chance-shaped activity. Such questions are beyond the scope of this chapter.

We are also aware that the study has some important limitations. Methodologically, there needs to be more systematic ways of recording subjective impressions that are the basis for the description of the phenomenal staging, and more work needs to be done to establish, either through observation of behaviour, or through carefully controlled self-report data, the kinds of effects that phenomenal staging can have on visitors. On both these counts, we have relied rather heavily on first-person observations from one of us. Our aim here was less to produce generalizable findings and more to make a case for the systematic understanding of the imaginative functioning of buildings.

In the end, what we have tried to show here is that attention to how differently motivated users actively see a given building, what they make of its visual environment, and how successful the design of the building is in manipulating all this, offers insights into aspects of its design that may not be easily revealed in studies of user perception or quantitative analyses of the structure of the visual environment. If nothing else, our effort should have illustrated the peculiar methodological difficulties inherent in developing systematic and reliable descriptive accounts of what is seen and perceived by different kinds of visitors. If the study is able to instigate others into more work on these methodological areas, we will consider it a useful contribution.

Notes

* This chapter was originally published as: Zook, Julie Brand and Sonit Bafna "Imaginative Content and Building form in the Seattle Central Public Library." Proceedings: Eighth International Space Syntax Symposium. 2012.
1 The Kunsthal is an art museum in Rotterdam, The Netherlands, designed by OMA and completed in 1992.
2 The Parc de la Villette, Jussieu Library, and Voluntary Prisoners of Architecture projects are other examples of a similar approach.
3 'Someone has built it before', retrieved from http://archidialog.com/tag/the-stacking-diagram/.
4 We should also note that in the studies cited above, integration and connectivity values are calculated using axial maps. However, as more recent studies have found (for instance, Peponis et al., 2008), the visual integration mapping which we use here is consistent with the axial mapping at the gross level that we operate in this chapter.
5 Depthmap assigns a value of '1' to the originating isovist in measures of mean depth; however, since from the perspective of our concern with turns, the originating position would rightly have a value of '0', we adjust the mean depth measure accordingly, subtracting 1 from it. We follow Peponis (2012) in this, although we do not use his terminology of purview and purview interface.
6 Part of the support for such background consciousness comes from experiments that show distinct capacities of the visual system to recognize 'where' specific features are located independently of knowing 'what' objects they belong to (Sagi and Julesz, 1985). The specific characteristics of information processing in background consciousness – high speed, independence

from the amount of visual information present in the visual field, and sensitivity to overall form, but not to colour – all correspond to the properties of a particular channel of information processing in the visual system (Livingstone and Hubel 1987). It is also this background consciousness that makes it possible for the overall experience of our visual environment to be seamless, and gaps in sight to be filled in imperceptibly and is quite likely utilized heavily by specific attentional mechanisms such as vigilance and visual search (Posner 1994).

7 We assume that the reader is generally familiar with the functioning of the human eye, and with the physiological and anatomical differences across the retina, but those wishing to brush up their knowledge will find Hubel (1995) wonderfully pertinent; naturally any standard handbook on vision will suffice as well.

References

Bafna, S., 2012. The imaginative function of architecture: A clarification of some conceptual issues. In: M. Greene, J. Reyes, and A. Castro (Eds), *Proceedings of the 8th International Space Syntax Symposium*. Santiago de Chile: PUC.

Bafna, S., Hyun, M., Lee, H., Antunez, C., and Yi, L., 2009. The analysis of visual functioning of buildings. In: D. Koch, L. Marcus, and J. Steen (Eds), *Proceedings of the 7th International Symposium on Space Syntax*. Stockholm: TRITA-ARK Forskningspublikation.

Benedikt, M., 1979. To take hold of space: Isovists and isovist fields. *Environment and Planning B: Planning and Design*, 6, 47–65.

Chanchani, S., 2002. Architecture and central public libraries in America, 1887–1925: A study of conflicting institutions and mediated designs. Ph.D. dissertation. Georgia Institute of Technology.

El Croquis, 2004. *OMA (I), 1996–2006*. 131/32, 34–5. Madrid.

Frankl, P., 1986. *Principles of Architectural History: The four phases of architectural style, 1420–1900*. Cambridge, MA: MIT Press. Translated by James F. O'Gorman from *Die Entwicklungsphasen der neueren Baukunst*. Stuttgart: B. G. Teubner, 1914.

Goffman, E., 1959. *The presentation of self in everyday life*. New York: Doubleday.

Grajewski, T., 1993. The SAS head-office: Spatial configuration and interaction patterns. *Nordic Journal of Architectural Research*, 2, 63–74.

Hoffman, D., 1998. *Visual Intelligence: How we create what we see*. New York: W. W. Norton and Co.

Hubel, D. H., 1995. *Eye, brain, and vision*. New York: W. H. Freeman.

Iwasaki, S., 1993. Spatial attention and two modes of visual consciousness. *Cognition* 49, 211–33.

Koolhaas, R., 1978. *Delirious New York: A retroactive manifesto for Manhattan*. New York: Oxford University Press.

Livingstone, M. S. and Hubel. D. H., 1987. Psychophysical evidence for separate channels for the perception of form, colour, movement and depth. *Journal of Neuroscience*, 7, 3416–68.

Mack, A. and Rock, I., 1998. *Inattentional blindness*. Cambridge, MA: MIT Press.

Marr, D., 1982. *Vision*. New York: W. H. Freeman and Co.

Moeser, S. G., 1988. Cognitive mapping in a complex building. *Environment and Behavior*, 20, 21–49.

O'Neill, M. J., 1991. The effects of signage and floorplan configuration on wayfinding accuracy. *Environment and Behavior*, 24, 411–40.

Palmer, S. and Rock, I., 1994. Rethinking perceptual organization: The role of uniform connectedness. *Psychonomic Bulletin and Review*, 1, 1, 29–55.

Penn, A., Desyllas, J., and Vaughan, L., 1999. The space of innovation: Interaction and communication in the work environment. *Environment and Planning (B): Planning and Design*, 26, 193–218.

Peponis, J., 2012. Building layouts as cognitive data: Purview and purview interface. *Cognitive Critique*, 6, 11–52.

Peponis, J., Wineman, J., Rashid, M., Bafna, S., and Kim, S. H., 1998. Describing plan configuration according to the covisibility of surfaces. *Environment and Planning B: Planning and Design*, 25, 693–708.

Peponis, J., Bafna, S., and Zhang, Z., 2008. Connectivity of streets: Reach and directional distance. *Environment and Planning (B): Planning and Design*, 35, 881–901.

Posner, M. I., 1994. The mechanism of consciousness. *Proceedings of the National Academy of Sciences of the United States of America*, 91, 398–403.

Psarra, S. and Grajewski, T., 2001. Describing shape and shape complexity using local properties. In J. Peponis, J. Wineman, and S. Bafna (Eds), *Proceedings of the 3rd International Space Syntax Symposium*. Ann Arbor, MI: University of Michigan, 28.1–16.

Rowe, C., 1976. *The mathematics of the ideal villa and other essays*. Cambridge, MA: MIT Press.

Sagi, D. and Julesz, B., 1985. 'Where' and 'what' in vision. *Science*, 228, 1217–9.

Scully, V., 1991. *Architecture: The natural and the manmade*. New York: St. Martin's Press.

Turner, P. A., Doxa, M., O'Sullivan, D., and Penn, A., 2001. From isovist fields to visibility graphs: A methodology for the analysis of architectural space. *Environment and Planning (B): Planning and Design*, 28, 193–221.

Turner, A., Penn, A., and Hillier, B., 2005. An algorithmic definition of the axial map. *Environment and Planning (B): Planning and Design*, 32, 3, 425–44.

Vialard, A. and Bafna, S., 2009. The structure of change in mid-twentieth century American house. In D. Koch, L. Marcus, and J. Steen (Eds), *Proceedings of the 7th International Symposium on Space Syntax*. Stockholm: TRITA-ARK Forskningspublikation.

7 Seattle Central Library as place

Reconceptualizing space, community, and information at the Central Library

Karen Fisher, Matthew Saxton, Phillip M. Edwards, and Jens-Erik Mai

Introduction

'Place' as a research phenomenon has occupied scholars in such fields as sociology, anthropology, and human and cultural geography for decades.[1] Of late, it has also proven a useful concept for understanding the multifaceted dimensions of libraries, how they are perceived and used by different stakeholders but most specifically, library users. Difficulties lie, however, in how 'place' is understood and operationalized by different researchers. Such confounding inhibits our knowledge of libraries' roles in society. In this chapter we address two primary frameworks for understanding libraries as 'place' by drawing upon findings from a field study of the newly constructed central building of the Seattle Central Library.

Early approaches to understanding 'place' tended to focus on describing its characteristics. Geographer Fred Lukermann, for example, in the 1960s – as highlighted by Relph – characterized 'place' as being where (1) location is fundamental, (2) nature and culture are involved, (3) spaces are unique but interconnected and part of a framework of circulation, (4) spaces are localized, and (5) spaces are emerging or becoming, and have a historical component (Relph, 1976, p. 3). While this framework is useful for an elementary understanding of place, it adds the complex, related notion of 'space' and does not address the myriad ways in which one may interpret 'place', such as a physical place (a lakeshore), an activity (e.g., place of worship) and a figure of speech ('she was put in her place'). 'Place' can also be explored in a cultural sense, as was the focus of Feld and Basso's *Senses of Place* (1996), which contains ethnographies of what 'place' means to such populations as the Apache of Arizona and the Kaluli people of New Guinea in terms of expressing and knowing. Lippard in *Lure of the Local: Senses of Place in a Multicentered Society* (1997) similarly discusses 'place' by blending history, geography, cultural/social studies, and contemporary art.

In the library and information science (LIS) literature, similar treatments of place have occurred, many of which resemble thought-pieces, polemics, or focus heavily on user satisfaction in addition to focusing on the library as a place of social, political, cultural, and physical dimensions. For example, Curry et al. (2004) surveyed over 500 library users in four branch libraries in British Columbia, Canada. The researchers asked library users about satisfaction with individual features and components of the building and facilities; the most highly ranked features across all settings were windows and lighting, particularly natural lighting. Numerous works thus abound of how libraries design diverse services and engage physical space and objects to address users' needs beyond those of such time-tested sources as monographs and serials. Allen

114 *Fisher, Saxton, Edwards, and Mai*

and Watstein (1996), Ginsburg (1997), Albanese (2003), Shill and Tonner (2003), and Engel and Antell (2004), for example, discuss college libraries; Weise (2004), and Ludwig and Starr (2005) focus on health libraries; Wagner (1992), Gosling (2000), St. Lifer (2001), Demas and Scherer (2002), McKinney (2002), Ranseen (2002), Saanwald (2001), Alstad and Curry (2003), Bryson et al. (2003), Bundy (2004), Wood (2003), and Worpole (2003) address public libraries; Crumpacker (1994) suggests ways that school libraries can be more inviting, while an entire issue of the regional journal *Alki* (December 1999) was devoted to professional renderings on 'the library as place'.

In introducing an issue of *American Studies* on 'The American Library as an Agency of Culture', Augst (2001) proposes that libraries function as place in three ways: as social enterprises, as part of the physical/public infrastructure, and as sites of collective memory. Thomas (1996) employs a social constructionist approach to discursively view academic, public, and school library practices architecturally. A different twist emerged from Block's (2003) interviews with non-LIS staff from the non-profit 'Project for Public Spaces' (http://www.pps.org). She reported that libraries' staunch internal focus relegates them to 'community living room[s], at best' as opposed to the community front porch – a place to launch activities and contacts with other people, instead. Four intrinsic qualities for great public spaces include access and linkages (easy to get to, connected to surrounding community); comfort and image (safe, clean, and attractive); uses and activities (has many things to do); and sociability (place to meet other people). Exemplar libraries were the New York Public Library, Multnomah County Library in Portland, Oregon, and the Beaches Toronto Branch Library.

In-depth studies of the ways in which individuals, families, neighbourhoods, and communities benefit from libraries have tended not to use 'place' as a framework. For example, Durrance and Fisher (2005) in *How Libraries and Librarians Help* discuss ranges of library outcomes as does Nancy Kranich in her edited work *Libraries and Democracy: The Cornerstones of Liberty* (2001, pp. 49–59) and Molz and Dain in *Civic Space/Cyberspace: The American Public Library in the Information Age* (1999). Fisher et al. (2004) use Fisher's related notion of information grounds (Pettigrew, 1999, p. 801) to interpret findings from their study of Queens Borough Public Library system and its immigrant users. Consequently, LIS does not have a robust framework for analysing the roles of libraries in terms of 'place' – a problem noted by Wiegand (2003) who laments the 'cost to LIS of ignoring "place" and "reading"', and by Gorman (2000) in emphasizing the wide-ranging values that the public attributes to libraries and yet is little systematically documented.

Leckie and Hopkins (2002) presented a 'place'-based framework in examining the public place of the Toronto and Vancouver central libraries. They conducted over 1,900 user surveys, 100 user interviews, staff interviews, and observational seating sweeps to gather individuals' perceptions and common usage patterns of library materials and facilities. In critiquing an interdisciplinary literature on the nature of 'public space', especially in terms of public rights, privacy, and access, they highlighted Oldenburg's (1999) assertion that 'highly successful public places' (aka 'third places'), comprise eight key characteristics. While Leckie and Hopkins did not revisit Oldenburg's framework in discussing their findings, they reported that (1) central libraries are unique, necessary, and heavily utilized places, (2) new information technologies augment as opposed to diminish the role of these places, and (3) the encroachment of private interests (e.g., ongoing commercialization) is threatening to 'transform the fundamental nature of libraries' as public places (Leckie and Hopkins,

2002, p. 360). Similarly, the notion of 'sense of place (SoP) in the context of regionalism' was highlighted by McCook (2004). Like Oldenburg, she defined sense of place as 'the sum total of all perceptions – aesthetic, emotional, historical, supernal – that a physical location, and the activities and emotional responses associated with that location, invoke in people' and further asserted that public libraries, having exemplary sense of place to its constituents, can help communities keep their distinct characters (McCook, 2004, p. 294).

Conceptualizing place

To understand library as place we selected two frameworks to guide our empirical investigation: Oldenburg's (2002) notion of the third place, and Cresswell's (2004) extended five-part definition of place. These frameworks illuminated the research problem by making core terms (e.g., place and space) explicit and operationalizable.

In his popular book *The Great Good Place: Cafes, Coffee Shops, Bookstores, Bars, Hair Salons, and Other Hangouts at the Heart of a Community(1999)*, Oldenburg introduced the phrase 'third place' and inspired the title of many community-oriented businesses such as Seattle's 'Third Place Books'. According to Oldenburg, public places such as cafes and hair salons function as 'third places', that is, where people can be found when they are not at home or work. A veritable and necessary social good, Oldenburg describes several third places and conceptualizes on their nature, which as neighbourhood locales must exhibit eight characteristics to be successful and attract people:

- Occur on neutral ground where 'individuals may come and go as they please, in which none are required to play host, and in which all feel at home and comfortable' (Oldenburg, 1999, p. 22).
- Be levellers, inclusive places that are 'accessible to the general public and does not set formal criteria of membership and exclusion' and thus promote the expansion of social networks where people interact with others who do not comprise their nearest and dearest (Oldenburg, 1999, p. 24).
- Have conversation as the main activity – as Oldenburg explains, 'nothing more clearly indicates a third place than that the talk is good; that it is lively, scintillating, colorful, and engaging' (Oldenburg, 1999, p. 26); moreover, 'it is more spirited than elsewhere, less inhibited and more eagerly pursued' (Oldenburg, 1999, p. 29).
- Are accessible and accommodating: the best third places are those to which one may go alone at most anytime and be assured of finding an acquaintance (Oldenburg, 1999, p. 32).
- Have 'regulars' or 'fellow customers', as it is these, not the 'seating capacity, variety of beverages served, availability of parking, prices, or other features', that draw people in – 'who feel at home in a place and set the tone of conviviality' while nurturing trust with newcomers (Oldenburg, 1999, pp. 33–5).
- Keep a low profile as a physical structure, 'typically plain', unimpressive looking from the outside, which 'serves to discourage pretension among those [who] gather there' and meld into its customers' daily routine (Oldenburg, 1999, p. 37).

- Have a persistent playful, playground sort of mood: 'those who would keep a conversation serious for more than a minute are almost certainly doomed to failure. Every topic and speaker is a potential trapeze for the exercise and display of wit' (Oldenburg, 1999, p. 37).
- Are a home away from home, the places where people can be likely found when not at home or at work, 'though a radically different kind of setting from home, the third place is remarkably similar to a good home in the psychological comfort and support that it extends' (Oldenburg, 1999, p. 42).

Oldenburg further espouses third places in terms of their personal benefits, which include novelty, perspective, spiritual tonic, and friendship; societal good in terms of their political role, habit of association, role as an agency for control and force for good, recreational spirit, and importance 'in securing the public domain for the use and enjoyment of decent people' (Oldenburg, 1999, p. 83) – in addition to the negative or downside of third places such as segregation, isolation, and hostility. In many ways, Oldenburg's work suggests that third places build social capital, popularized by Putnam and Feldstein as 'making connections among people, establishing bonds of trust and understanding, and building community' (Oldenburg, 1999, p. 1). Oldenburg, however, omits libraries as a potential third place, including from his 2002 edited work of 19 examples of third places from across the country that include coffee shops, a bookstore, a gym, and urban streetscape. Putnam, on the other hand, acknowledges the pivotal role of public libraries in building and maintaining social capital in his case study of the Chicago Public Library's Near North Branch Library (Putnam and Feldstein, 2003).[2]

Oldenburg's strict focus on the public or social dimensions of place alerts one to the need for addressing other nuances. In this respect we turn to Cresswell, a professor of social and cultural geography at the University of Wales who crafted *Place: A Short Introduction*. He asserts that place can be defined in five ways, the first three of which he borrows from political geographer John Agnew (1987):

1. Location: the fixed objective position or coordinates (Cresswell, 2004, p. 6).
2. Locale: 'the material setting for social relations – the actual shape of place within which people conduct their lives as individuals' (Cresswell, 2004, p. 7).
3. Sense of Place: 'the subjective and emotional attachment people have to place' (Cresswell, 2004, p. 7).

To these Cresswell adds:

4. Space: a more abstract concept than 'place', space separates places and is 'a realm without meaning' (Cresswell, 2004, p. 10).
5. Landscape: 'the material topography' whether natural or human-made, people do not live in landscapes, they look at them (Cresswell, 2004, p. 11).

In terms of libraries, Oldenburg's and Cresswell's frameworks offer insightful orientations for understanding the roles of libraries within society. Whereas Cresswell discusses five distinct facets of place, Oldenburg focuses more specifically on the social side. Noticeably absent from both frameworks if applied to a library setting, however, is the concept of information. Although information may be loosely equated with Oldenburg's third concept of conversation and books may be regarded as part of Cresswell's locale (i.e., the material setting), neither framework explicitly incorporates information seeking and consumption as a core aspect of place. Thus the current study may contribute to the foregoing frameworks by adding 'information' to the repertoire of place.

The current study

To better understand the perceptions of Seattle's denizens toward the new building, considered the world's most avant-garde public library, we drew upon the earlier frameworks of 'place' to derive the following primary research question:

> What does the Seattle Central Library mean as 'place' – socially, politically, culturally, and economically – to library users and passers-by?

In addition, we wanted to examine the impact of the book spiral. Some of its presumed advantages were ease of access, especially for disabled users, and ease of maintenance for library staff.[3] Thus, a secondary research question comprised:

> How does the book spiral affect users' understanding of how the collection is organized?

Methodology

We interviewed three groups of informants: (1) people in the book spiral, (2) people in other parts of the library, and (3) people walking by outside (passers-by), who could be users or non-users. This pool purposefully included different segments of the service population, including residents, commuters, and visitors. Users were asked 30 open and closed questions; passers-by were asked 17 of the same. Questions reflected three categories of people's perceptions of the Seattle Central Library[4], as a

- *physical place* (i.e., what they liked or disliked about the structure and its surroundings);
- *social place* (i.e., how they interacted with other people, sense of community); and
- *informational place* (i.e., perceptions of library materials and specifically the design and structure of the book spiral).

Following questions about visit frequency, participants were asked about the building and the role of the Seattle Central Library in their daily lives, finishing with free association to discover the concepts that they associated with eight basic terms: *architecture, books, community, free speech, learning, librarians, reading,* and *technology.* Participants were encouraged to respond to the free association terms with a phrase. The sequencing of the terms, however, varied across interviews to control response bias.

Rooted in early experiments by Galton in the 1880s, free association is a popular social science research method but has been rarely used in LIS. In one of the earliest descriptions of the free association method, Wheat (1931) said that difficulty lay with selecting words that could be understood in the same way by all people, especially as

118 *Fisher, Saxton, Edwards, and Mai*

ethnicity, regionalism, and English as a second language can affect word interpretation. He also noted that word types can make a difference in responses as nouns result in more common responses while verbs, prepositions, and conjunctions cause more abstract and less common answers. More recently, Nelson et al. (2000) assert that people who have similar experiences and come from similar social units are likely to have shared associations between stimulus and response words that should not be expected from others.[5] After the free association terms, the interviews concluded with demographic questions to determine how well the sample resembled a cross-section of the Seattle population in terms of age, gender, ethnicity, income, education, and occupation.

Data collection was randomly scheduled during the mornings, afternoons, and evenings to reflect the Seattle Central Library's opening hours over three weeks (8 October–7 November 2004). This time period was considered typical as schools and colleges were in session and no federal holidays occurred. Rather than drawing a proportionately representative sample, we sought a diverse sample to maximize the different perspectives available and thus utilized a non-random-sampling technique. Interviewers varied who they approached by alternating between sexes, ages, styles of dress, and apparent ethnicity. As an incentive to participate, respondents received a Starbucks espresso coupon. Two uncontrollable factors, however, may have affected people's perceptions of civic institutions, needs for information, and sense of community; namely the co-occurrence of (1) the US presidential election, which may have resulted in greater awareness and interest in political issues (e.g., the term 'free speech' during the free association component), and (2) controversial US military operations in Iraq – the perceptions and attitudes of the Seattle population toward government may have been more personally affected given the numerous military installations in the surrounding counties. Interviewers recorded responses as phrases and key words using the informant's own words, which were entered along with field notes (operational, methodological, theoretical) into QSR NUD*IST 5 (qualitative data management software). Through content analysis, we identified themes that reflected our theoretical frameworks as well as emergent themes, counterexamples, and anomalies. Following an overview of our respondents' socio-demographic characteristics, we address their perceptions of the Seattle Central Library as a physical, social, and informational place in downtown Seattle to determine what, if any, symbolic or practical meaning they attribute to the library. We conclude revisiting our two theoretical frameworks and sharing suggestions for future research.

The Seattle Central Library: its users and passers-by

We conducted 226 interviews over three weeks; 259 people declined to participate, resulting in a response rate of 46.6 per cent (about twice the response rate for a typical survey). Two thirds of the interviews occurred with users inside the building (151 interviews), and one third occurred with passers-by (75 interviews).

Almost 80 per cent had an SPL library card, indicating that the sample largely comprised library users. Participants were evenly split between men (51.7 per cent) and women (48.3 per cent). The majority was White (67.3 per cent) and spoke English as the primary language at home (86.7 per cent). Asian (12.4 per cent), Black (7.5 per cent), and multiracial (6.1 per cent) persons also participated. Ages ranged from 18 to 82, representing individuals from diverse stages of life. Education levels reflected the larger Seattle population (*American Community Survey*, 2003): 96.0 per cent graduated from high school and 56.2 per cent had a four-year degree. Participants' occupations varied, though many were students (14.1 per cent), unemployed (11.5 per cent), or retired individuals (9.7 per cent). Almost half earned less than $30,000, and close to a third earned between $30,001 and $75,000.

Seattle Central Library as physical place: structure and architecture

> I'm a warm and cozy person, so when I first saw it, it seemed cold. But now that we're here, we've made it our own place.

The preceding quote best typifies the reaction expressed by many regarding the theme of the Seattle Central Library as physical place. The architecture of the library is modern, challenging in terms of being unlike any other place in Seattle, and presents an environment that cannot be assimilated all at once. Even after a dozen visits to the site, we found new features, rooms, and spaces of which we were previously unaware. The great majority of all users and passers-by expressed strong feelings about the new building, regardless of whether they 'loved it' or 'hated it'. In their responses, participants frequently used superlatives (e.g., greatest, ugliest, most exciting, coldest, and loveliest) to describe their feelings and reactions to the physical structure. However, regardless of whether they initially admired or despised the structure, most expressed a sense of ownership of the space and recognized that this was 'their' library.

One of the most common emergent themes was that of civic pride and the role of the Central Library building as a symbol of modernity and forward thinking. Such comments were more common from passers-by, those who live and work in the vicinity of the structure, but were also echoed by those within the building. While perhaps such comments may initially sound cliché – such as one might hear from a city 'booster' – they were nonetheless the exact terms and sentiments expressed by most informants. Far from being labelled as an archaic institution in the age of the internet or being associated with a pre-digital past, the library was identified as 'new', 'modern', 'vibrant', 'exciting', 'innovative', and 'visionary', as explained by the following respondent:

> Sometimes we get stuck in notions of how things ought to be – what's appropriate and what's not. This gives us an opportunity to go out of the mode of what we think of as urban structures. Not a lot of embellished finishes. Things are open and exposed. Don't have to have all that to make it a great space.

The informants also recognized the structure as a 'spotlight', 'showcase', 'attraction', 'landmark', and 'icon'. Following the Space Needle as a city icon, the Seattle Central Library has captured the public's imagination as a unique element of the city's landscape and a point of interest for locals and visitors alike. As a respondent observed, 'This is one of the greatest additions to Seattle that I've seen in a long time. Sometimes, I purposely walk by just to pass it.' Another echoed these thoughts with, 'It's a change from how people think of libraries. I keep coming back. Sometimes, I walk through just to walk through the library.'

120   *Fisher, Saxton, Edwards, and Mai*

Focusing on the interior of the structure, another popular theme to emerge is the sense of light and spaciousness throughout the structure. Glass walls provide a sense of openness on all floors. Even within the stacks of the book spiral, a glance to the right or left will provide a vista of the streetscape and neighbouring towers. Many observed that this had an inspirational effect, using terms such as 'inspiring', 'bright', 'airy', 'never crowded', and 'open' to describe the atmosphere. One stated, 'I like the transparency between the inside and the outside. Still feels like it's part of the city even though it's a huge building.' Far from the idea of a library as a place of separation or seclusion, the structure gives the reader a feeling of greater connection with the surrounding city.

The visitor is presented with balconies and open views to the main floor at a number of places, resulting in mixed responses of delight and uneasiness, as expressed in the following observations. One expressed, 'You can go up nine to ten levels and look down over the rail. The rail comes up to my hip. You know how you get that stomach feeling, when it lurches? I love that!' while another had a negative reaction, stating, 'I was immediately taken by the suicide platform at the top.' While agoraphobics may seek out spaces toward the interior of the building that are less exposed, most informants expressed pleasure with the spacious views and grand open spaces within the structure.

The minority of informants who disliked the structure almost exclusively referred to a sense of coldness or bleak quality in the modern style. They used terms such as 'cold', 'uncomfortable', 'unfinished', 'austere', 'intimidating', and 'grey' to describe their perceptions. The predominance of 'concrete' and lack of carpeting contributed to this feeling. The building was likened to a 'warehouse' and a 'minimal security prison'. Several of these respondents sought to soften their criticism by suggesting that they didn't 'care for modern architecture' regardless of purpose or setting, and went on to make many complimentary statements about how important the library was to them. This distinction between the library as a structure and the library as a service organization indicates a depth of thought and reflection on the purpose of library in the community. One observed, 'The building isn't worth it, but the library is.'

During the word-association exercise, both positive and negative responses to the term 'architecture' were consistent across both users and passers-by alike (Table 7.1).

The last theme to emerge is the identification of the new library as an improvement over the old. Subjects described the old facility as 'tired', 'crowded', 'worn', 'deplorable', and 'falling apart'. Such criticisms of the old building are probably vocalized more frequently now as users make mental comparisons to the new structure. Beyond the aesthetic considerations of the architecture itself, informants recognized the new facility as providing more technology, more space, and more resources than the previous facility. The building draws new users, as one indicated, 'I know more people who have come to this library than the old one. They're excited about this library.' Whether the impressions regarding the size of collections are justified or not, users expressed a sense that the new building has more books, more magazines, and more CDs to offer than the old facility. Despite the ease with which materials can be shipped to any branch, several informants noted their primary motivation to visit the downtown library is to review sources that are not available at their local branch, indicating that they value 'seeing' items all in one physical space. Informants also reaffirmed the downtown location as a 'convenient' site for the library in that it provides access to both public transport and local freeways. The library has been located on this specific block in Seattle for over a century, and the residents continue to value its central location in the prime commercial heart of the city.

Seattle Central Library as place   121

Table 7.1 A sample of responses from word association – 'architecture'

	Users	Passers-by
Positive	Adventuresome	Amazing
	Amazing	Beautiful
	Artistic	Creative
	Beautiful	Cutting edge
	Brilliant	Daring
	Crazy (good)	Discovering
	Delightful	Exciting
	Funky! It's free-spirited	Eye catching
	Futuristic	Fantastic
	Inviting	Fascinating
	It fits in	Form of art
	Liberating	Functional
	Modern	Hope
	Outstanding	Inspiring
	Spectacular	Stimulating
	Tripping	Striking
	Unique	Superb
	Very sharp	Unique
	Wonderful	World class
Negative	Brutalism	A freak
	Funny looking	Atrocious
	Futuristic	Dangerous
	Ingenuous	Egotistic
	Overblown	Expensive
	Striking	Imposing
	Ugly	
	Unfinished	

At the end of the interview, users were asked if they had anything else they wanted to say to the City Librarian or Board of Trustees. One subject noted, 'I congratulate them for having the courage to make this happen', and another said, 'It means a lot for Seattle to support something that was so controversial and to move on through it… It is a testament to accomplishing things and realizing the public sector deserves the best that we can give them.' Several echoed this sentiment of courage as reflected with the decision to go with a modem architectural style and to build such a grand structure for a public institution in the face of a weakening economy. The building becomes a statement about the values and priorities of the city's residents, and the determination and strength it requires to make those priorities real in a physical sense.

The Seattle Central Library as social place

I will bring a friend next week for the very special purpose of seeing the building and each other. It's a destination, a very special building.

To come here is a kind of a social event for me. People are checking it out, which is good but it's not like I come here to find dates. Not yet, at least.

122 *Fisher, Saxton, Edwards, and Mai*

While public library mission statements have long focused upon educating the masses, librarians have been well aware of the social functions that libraries play, from the toddler who learns to share books at baby story times to the teenager who meets rambunctiously with peers in the computer room, and from the homeless who seek nooks for rest to the seniors whose only public outing may be the weekly book club meetings. Aside from a few key works (e.g., Durrance and Fisher, 2005; McKechnie and McKenzie, 2004), however, little basic research has systematically addressed the social role that the public library plays in the lives of its users. The new Seattle Central Library building was designed with the express purpose of bringing people together via its meeting rooms, collaborative work spaces, coffee stand, atria, use of colour, lighting, and furniture. Indeed, the third floor of the Seattle Central Library is called the 'Living Room'. But how effective are these efforts?

Our survey comprised several questions regarding the social effects of the new Seattle Central Library. First, we were interested in whether people came to the Seattle Central Library with other people; meaning was there a social aspect in the simple act of visiting the Seattle Central Library? Of the users, 76.2 per cent said that they had come alone that day while 23.8 per cent had been accompanied by someone else. However, when asked if they *ever* come with others, over half (53.6 per cent) replied 'yes'. Analysis determined that these companions were invariably close family, friends, or associates. Others included roommates, elderly neighbours, co-workers (en route to or from work), paid caregivers, and out-of-town visitors. The heartening finding here is that the Seattle Central Library serves as a connector, providing social opportunities for people to interact across the generations. As shown in Table 7.2, responses regarding *why* people come to the Seattle Central Library together ran the gamut: from using services and obtaining materials to sharing an experience to the pragmatic of saving parking fees. These themes were typified by users who said, 'I came with visitors from out of town; they read about the library in the newspapers and wanted to see it', 'I visit with friends at the library', 'I come with my children and husband for schoolwork. We take turns watching the kids and using the library', and 'I come with my wife and the other members of the genealogy club'.

Respondents were further asked 'Do you ever come to do things for other people?' Of the 32.5 per cent who said 'yes', the recipients of their generosity included family members, friends, roommates, and neighbours as well as students and members of groups such as the Sci-Fi Museum, book clubs, and community-based organizations. Activities that users perform on behalf of others ranged from borrowing and returning materials (books, movies, CDs), doing research using the collection, using the computers to search the web, check email, write and print documents, and working on school projects. Most representatively and memorably we were told:

- 'I look at Arab books for my woman.'
- 'Sometimes I compare financial news for friends.'
- 'My sister's in jail because of her manic depression condition. I want to help her get treatment and want to learn about what it's like for her.'
- 'I used the computers to produce a newsletter for a volunteer position I hold.'
- 'I have an invalid friend and I sometimes get CDs for her.'
- 'I come to do things for my son because he has a very busy schedule and my parents because they are home bound.'

Table 7.2 Reasons that people come to the Seattle Central Library with other people

Part of looking after children who are not in school
To use the computers/internet
To look for books, magazines, movies (kids have a bigger selection than at branches)
To read to children
To go to an activity such as baby story time
So kids can work on school projects
Friends come together to work on projects, do research (e.g., genealogy)
For 'transportation practice'
To date or to study
To visit/socialize
To have lunch together, run errands
Part of sightseeing
Parking is easier
To translate for someone who speaks/reads English poorly

Like many libraries, the Seattle Central Library features regular presentations for the public on an array of topics. Of our respondents, however, only 9.4 per cent had ever come to a public presentation – which was not surprising given how recently the building had been opened. The types of presentations they attended included children's story time, the Opening Day Welcoming Ceremony, Chinese dancing, music concerts, the Warsaw Uprising 60th Anniversary, and the September Project.

One third of users indicated that they used the Seattle Central Library for work. While the most frequent reason was to find a job, other responses included for research, to print documents, use the computer, get materials, and write documents and presentations. Our examples show that people who work in varied positions rely on the Seattle Central Library to get the job done. Occupations for which the library was a key resource included teachers, who use it to get materials for their lessons ('I'm a teacher, I look for children's books on various subjects'), chefs ('I'm looking for recipes of Thai food to cook in the restaurant where I work' and 'for work, I'm checking on specialized cooking for Italian or French cooking'), and business owners ('My business is container gardening so I look for books on this subject'). Other respondents described their work-related uses as 'I looked up stuff about the Americans with Disabilities Act and ASL – American Sign Language', 'I [used the computer] to get an application for a professional exam', 'I'm here to get educational material, technical information related to my job', and 'I research patents, children's book ideas on bees, and textile resources'. Two separate authors said that they use the Seattle Central Library as a place 'to write' and to meet with editors.

Thus far we have addressed the more obvious social aspects of the Seattle Central Library such as with whom people visit and why. Deeper understanding of the Seattle Central Library's social dimensions, however, lurks in the undercurrents of people's views of the Seattle Central Library and community, its architecture, its books and librarians, and the relationship between the Seattle Central Library and freedom of speech. Results from the word-association method using the term *community* were rich and mainly positive. Users and passers-by alike replied that together 'SPL and community' largely signified an important melding of varied people in a warm environment. Illustrative remarks ranged from the basic: 'Everybody gets together here',

124 *Fisher, Saxton, Edwards, and Mai*

'It's good for the community to have a library', 'This is a good service to the community', 'It brings everybody together, you feel like you're part of something', 'It's a building that brings different populations together', 'It feels like a place where people come together', and 'Lends itself to community; good informal public spaces', to the more analytic, such as, 'Buildings always represent community. This is a community that is really out there and willing to test the waters. Many communities would never have let this happen. [SPL] is forward looking' and, 'I think of the library when I think of the city... it's a major component. I'm trying to learn to use it better.' The few negative observations were along the line of the following: 'This library is trying to be conducive to building community, but there's a lack of information about the events here. They have the right idea, but they don't market it very well. I see advertisements about what's going on at Kane Hall [auditorium at the University of Washington] but not here. I don't know what's coming', and '[It's] forced. They're trying to create a sense of community, but forgetting some groups of people. I think this building represents a narrow-minded sense of community.'

While architecture and the trappings of physical comfort à la furniture, open space, greenery, lighting, and refreshments can do wonders for the heightening of a building and its inhabitants' sociability – as discussed earlier under 'architecture' – to people who truly know books and librarians, the latter are also intrinsic elements in the social life of a library. While responses to the word-association method regarding 'books' are shared in our discussion of physical place, they also bear mentioning here because of the pervasive ways in which both users and passers-by spoke frequently of books as their 'friends' – friends that you could meet at the library or friends that could accompany you home or elsewhere, courtesy of the library. Moreover, respondents spoke about books using such terms as 'love', 'exciting', 'needed'. and 'take you away'. As a 37-year-old female library user gushed, 'anything you want is in a book except human contact, and even then if you're engrossed in the story that is a form of contact'.

Users and passers-by's views of librarians were somewhat similar if in a less openly emotive way. As a social type librarians were invariably cast as nice, kind, friendly, helpful, educated, knowledgeable, and, yet, quiet women who wear glasses and provide people with advice and aid in searching. While the users provided more comments on 'librarians' than their passer-by counterparts, their tenor was similar. A more colourful remark 'They know everything! If l say, "I read this book once and it had this girl in it", they're like "I know that book, it's right over there".' General confusion over who exactly a librarian is from amongst all of a library's staff, however, still exists in the minds of at least some users, which results in negative comments. For instance, one passer-by said 'They don't know how to use the equipment, a lot of them haven't been trained', while a user sniped 'Too overzealous. Every time I go to have a smoke I have to hide books or they stash them in a back room for a couple of days.' Another theme was that respondents felt that they did not see or interact enough with librarians. Responses along these lines included: 'Librarians are very talented... I wish there was more opportunity for us to have one-on-one contact with librarians', 'Haven't met one in this library but I admire librarians', '[Librarians are] concentrated on the fifth floor, I wonder how visible they are', 'They've been nice to me but I don't have much contact with them', and 'Unlike many of the public places that I go where I know people's names and addresses, I haven't yet gotten to know any of these librarians or their names'.

On the one hand, this suggests that the public is savvy; they know that the person behind the circulation desk or providing security is not a librarian; on the other hand, it further suggests that perhaps librarians have become invisible, that the few who haven't been replaced by technicians or paraprofessionals are mainly behind the scenes, and that a lack of name badge or other prominent signage is keeping them from being easily identified. Whatever the reasons, the public – at least those of the Seattle Central Library – admire their librarians, know their worth, and want to see and interact with more of them.

The final element in our analysis of the social dimensions of 'Seattle Central Library as place' relate to the notion of free speech. Long considered a fundamental principle of library service by librarians and those who have benefited from librarians' support of free speech, such as film director and author Michael Moore, whose work *Stupid White Men* (2001) was only published due to the efforts of librarians, freedom of expression is a nebulous concept that we were unsure that the public might connect with libraries. Results from the word analysis method indicated that this was somewhat the case in that many comments pertained to the notion of free speech itself and not in connection to free speech in terms of the Seattle Central Library. Moreover, due to the overlap in timing of our study with the national election, several responses reflected anti-Bush and anti-Republican fervour in the predominantly Democrat stronghold of Seattle. However, many respondents did have lengthy remarks that clearly illustrated an understanding of the relationship between freedom of expression and libraries. On the negative side, one user said that 'You're not allowed to talk in the library', while another asserted that free speech was 'ignored' and added 'a display on the first floor is very offensive to the President, the Republicans and our participation in the war. I have complained about it. I also asked for a typewriter to be available but never heard from anyone.' On the positive side of the relationship between the Seattle Central Library and freedom of speech, many comments were made, from the basic 'That's what libraries are for', 'Ask questions, they'll freely help you here, Very helpful in there', 'No problems with free speech at the library', 'Relates to library policy of non-discrimination', and '[They have] literature of different opinions', 'Definitely, [Seattle Central Library] is a public space, at least on the first floor. You can talk freely there', and 'It's pretty good, I liked the September project, the painting'. Other responses centred on the SPL's practice of not divulging borrowers' records, for example: 'I think it's terrific they don't give out patrons' records. Who's that guy? Ashcroft? I think he's a Nazi', and 'It's good, [the library is] protected, records are destroyed'. Perhaps the most illustrative if not oddest came from the user who said:

> I yelled at a librarian the other day. Actually he was a technician. I couldn't get logged in and he said that the computer was reserved. I said I only wanted it for 5 minutes and he said 'okay', but by that time someone else had taken it and there were no others for me. So I yelled at him, I didn't get kicked out, so I guess that's free speech.

From the responses of participants, it is very clear that the public using the Seattle Central Library have not only a wide-ranging understanding of multifaceted aspects of free speech, but also see the library as a place where free speech is practised and upheld in a variety of different ways.

Seattle Central Library as informational place

Informants readily identified the Central Library as a place for obtaining information, reading for pleasure, and learning. While this observation is not surprising, the comments of those interviewed indicate a deep recognition of the importance of information and education in their lives and also illustrate a high social value placed on learning both for themselves and for the community as a whole. Coupled with this recognition, the concept of free access was also highly valued and frequently mentioned by those surveyed. While they did not use a term such as 'digital divide', users and passers-by alike identified the communal social benefit to providing access to the internet and access to computers to all segments of the population regardless of the ability to pay.

One of the most common terms used by all subjects was 'find', regardless of what it was being sought. Informants were highly aware of the library as a place to 'find', 'seek', 'locate', 'get', 'explore', 'discover', or gain 'access' to information, or as one informant worded it, 'things you need'. They used terms such as 'gateway' and 'catalyst' to describe the library's function. As one user commented, 'It's like a treasure for me. I can get anything I want if I have time.' Another stated, 'There are more computer terminals than I've seen anywhere else. It's a real tool.' These quotes reflect two important characteristics. First, the library is perceived as an endless source of information, a thought echoed by another informant who used the term 'no boundaries' to describe what the library meant to them. Second, the informant recognized the library as a place where they must commit something of themselves, in this instance 'time', or use a 'tool' in order to gain benefit.

One evident difference between the perceptions of users and passers-by appeared in how both groups characterized what people wanted to find. Passers-by tended to define the search in terms of objects. They described the library as a place to find 'books', 'newspapers', or 'CDs'. In contrast, users more frequently spoke of 'information', 'research', or 'knowledge'. One explanation may be that users who frequent the physical library may come to know the resources and collections better than the casual observer. This difference may indicate deeper reflection on the part of the users, or perhaps a problem-solving perspective that is not necessarily shared by non-users. While passers-by placed a value on the library as a warehouse of materials, users tended to focus on what they gain from these materials. One commented, 'At this point in my life, it's a place for seeking and understanding'. This thought illustrates that the library is associated with the process of thinking and not only obtaining information.

Many of those interviewed also described the role of librarians and staff in helping them find information. Almost all statements were favourable (informants who felt free to criticize the building may have been less willing to criticize individuals) and many expressed gratitude for the assistance they have received. While it's possible that responses about libraries and librarians may be influenced by a halo effect, numerous participants gave concrete explanations of why they were pleased with assistance. One typical comment was, 'Librarians deserve whatever break they can get. The go out of their way to be helpful.' The librarian is perceived as doing more than expected in terms of finding information. Another shared perception was that librarians are patient and tolerant of those who don't know 'simple' things, as explained by the following respondent: 'I'm sure they are asked many simple questions like how to find this [he holds up a piece of paper with a call number on it] and they never seem to

Seattle Central Library as place 127

mind answering. I've never had problems getting help.' Such observations are in direct contrast to the stereotype of the librarian that permeates popular culture as an impersonal, condescending, and rule-bound individual.

In addition to finding and seeking, participants frequently discussed themes related to lifelong learning, learning resources, and learning environment. Users were far more likely than passers-by to discuss the library as a place for learning. While both groups commented on the nature of learning as a 'lifelong' process, users were more likely to describe learning as something that is 'constant' or occurring 'each day'. One user commented it was the 'main reason I come to the library'. An analysis of responses to the term 'learning' during the word-association exercise indicates that the library as a place supports learning by providing resources and creating a conducive place for learning. Both users and passers-by noted the importance of collections as sources for study, but users were more likely to comment on the environment within the building. As one stated, 'The most important aspect of the library for me is that it is a playful place. It redefines libraries and it links libraries to exploration.' The connection between place and learning is clearly recognized by the library's users.

A second emergent theme pertaining to learning involves the concept of education as a public social good and the importance of providing the opportunities for learning to the community. Respondents used terms such as 'necessary', 'fundamental', 'progressive', 'growing', and 'empowering' to describe the library's contribution to learning. One noted, 'I think it provides the opportunity for everyone in the city to attain individual growth'. Special emphasis was placed on the importance of the library as a learning place for children, as typified by one who stated, 'For me and my children, it represents a learning tool to give my children an opportunity for higher education. We couldn't live without it. They love school now.' In this quote, the notion of library as 'tool' is again illustrated. The concept of place for learning is closely tied to the concept of a place for free access. One commented that the library provides 'the opportunity to improve yourself at no charge. A free public education.'

Informants were highly vocal in how they emphasized the need for 'free' access. When asked whether the library building was worth the cost, the overwhelming majority responded affirmatively and used terms such as 'bargain', 'opportunity', and 'free' to explain their reasoning. As one participant concisely stated, 'It is less than the cost of buying books each year'. Reasons for justifying cost fell into three categories: assisting people with low income, personal savings, and cost effectiveness for the community. First, many observed the importance of free access promoting equity in the community, especially for the economically disadvantaged. Statements such as 'Poor people can use the internet' and 'Everyone can have a membership' exemplify this concern. Another responded to questions about cost by saying, 'A society without public libraries is going nowhere'. Social good, above and beyond personal benefit, is perceived as a core value in favour of spending on libraries. Others voiced a second, more pragmatic rationale explaining that the library saved them much more than it cost in terms of purchasing books and movies. As one person observed, 'Books and movies are expensive', and users and passers-by alike identified the trade-off of borrowing versus purchasing items for oneself. This was recognized most clearly by those who also expressed a large appetite, as one who stated, 'I like to read fiction, but if I bought all the new romances, it would burn a hole in my pocket... I'm very grateful that membership at the library is free.' A third argument was voiced by those who

128 *Fisher, Saxton, Edwards, and Mai*

suggested the cost was 'cheap' in comparison to other public expenditures, such as the amount spent on a sports stadium or the proposed monorail project aimed to improve public transportation. Others noted that they 'spend more on lattes' each week than the estimated per person annual cost of building the new library.

The most common criticism related to cost pertained to hours of operation. Rather than decrease the quality of service or reduce levels of staffing, the Seattle Central Library has addressed past cuts in the operating budget by closing all facilities for two weeks each year (once in winter and once in spring). A small number of informants suggested that the library should have increased hours rather than build a new facility. These observations may be naïve given that the cost of construction came from bond funds rather than operating funds, but such comments do indicate that the closures have the desirable effect of making budget cuts visible to a public that keenly desires more services and access, and feels the temporary loss.

Discussion

At the outset of this chapter we introduced two frameworks for understanding libraries – the Seattle Central Library specifically – as 'place': Oldenburg's notion of the third place and Cresswell's five component lens. Conceptually we found that that both frameworks served their primary purpose of orienting us toward our research phenomenon, meaning they helped us understand nuances among different cognate terms such as 'place', 'space', and 'landscape'. Along this vein, they also provided initial insights into how data analysis might be approached. We now return to these frameworks to discuss how well they served in these capacities and how we potentially enriched them in the course of this research.

Oldenburg's third place framework, which, as noted, has been cited severally by LIS researchers but not applied in depth, was of primary interest for its focus on the social aspects of libraries as place. While we heartedly agree that libraries are a veritable and necessary social good, our data did not support all of Oldenburg's eight propositions in establishing libraries, at least the Seattle Central Library, as a third place. Thus, in answer to the broad question 'Is the Seattle Central Library a third place?' results from our study suggest that while it may be a third place in spirit, it fully meets few of Oldenburg's criteria. For example, our data supports the following assertions:

- Occurs on neutral ground, where 'individuals may come and go as they please, in which none are required to play host, and in which all feel at home and comfortable'.
- Be levellers, inclusive places that are 'accessible to the general public and do not set formal criteria of membership and exclusion' and thus promote the expansion of social networks where people interact with others who do not comprise their nearest and dearest.
- Are a home away from home, the places where people can be likely found when not at home or at work, 'though a radically different kind of setting from home, the third place is remarkably similar to a good home in the psychological comfort and support that it extends'.

However, the following criteria or propositions were not borne out (or partially at best) by our analysis:

- Have conversation as the main activity – while conversation occurs freely, it is not the central activity featured at the Seattle Central Library, notwithstanding the library's efforts at facilitating conversation via its third-floor living room and other communal areas.
- One may go alone and be assured of finding an acquaintance – while groups may meet at the library, visitors cannot always expect to find a friend or acquaintance, especially given the sheer size and complexity of the building.
- Have 'regulars' or 'fellow customers' who nurture conviviality and trust with new-comers – persons may frequent the library and get to know others who regularly visit at the same time, but little or no special outreach is made to the new visitor.
- Keep a low, unimpressive profile as a physical structure – Koolhaas, the architect, intended to make a bold statement with the design of the structure, and the visitor is meant to experience the physical nature of the building as well as use the library's resources.
- Have a persistent playful, playground sort of mood – users clearly indicated the serious nature of the work and learning they performed in the library, and while some commented that the place was fun or playful, the mood was one of productivity, study, and reflection.

While our analysis of the Seattle Public Library does not support the third place propositions noted above, it is consistent with other third place characteristics that Oldenburg notes, such as offering such personal benefits as novelty, perspective, spiritual tonic, and friendship via its collection, staff, services, and clientele. In addition, the Seattle Central Library was highly regarded by our respondents as a societal good in terms of its political role, habit of association, recreational spirit, and importance 'in securing the public domain for the use and enjoyment of decent people' (Oldenburg, 1999, p. 83). We found little evidence, other than the odd respondent who felt that the homeless should be barred from the library, that the Seattle Central Library harbours such negative third place characteristics as segregation, isolation, or hostility. In this sense, our analysis also supports Putnam and Feldstein's (2003) observation that libraries foster social capital by facilitating human relationships via trust and understanding and hence nurture community. More significantly, we found that the Seattle Central Library supports two distinct forms of social capital, bonding and bridging, because in addition to linking together people of similar ilk they also promote diversity by assembling people of different types – themes that echo Putnam and Feldstein's (2003) observations of the Chicago Public Library's Near North Branch. Given the misfit between Oldenburg's framework and the Seattle Public Library (strong agreement on only three of the eight criteria), we ask to what degree might the framework better account for the nature of a library branch? In other words, might the smaller scale and tighter cohesiveness of a branch library make it more fully reflect the attributes of a third place? According to Oldenburg, bookstores fit the bill as a third place (Oldenburg, 2002), so why not a branch library?

Our second framework, Cresswell's five-part definition of 'place', was useful for helping clarify the differences among overlapping terms. Using this framework, responses can be classified as follows:

Location: This concept was of particular interest given the history of the site being used for the downtown Central Library for over a century. Respondents confirmed the importance of the location in terms of ease of accessibility and prominence in the heart of the city. The site is well situated for low-income residents, who were recognized as primary beneficiaries of the services, collections, and technology.

Locale: The variety of the settings within the structure accommodate a range of user's needs and purposes, including interacting with others or individual efforts. Users frequently commented on material features (plants, lights, furniture, coffee stand, colours, etc.) as they related to the activities they were conducting.

Sense of place: Respondents expressed a range of feelings and emotions associated with the building, specific structural features, collections, and the importance of the library in their own lives.

Space: Cresswell's discussion of space helped differentiate our understanding of place, but does not apply to the analysis of individual responses concerning the Central Library as a single place.

Landscape: Respondents shared their thoughts and feelings regarding how the Central Library fits into the greater topography of the city and the downtown area.

Cresswell's framework, like Oldenburg's, is a useful lens for understanding the importance of libraries as places within contemporary society. Neither, however, adequately addresses the concept of information as it figures in the broader notion of place. While information may be loosely equated with 'conversation' in Oldenburg's framework and 'books' may be regarded as part of 'locale' or material setting in Cresswell's terms, neither framework explicitly incorporates information seeking and consumption as a core aspect of place. Thus the current study may contribute to the foregoing frameworks by adding an 'informational' component to the place-based characteristics noted in these frameworks. We suggest that an 'informational place' can be operationalized as comprising all themes regarding information finding and seeking, reading, lifelong learning, learning resources, and learning environment.

Beyond extending past research on the roles that libraries play in people's lives and the values ascribed to them by employing a strong place-based framework, our study examined the perceptions of both users and passers-by in addition to employing the free association – a population and method rarely included in past studies. Moreover, the study was timed to occur a few months after the opening of the new Seattle Public Library, an unprecedented effort in library design and hence a unique opportunity for field research.

Notes

* This is a reprint and was originally published as: Fisher, Karen E., Matthew L. Saxton, Phillip M. Edwards, and Jens-Erik Mai. 'Seattle Public Library as Place: Reconceptualizing Space, Community, and Information at the Central Library.' In _The Library as Place: History, Community, and Culture_, edited by John E. Buschman and Gloria J. Leckie, 135–60. Westport, CT: Libraries Unlimited, 2007.

1 We wish to thank the Seattle Public Library (SPL) Foundation for supporting this study through providing participant compensation. We also wish to thank SPL staff Deborah Jacobs, Michele D'Allesandro, Andra Addision, and Lois Fenker for their invaluable assistance, and especially our MLIS student assistants: Peter Cole, Amy A. Dobrowolsky, Grace Fitzgerald, Betha Gutsche, Robyn Hagle, Sumi Hayashi, Carol Landry, Sarah Merner, Anne Miller, Hannah Parker, Jennifer Peterson, Christopher Rieber, and Kristen Shuyler.

2 As Jean Preer (2001) astutely lamented, Putnam omitted libraries from his popular monograph *Bowling Alone: Collapse and Revival of American Community* (2000) – an oversight he corrected after discussion with library professionals at the 2001 annual American Library Association meeting by including the Chicago Public Library as a case study in his book with Feldstein in which he discusses the importance of branch libraries in bringing people together and enabling access to electronic information across the digital divide.

3 "The majority of the nonfiction collection – 75 per cent of the entire collection – is located on the Book Spiral. This allows the nonfiction collection to be housed in one continuous run, and avoids the problem of having to move books into other rooms or floors when various subject areas expand. The spiral is an architectural organization that allows all patrons – including people with disabilities – the freedom to move throughout the entire collection without depending on stairs, escalators and elevators. Book shelves are not filled to capacity, so there is room for the collection to grow." ("Central Library" par. 17).

4 "Interview guides for users and passers-by are published on pp. 154–157 of: Fisher, Karen E., Matthew L. Saxton, Phillip M. Edwards, and Jens-Erik Mai. 'Seattle Public Library as Place: Reconceptualizing Space, Community, and Information at the Central Library.' *In The Library as Place: History, Community, and Culture*, edited by John E. Buschman and Gloria J. Leckie, 135–60. Westport, CT: Libraries Unlimited, 2007."

5 Numerous other works such as Crosland (1929); Siipola et al. (1955); Bilodeau and Howell (1965); Cramer (1968); Gerow (1977); Szalay and Deese (1978); Mefferd (1979); Silverstein and Harrow (1983); and Craighead and Memeroff (2001) also provide guidance in the selection and analysis of free association terms.

References

Agnew, John. *Place and Politics: The Geographical Mediation of State and Society*, Boston, MA: Allen and Unwin, 1987.

Albanese, Andrew Richard. 'Deserted No More'. *Library Journal* 15 April (2003): 34–6.

Allen, Frank R. and Sarah Barbara Watstein. 'Point/Counterpoint: The Value of Place'. *College and Research Libraries News* 57.6 (1996): 372–73, 383.

Alstad, Colleen and Ann Curry. 'Public Space, Public Discourse, and Public Libraries'. *LIBRES Library and Information Science Research Electronic Journal* 13 (2003). Retrieved 15 September 2005 from http://libres.curtin.edu.au/libres13n1/pub_space.htm.

American Community Survey. 2003. Retrieved from https://www.census.gov/programs-surveys/acs/.

Augst, Thomas. 'American Libraries and Agencies of Culture'. *American Studies* 42.3 (2001): 5–22.

Bilodeau, Edward and David Howell. *Free Association Norms by Discrete and Continued Methods*. Washington, DC: US Government Printing Office, 1965.

Block, Marylaine. 'How to Become a Great Public Space'. *American Libraries* April (2003): 72–6.

132   *Fisher, Saxton, Edwards, and Mai*

Bryson, Jared, Bob Usherwood, and Richard Proctor London. 'Libraries Must Also Be Buildings? New Library Impact Study'. Museums, Libraries, and Archives Council Information, Centre for Public Libraries and Information in Society. March (2003). Retrieved 15 September 2005 from http://www.mla.gov.uk/documents/sp024rep.doc.

Bundy, Alan. 'Places of Connection: New Public and Academic Library Buildings in Australia and New Zealand'. *Australasian Public Libraries and Information Services* 16.1 (2004): 32–47.

Craighead, W. Edward and Charles B. Nemeroff. *The Corsini Encyclopaedia of Psychology and Behavioral Science*. New York: Wiley, 2001.

Cramer, Phebe. *Word Association*. New York: Academic Press, 1968.

Cresswell, Tim. *Place: A Short Introduction*. Malden, MA: Blackwell, 2004.

Crosland, Harold. *The Psychological Methods of Word-Association and Reaction-Time as Tests of Deception*. Eugene, OR: University of Oregon Press, 1929.

Crumpacker, Sara. 'The School Library as Place'. *Wilson Library Bulletin* 69.1 (1994): 23–5.

Curry, Ann, Denisa Dunbar, Ellen George, and Diana Marshall. 'Public Library Branch Design: The Public Speaks!' Canadian Library Association/British Columbia Library Association Joint Annual Conference. Victoria, BC, Canada, 16 June 2004.

Demas, Sam and Jeffrey Scherer. 'Esprit de Place: Maintaining and Designing Library Buildings to Provide Transcendent Spaces'. *American Libraries* April (2002): 65–8.

Durrance, Joan C. and Karen E. Fisher. *How Libraries and Librarians Help: A Guide to Identifying User-Centered Outcomes*. Chicago, IL: American Library Association, 2005.

Engel, Debra and Karen Antell. 'The Life of the Mind: A Study of Faculty Spaces in Academic Libraries'. *College and Research Libraries* 65.1 (2004): 8–26.

Feld, Steven and Keith H. Basso, eds. *Senses of Place*. Santa Fe, NM: School of American Research Press; Seattle, WA: distributed by University of Washington Press, 1996.

Fisher, Karen E., Joan C. Durrance, and Marian Bouch Hinton. 'Information Grounds and the Use of Need-Based Services by Immigrants in Queens, New York: A Context-Based, Outcome Evaluation Approach'. *Journal of the American Society for Information Science and Technology* 55.8 (2004): 754–66.

Gerow, Joshua. 'Instructional Set and Word Association Test (WAT) Responses of Children and Adults'. *Journal of Genetic Psychology* 130.2 (1977): 247–54.

Ginsburg, Judith Renee. Placemaking: Case Study of How Participants Understand the Design, Development, and Function of an Academic Library'. Dissertation, University of Oregon, 1997.

Gorman, Michael. *Our Enduring Values: Librarianship in the 21st Century*. Chicago, IL: American Library Association, 2000.

Gosling, William. 'To Go or Not to Go? Library as Place'. *American Libraries* November (2000): 44–5.

Kranich, Nancy, ed. *Libraries and Democracy: The Cornerstones of Liberty*. Chicago, IL: American Library Association, 2001.

Leckie, Gloria J. and Jeffrey Hopkins. 'The Public Place of Central Libraries: Findings from Toronto and Vancouver'. *Library Quarterly* 72.3 (2002): 326–72.

Lippard, Lucy R. *Lure of the Local: Sense of Place in a Multicentered Society*. New York: New Press, 1997.

Ludwig, Logan and Susan Starr. 'Library as Place: Results of a Delphi Study'. *Journal of the Medical Library Association* 93 (2005): 315–26.

McCook, Kathleen de la Pena. *Introduction to Public Librarianship*. New York: Neal-Schuman, 2004.

McKechnie, Lynn and Pam McKenzie. 'The Young Child/Adult Caregiver Storytime Program as Information Ground'. Library Research Seminar III. Kansas City, KA, 15 October 2004.

McKinney, William Allen. 'Policy and Power: The Role of the Neighborhood Library in the Community and the Forces that Add to or Detract from Its Efficacy'. Dissertation, Temple University, 2002.

Mefferd, Roy, Jr. 'Word Association: Response Behavior and Stimulus Words'. *Psychological Reports* 45.3 (1979): 763–67.

Molz, Redmond Kathleen and Phyllis Dain. *Civic Space/Cyberspace: The American Public Library in the Information Age*. Cambridge, MA: MIT Press, 1999.

Moore, Michael. *Stupid White Men – and Other Sorry Excuses for the State of the Nation!* New York: Regan Books, 2001.

Nelson, Douglas, Cathy McEvoy, and Simon Dennis. 'What Is Free Association and What Does It Measure?' *Memory and Cognition* 28.6 (2000): 887–99.

Oldenburg, Ray. *The Great Good Place: Cafes, Coffee Shops, Bookstores, Bars, Hair Salons, and Other Hangouts at the Heart of a Community*. New York: Marlowe, 1999.

Oldenburg, Ray. *Celebrating the Third Place: Inspiring Stories about the 'Great Good Places' at the Heart of Our Communities*. New York: Marlowe, 2002.

Pettigrew (Fisher), Karen E. 'Waiting for Chiropody: Contextual Results from an Ethnographic Study of the Information Behavior among Attendees at Community Clinics'. *Information Processing and Management* 35.6 (1999): 801–17.

Preer, Jean. 'Where Are Libraries in Bowling Alone?' *American Libraries* August (2001): 60–3.

Putnam, Robert D. *Bowling Alone: Collapse and Revival of American Community*. New York: Simon and Schuster, 2000.

Putnam, Robert D. and Lewis M. Feldstein. *Better Together: Restoring the American Community*. New York: Simon and Schuster, 2003.

Ranseen, Emily. 'The Library as Place: Changing Perspectives'. *Library Administration and Management* 16.4 (2002): 203–7.

Relph, Edward. *Place and Placelessness*. London: Pion, 1976.

Sannwald, William, 'To Build or Not to Build'. *Library Administration and Management* 15.3 (2001): 155–60.

Shill, Harold B. and Shawn Tonner. 'Creating a Better Place: Physical Improvements in Academic Libraries, 1995–2002'. *College and Research Libraries* 64.11 (2003): 431–66.

Siipola, Elsa, Nanette Walker, and Dorothy Kolb. 'Task Attitudes in Word Association, Projective and Nonprojective'. *Journal of Personality* 23.4 (1955): 441–59.

Silverstein, Marshall and Martin Harrow. 'Word Association: Multiple Measures and Multiple Meanings'. *Journal of Clinical Psychology* 39.4 (1983): 467–70.

St. Lifer, Evan. 'What Public Libraries Must Do to Survive'. *Library Journal* 1 April (2001): 60–2.

Szalay, Lor and James Deese. *Subjective Meaning and Culture: An Assessment through Word Associations*. Hillsdale, NJ: Lawrence Erlbaum Associates, 1978.

Thomas, Nancy Pickering. 'Reading Libraries: An Interpretive Study of Discursive Practices in Library Architecture and the Interactional Construction of Personal Identity'. Dissertation, Rutgers, State University of New Jersey, 1996.

Wagner, Gulten S. 'Public Library Buildings: A Semiotic Analysis'. *Journal of Librarianship and Information Science* 24.2 (1992): 101–8.

Weise, Frieda. 'Being There: The Library as Place'. *Journal of the Medical Library Association* 92.1 (2004): 6–13.

Wheat, Leonard. *Free Associations to Common Words: A Study of Word Associations to Twenty-Five Words Picked at Random from the Five Hundred Most Commonly Used Words in the English Language*. New York: Teachers College, Columbia University, 1931.

Wiegand, Wayne A. 'To Reposition a Research Agenda: What American Studies Can Teach the LIS Community about the Library in the Life of the User'. *Library Quarterly* 73.4 (2003): 369–82.

Wood, Mark, et al. 'Better Public Libraries'. Museums, Libraries, and Archives Council Information, Commission for Architecture and the Built Environment. 2003. Retrieved 15 September 2005 from http://www.mla.gov.uk/documents/id874rep.pdf.

Worpole, Ken. '21st Century Libraries: Changing Forms, Changing Futures'. Commission for Architecture and the Built Environment, 2003.

Part III
The library and its users

8 Emotional responses to locations in the Seattle Central Library

Saskia Kuliga

People respond to and interact with buildings. We form opinions about building function or how spaces feel to us, we reason about building layout or the intentions the architect might have had, and we may become confused (or even lost) in certain locations in a building that do not meet our expectations. This reciprocal human–environment interaction is a key topic of environmental psychology, which studies how people experience, behave in, and understand natural or built environments. This chapter invites you, the reader, to take a journey through different aspects and measurements of how building users, unfamiliar with the Seattle Public Central Library, experienced it. It presents the results of a post-occupancy evaluation that focused on the extent that users' emotional and aesthetic responses to key locations corresponded with their associated spatial properties. Before we continue, we need to introduce two important theoretic ideas.

First, the spatial features of inhabited space can be objectively and formally quantified, represented, and analysed. Space syntax, a set of theories and techniques for spatial representation and analysis (Hillier and Hanson, 1984; Hillier, 1996) can be applied usefully to the task of understanding what users perceive in an environment. For example, by examining all possible fields of view or sightlines from a given location to any other location in a building, it can quantify spatial intervisibility. Space syntax has been a good predictor of human movement patterns; particularly in relation to anticipating a user's free exploration and search for destinations in an as yet unknown environment (e.g., Haq and Zimring, 2003; Hölscher et al., 2012).

Second, spatial experience arises to a large extent from our visual perception of physical spatial features (Herzog, 1992; Kaplan and Kaplan, 1989; Appleton, 1975). It should therefore be possible to relate subjective user experience to measurable spatial properties. However, people perceive and process all available environmental information *holistically*. For example, while searching for a destination in the Seattle Public Central Library, people may be influenced by certain preconceptions about 'how a typical library looks'; or they may be drawn towards the vibrant colours of the brightly coloured escalators. People *holistically* perceive and process environmental information: not only spatial properties (such as specific views or unimpeded lines of sight, as space syntax represents and analyses), but also all other available environmental information and sensory input (such as colours, materials, or architectural style). For the remainder of this chapter, we thus assume that holistic user experience works as an interplay between the individual and environmental characteristics, which, in unison, form users' subjective impressions of space.

138 *Saskia Kuliga*

If we look at psychological research about environmental appraisal from the past, we learn that people may have subconscious preferences for certain spatial configurations that offer potential advantages for survival (Appleton, 1988); such as providing shelter and protection (enclosure) or facilitating orientation (prospect). Space that is perceived as rather open and well structured may be aesthetically preferred (Herzog, 1992). These environments are assumed to offer the chance to gain the advantage of a 'prospect', or overview, to other areas (Herzog and Leverich, 2003). Environmental characteristics, such as the degree of *complexity* (informational richness), *legibility* (ease of identification of environmental elements), *coherence* (sense of order and organization), and *mystery* (promise that additional information is available as one moves further into the scene) may relate to our intrinsic human need for environmental understanding and exploration (Kaplan and Kaplan, 1989). Franz and Wiener (2005) applied these concepts to a virtual, indoor environment and asked participants to find the best indoor outlook or the best refuge place. They found that eye-level views through a space do not only influence participants' behavioural judgements of indoor sites, but also correlate with their spatial experience in terms of perceived complexity, interest, and clarity of the environment.

An additional concept to spatial experience in terms of evolutionary-based preferences (Appleton, 1988) or intrinsic needs related to information processing (Kaplan and Kaplan, 1989), namely 'aesthetic and emotional experience', has been discussed as 'cognitive and emotional processes evoked by the aesthetic processing of an object' (Leder et al., 2004), or as a 'special state of mind that is qualitatively different from the everyday experience' (Marković, 2012). Furthermore, the authors of Chapter 6 in this book, Zook and Bafna, refer to the phenomenal impression of space that works both on the functional level (asking whether a building support user needs/tasks), as well as on a reflective level (actively thinking about spatial design).

Zook et al. (2012) raised the question of whether formal space syntax methodologies could be extended towards this phenomenal impression and imaginative experience that buildings could arguably evoke. The authors calculated a number of space syntax measures to infer what phenomenal aspects users might possibly experience while pursuing 'library-typical tasks', such as checking out a book, attending a meeting, and meeting a friend to work together. Additionally, Zook and Bafna 'cognitively walked' along each of the presumed routes and presented a personal, subjective description of the phenomenal and visual experience of the building, describing possible vistas, colours, surfaces, and materials along the way. They argued that the Seattle Central Library 'Sets up an absorbing and imaginative experience that decenters the visitor and excites exploration' (2012, p. 8087), but noted that their study's key limitation was the lack of actual user data. This chapter contributes a set of subjective spatial experience data to this ongoing discussion between the space syntax community and environmental psychologists.

Summing up, in order to understand the user experience of the Seattle Public Central Library, the work presented in this chapter assessed users' spatial experiences (relating to quantifiable concepts, such as spaciousness), as well as their emotional responses to key locations in the building (relating to subjective concepts such as pleasure). We examined whether users' self-reported ratings corresponded with syntactic spatial measures, in order to understand how subjective user experience and objective spatial properties may be perceptually linked.

Public reception of the Seattle Central Library

Surrounded by an eccentric exterior shape, the interior of the Seattle Central Library sets up a vibrant tone with neon escalators, black boxes that hide staircases, quasi-theatrical lighting, modern furniture and carpets with macro-prints of plants, wide-angled views of the outer structure, and dizzying heights when one looks down to the atrium from the tenth floor. Possibly due to its, at times, bewildering and cognitively complex design, the building received divided feedback from the public: voted *Time Magazine's Building of the Year 2004* (Lacayo, 2004) and awarded the *American Institute of Architects Honor Award for Architecture 2005* (*Architecture Week*, 2005), the library was also criticized for functional and navigational flaws. Shortly after the opening, local media commented that people were getting lost too often and that some parts of the building resembled a labyrinth (Murakami, 2006).

To assist library users to find the escalators, stairs, and restrooms, temporary posters with directions were installed to overcome the effects of missing signage (as described in more detail by Dalton in Chapter 3). Before long, a professional wayfinding company (Wayworks LLC) was hired to install a new signage system. Bright-yellow directories now provide a global overview of the floors and their local functions, and blue freestanding columns (also known as signage totems/monoliths) offer directions to local destinations. The previously designed super-graphics on the underside of escalators and fronts of information desks remained as augmented artwork.

Nevertheless, critics did not wait long to call for a reassessment of the library, suggesting that a post-occupancy evaluation would not only address the functional limitations of the building, but, according to one journalist, also

> a region few architects know how to talk about: how a building feels. This one feels, in varying places, raw, confusing, impersonal, uncomfortable, oppressive, theatrical and exhilarating. Ponder any spot in this vast building, and two, three or more of those adjectives inevitably swirl together.
>
> (Cheek, 2007)

Some research indeed suggests that architects can predict users' aesthetic reactions to particular buildings only vaguely or even inaccurately (Brown and Gifford, 2001). For example, while architects appreciate the use of concrete (one reason being its potential for sculpting form), non-architects do not appear to share this perspective and often rate concrete based mainly on their visual impressions (Benz and Rambow, 2011).

The question of how users experience a building is therefore non-trivial to design researchers and practitioners. In an argument that environmental research and design should be based on building users' eye-level experience as they move through space, and users' self-reported preferences, Thiel noted that 'we [design professionals] will certainly thrill to the poetic, practical, and proleptic fruits of our imagination. But... with their wonderfully various backgrounds, manifold preoccupations, and differing situations, will they [the users] – and should they – respond as we do?' (Thiel, 1997, p. 36). Taking the user perspective into account is a key concept of evaluating building functionality and the user experience of built space, and this chapter looks specifically at self-reported, subjective user experiences of the Seattle Public Central Library.

Emotional response research

The research questions for this study were formulated as: 1) how do users describe their appraisal of key locations of the Seattle Central Library (e.g. what words do they use and which topics do they address?) and what difficulties for functionality of the building do they identify (e.g. where and how do difficulties in understanding the library's unconventional circulation arise for library visitors)?; and 2) to what extent do configurational measures such as isovist area, connectivity, and integration correspond with user statements (e.g. is there a measure of spatial configuration that could explain why certain locations are found troubling by users)?

Thirty-six participants (18 males, 18 females) were recruited via a local online advertisement and received a compensation of $30 for this two-hour study. Participants were 18–61 years old (M=30.39, SD=10.59), and one third of them were 20–5 years old. Almost all participants were US American (n=31) and all participants spoke English fluently. Three participants were students; the remaining participants worked in finances/accounting, creative businesses, or social and educative fields of work.

The advertisement specifically invited people who had never been to the Seattle Central Library, because, in this study, user experience was being assessed in the context of a larger wayfinding study, which evaluated how the library supported wayfinding for people without prior knowledge of the complex layout, and what strategies naïve users applied to find locations. However, only half of the sample reported that they were visiting the building for the first (n=4, 11 per cent) or second time (n=11, 30 per cent) in their lives, and most participants had visited the library three to six times (n=13, 32 per cent). Three participants who had visited the building 10, 30, and 120 times, respectively, were excluded from further analyses (to arrive at a consistent data set), leaving a sample of 33 participants. On a six-point scale, only two people (6 per cent of the sample) felt very or highly familiar with the building; three others felt neither familiar nor unfamiliar with the library (9 per cent), and the remaining participants (n=28, 84 per cent) did not feel at all familiar with the building. The distribution for how familiar participants felt with the architecture of the library was similar.

In order to approach the first research question and assess user impressions of the Seattle Central Library, this study made use of six navigation tasks, along with participants' ratings on a questionnaire about environmental appraisal and a 'reaction card' task (see later for task description), and their verbal comments about the building and its floors during a semi-structured interview. The behavioural outcomes from the navigation exercises are part of an article in preparation, and are only used as *context* for the qualitative user data and so will not be described in detail here.

Questionnaire for emotional responses

The semantic differential scale (Osgood, 1957) has previously been implemented to assess users' spatial experience in buildings (e.g. Benz and Rambow, 2011; Wiener et al., 2007; Hershberger and Cass, 1974). In this study, environmental appraisal was assessed via a standardized questionnaire by De Kort et al. (2003) with 27 binary adjectives, with six-point intervals on a semantically differential scale (e.g., 'meaningless to impressive'). The questionnaire was extended by nine additional items provided by the researcher that were intended to be relatable to space syntax measures and terms from environmental psychology ('unstable–stable', 'functional–non-functional',

Emotional responses 141

'confusing–comprehensible', 'narrow–spacious', 'simple–complex', 'unclear–clear', 'mystifying–clearly defined', 'arousing–calming', and 'novel–familiar'). Participants could also provide free-text comments for each location on the questionnaire. The questionnaire aimed at rating the key floor levels of the library (the two entrance levels, the meeting rooms, and the book spiral), instead of all 11 floors separately, due to the restricted time frame of the study. In the final part of the questionnaire, participants were encouraged to rate the whole library as they had experienced it during the study, and to what extent viewing the outside structure of the building had given them an understanding of the geometry and building structure once they were inside the building.

Reaction card task

An alternative activity to measuring usability via a questionnaire is the 'Product Reaction Card Desirability Toolkit' developed by the Microsoft Corporation in 2002. It consists of 118 'product reaction cards' with words such as 'creative', 'gets in the way', and 'flexible' (Benedek and Miner, 2002). Following instructions for subsamples of this test, the authors selected 76 positive and negative words that, in their opinion, had the potential to describe building characteristics (see Figure 8.1). This set has successfully been used for other projects that aimed at building evaluation

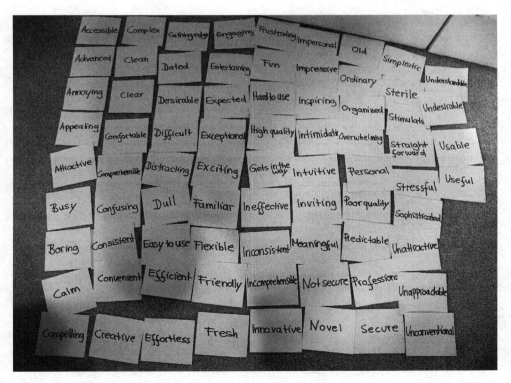

Figure 8.1 Alphabetically sorted 76-word subset for the 'reaction card task'.

(Bartle, 2012). According to Barnum and Palmer (2010), the toolkit can 'Prompt users to tell a rich and revealing story of their experience' (Barnum and Palmer, 2010, p. 4703), which was deemed useful for this study, as it provided participants with a wider vocabulary to describe their experiences in the library than they might have otherwise used.

One method to approach what words participants chose from the card-sorting task and whether there was a trend of common words that all participants chose is the use of word clouds. Following McNaught et al.'s definition, 'a word cloud is a special visualization of text in which the more frequently used words are effectively highlighted by occupying more prominence in the representation' (McNaught et al., 2010, p. 630). These 'Wordles' appear to be especially useful when they are supplemented with other research data (McNaught et al., 2010; William et al., 2013) and are transformed into a 'meaningful state' first (Ramsden and Bate, 2008), e.g. by analysing positive and negative feedback separately (Williams et al., 2013). While several programmes are freely available online, the authors used *Wordle.net*, a web-based tool for visualizing text (Viegas et al., 2009).

Semi-structured interview

After participants had filled out the questionnaires, they were asked to think back to each task and elaborate how they had oriented themselves to find the destination and where they thought navigation was difficult. These comments were used as supplementary data to assess how users subjectively perceived certain areas of the library. Due to library restrictions, participants were not allowed to verbalize their experience directly while navigating ('thinking aloud') as we might have instructed them to do in other, non-library buildings; however, retrospective reports immediately after a task and with a retrieval cue can give an approximation to actual memory structures (Ericsson and Simon, 1987). Therefore, photographs of the key locations were shown as an 'anchor' for a short time before they were turned upside-down (Figure 8.2).

Procedure

After completing the navigation tasks (not covered in this chapter), participants received the set of questionnaires for the environmental evaluation in a nearby café. For the reaction card task, the cards were spread out in a random pattern on a separate table and each participant was asked to choose the six adjectives (from the cards) that, in their opinion, would best describe the Seattle Central Library. They returned to their table and were encouraged to place the words in a descending order from describing the building best to least well. This served as a basis for the semi-structured interview about the tasks and the library, which rounded up the study.

Data analyses

Pearson correlation coefficient and Spearman rank correlation coefficient Rho were conducted to compare the syntactic variables to the six most significant adjectives that were selected by the participants. Furthermore, participants' verbal and text data were sorted by key location (e.g. third floor) and content (e.g. orientation, navigation,

Emotional responses 143

Figure 8.2 Photographs used as an 'anchor' during the questionnaire.

and signage) and linked to the statistical outcomes of the questionnaire (e.g. narrow–spacious). For the reaction card task data, 'Wordles' were created and participants' further comments about these words were used for interpretation.

Results from the questionnaire and participants' free-text answers

The first floor entrance: when participants thought back to the first floor, they felt that it was the most open of all rated sections (mean, or M=5.47, standard deviation, or SD=.92), as quite spacious (M=4.88, SD=1.01), stable (M=5.19, SD=.84) and more functional (M=5.15, SD=.89) than the meeting rooms (M=4.29, SD=1.51). The floor was also perceived as safer (M=5.12, SD=.94) than the meeting rooms (M=4.35, SD=1.57), which might be attributed to the security checkpoint in this section. The floor felt more public than private (M=1.69, SD=.98), legible (M=5.03, SD=.96), and accessible (M=4.88, SD=.96), although less accessible than the third floor (M=5.44, SD=.61). Participants' opinions on attractiveness diverged, but some mentioned on the free comment section of the questionnaire that it was their least favourite floor because of the concrete; one user commented: 'it feels more like a parking garage'.

The third floor entrance: this area was rated as the most impressive of all key locations (M=5.18, SD=.79), except the meeting rooms (M=5.26, SD=.89). It felt more inviting (M=4.74, SD=.83) than the first floor (M=4.00, SD=.12), was most attractive

144 *Saskia Kuliga*

of all rooms (M=4.82, SD=.94) and quite pleasant (M=4.88, SD=.88: 'great window views!'). The concrete elevator shaft was both loved ('I love the centre column contrasting the slanted windows') and hated ('the glass makes it much more beautiful; still too much concrete and the colour is ugly'). The area was further perceived as safe (M=5.18, SD=.72) and functional (M=5.12, SD=.84).

The book spiral: participants commented: 'Confusing – I'm still unclear as to the easiest way to traverse the stairways', and even more negative: 'I got dizzy and lost'. They felt that the book spiral was the narrowest section in the library (M=1.97, SD=1.41), most closed of all rooms (M=2.26, SD=1.07, p<.008), more monotone than the first and third floors (M=2.71, SD=1.33, p<.001), and most bare in terms of decoration (M=2.65, SD=1.09: 'I like the shelves and being able to see some wood; the concrete still feels kind of industrial'). The spiral was also judged, without further context, as 'A little frustrating' by one user.

The meeting rooms: this all-red floor led participants to comment in a more emotive manner; in one case feeling revolted ('What? I never want to go back there!'), in another devoted ('I love the fourth floor red meeting rooms'). The colour was highly criticized by many participants; e.g. 'Red is not a calming or soothing colour'; 'Monotone red is intimidating'; 'Overwhelming, unpleasant [and] too red'; and 'Hideous red, very dark overall impression; narrow hallway when doors open out into it'. This comment referred to a staircase that had been designed as an emergency exit, but was later opened for public use due to navigational issues. Two participants found analogies: 'It made me feel like I was a little kid again, trying to walk through those tubes', and 'I felt like I was inside building blocks or a toy'. Participants judged the meeting rooms as equally impressive as the third floor (M=5.26, SD=.89) and most interesting of all the rooms except the first floor (M=5.21, SD=.98). Although opinions were divided, the meeting room floor was also rated as most arousing (M=2.65, SD=1.41), most artificial (M=1.88, SD=1.27), and the most mystifying of all rooms (M=2.91, SD=1.44) and, similar to the book spiral, the most monotone area (M=2.35, SD=1.53), bare (M=2.88, SD=1.66), and closed (M=2.91, SD=1.24).

Appraisal of the whole library: in general, seven participants (21 per cent of this sample) stated that viewing the outside structure of the building had given them an understanding of the geometry once they were inside the building; 23 persons felt that viewing the exterior did not help (70 per cent), and three participants (9 per cent) did not report an opinion. To most participants, the interior felt quite impressive (M=5.33, SD=.98). While some users appreciated the building's complexity (M=4.94, SD=1.09; 'Amazing, I had no idea it was so complex'), other users criticized this aspect ('I was surprised how non-intuitive it was for me to find my way'). Signage and spatial differentiation were also mentioned as critical factors (e.g., 'It [was] hard to form a cohesive picture of the library and its layout in my head – Extremely interesting to walk through, but it does make it difficult to find things'). The comments on the interior of the building can usefully be compared to Seamon's exercise in Chapter 5, in which he showed students images of the exterior and asked them to write three words describing it.

On an aesthetic note, most, but not all, participants found the library attractive (M=4.81, SD=1.11), pleasant (M=4.83, SD=1.03), tasteful (M=4.81, SD=1.03), and interesting (M=5.33, SD=.71). The building felt open (M=5.03, SD=.87) and light (M=4.97, SD=.97). It could be observed that some participants strongly liked certain aspects of the building, but strongly disliked others (e.g., 'I really love all the areas with glass, natural lighting, carpets and plants; like the third floor or the top floor. But I dislike all the concrete areas and the loud colours, and especially the escalator decorations'). Some participants appeared to experience a tension between aesthetics and functionality: 'Overall it's a beautiful library, but it takes getting used to. I enjoy exploring new spaces, so I have fun figuring out the layout on my own.' Yet others felt that the library was built from a 'Very strange architecture, not user friendly for a first time visitor' and that the circulation was 'Confusing, but okay if you go with the flow'.

Results from the reaction card task

The six words that participants selected that in their opinion would describe the Seattle Central Library best were visualized for positive (70 per cent) and negative feedback (30 per cent) separately (see the Wordle in Figure 8.3). Nine participants (25 per cent) chose solely positive words and two participants (5 per cent) chose solely negative words; in all other cases feedback was mixed, e.g. participants found that the library was, for the most part, innovative but also confusing.

Figure 8.3 Results from the 'reaction card task'. Above: positive words; below: negative words.

146 *Saskia Kuliga*

From the positive words, impressive, creative, stimulating, innovative, and attractive were most often chosen to describe the library, followed by cutting-edge, entertaining, engaging, and high-quality. From the negative words, participants most frequently chose confusing, complex, inconsistent, and overwhelming, followed by frustrating, intimidating, busy, stressful, and sterile. Participants were also asked to verbally elaborate on why they had chosen those particular word cards. For example, unconventional was interpreted positively; e.g. noting that floors were different, staircases would lead to different levels, and unexpected vistas would emerge. Participants also perceived that looking down from the highest point on floor 10 towards level 3 as giving them a better understanding of the structure of the library (in reality, this view provides few clues as to the general layout of the building).

Participants chose 'innovative' because the library felt more sophisticated and creative than traditional libraries. The size of the library was the main reason participants chose the word 'impressive'. The building felt stimulating and creative; 'it makes your mind work on a different level. Neon green and red [is] more awakening than most buildings.' The words 'attractive' and 'cutting-edge' also referred to colours, angles, and the exterior 'shell'. Participants felt that the building stimulated a more 'active' approach, encouraging exploration and further engagement; e.g. 'It made me really curious to see what's going on throughout the whole thing' and '[It] begs to be explored'. The unconventional layout was 'thought-provoking. I actually feel like there was more relational involvement in this building than in other buildings. This one had a lot more character and interaction.'

On the negative side, the library felt inconsistent, 'Because the layout on every floor is a little different than the layout on other floors', and because 'Escalators were located on different like sides of the floor. It felt really random.' Participants also complained that they could not use the same strategy twice during the wayfinding tasks and that the building 'Got in the way'. The word impersonal was chosen because of the size of the library ('It loses that comfortable feeling') and due to the use of concrete.

Results from the semi-structured interview

Orientation, navigation and signage: participants generally reported a positive aesthetic experience, but uncomfortable navigation; for example, they pointed out that the staircases were clearly labelled, but located at unexpected and hard-to-find locations; escalators surprisingly skipped whole floors, and participants missed a 'Central location for all floors to get from one floor to the next' (which was the original function the architects had assigned to the 'Mixing Chamber'). 'Going up' the building felt easy, but 'Going down' remained unclear, because there was no down escalator and the staircases were not always visible. It also was 'Intimidating' that the floors were all different: 'Almost like a maze'. The book spiral was especially difficult to understand, 'Because I went up those stairs and I thought that would be a whole another level', it felt 'Cluttered, uneven and unpredictable', 'Winding around like an accordion'.

To find the destinations for the wayfinding tasks, participants reportedly followed signs and used directories, tried to first find the correct floor, or simply explored space by 'wandering around' until the correct destination was found. Participants complained that the signage felt illogical, unfamiliar, and confusing ('I was very surprised today that it wasn't more obvious how it works'); missed details, and the arrows on the blue columns (signage totems) and the maps provided on the third floor did not help. Furthermore, exits and entrances did not appear clearly defined and the library felt like a 'space that has a lot of different spaces within it'. Noting that she never felt any sense of orientation in the building, one participant believed that wayfinding would be easier if visitors spent more time reading the signs and super-graphics instead of 'breezing past, trying to figure the way out on their own'.

Aesthetics and emotion: many participants appreciated the building's design and intended to return later to explore the building further. Some perceived a tension when asked to rate the library, because everything felt extreme to them. On the rather emotive side of the ratings, some participants stated that they had perceived the library as daunting, intimidating, and claustrophobic. From an aesthetic point of view, the use of concrete was generally disliked for being sterile and cold. One participant remembered 'bright lime green, red, pink, and huge rooms with windows and views, both to the skyscrapers around and the town below', while another saw 'either concrete, or one colour'. From this statement and the general tone of several others, one could argue that by its unconventional design, the library evokes a tension between functionality and aesthetics that some participants appreciate: 'the planning of the building is weird; you kept going in circles; up on floors you've been on. But that makes it kind of cool also!' Another participant felt a void between exploration and functionality, because the building felt so highly artistic and expressive that it would hinder the accomplishment of tasks. Exploration and functionality, according to him, 'don't seem entirely integrated, although they do coincide and help each other out'.

In summary, the general tone of the questionnaire, reaction card task, and interview data appeared to reveal quite mixed user opinions about the library. In order to develop an understanding of how these user opinions could be related to the building's spatial structure, in the next section, a detailed visibility graph analysis (VGA) and convex space analysis was conducted, and a subset of six questionnaire items that showed the highest variance in user ratings and significantly differed between library areas (Figure 8.4) was used for subsequent correlation analyses.

Space syntax analysis: the challenge of performing the space syntax analysis for this study was to select measures that could be used to define the spatial properties of specific point locations, such as the first floor entrance, whilst also being used to measure the aggregate properties of larger regions, such as the book spiral. A combination of convex space analysis, VGA, and point isovist analysis was used. A convex space breakup was performed for all public floors of the library. For each individual location (from which the 'anchor' photographs were taken), the measures of convex space connectivity, mean depth, real relative asymmetry, relative asymmetry, and total depth were calculated. For the larger regions, the average value was calculated for all the convex spaces constituting that region (Table 8.1).

A similar exercise was performed for isovists and VGAs: for the larger regions, a number of isovist points were selected and the average value for the entire set of points constituting the region was calculated and the configurational and geometric measures 'mean isovist integration', 'mean isovist area', 'mean isovist connectivity', 'mean isovist visual control', and 'mean isovist maximum radial length' were calculated. For the specific locations from which the photographs were taken, full $360°$ isovists (the 'standard' isovist) and partial $120°$ isovists (namely the angle most closely

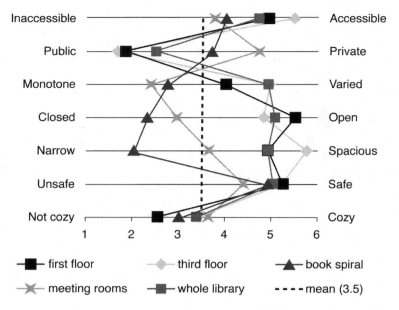

Figure 8.4 Subset of six questionnaire items.

approximating the camera lens used to take the 'anchor' photographs) were generated (Table 8.1; partial isovists displayed in Figure 8.5). The VGA was produced using the Depthmap software (Turner, 2001, 2004, 2007).

Correlation analyses: Pearson's correlation analysis revealed that the VGA measures (excluding the partial isovist with mean isovist connectivity, visual control, and mean maximum radial length; and point isovist with mean maximum radial length; <.89, p<.01) correlated significantly with each other (r>.95, p<.01). The convex space measures (except convex connectivity with any other measure) were significantly intercorrelated at p<.01. The six subjective ratings correlated among each other at p<.05 (Table 8.2, upper part).

In order to assess the strength of association between the six-item subset (Figure 8.4) and the syntactical measures for convex spaces and isovists (Table 8.1), Pearson's correlation and non-parametric Spearman rank correlation Rho were computed and averaged over an aggregated larger region, and at the level of the partial isovist (photograph) location, respectively. As both Pearson and Spearman Rho correlation analysis showed a similar correlation pattern, only the non-parametric Spearman-Rho's correlation coefficient is reported here, as it is more appropriate for rating data that is not normally distributed around a mean. The individual participant ratings of the four areas of each of the 33 participants were correlated with the syntactic measures; yielding N=132 data points.

Spearman Rho correlation analysis between the syntactic VGA measures and the subjective participant ratings indicated that mean isovist integration and mean isovist area explained the largest proportion of the variance in participants' ratings of the four library regions (Table 8.2, middle). As mean isovist connectivity, mean

Table 8.1 Results from the convex space analysis and the visibility graph analysis

Area	Convex space analysis (larger area)					Convex space analysis (point of photograph)				
	Mean connectivity	Mean depth	Real relative asymmetry	Relative asymmetry	Total depth	Connectivity	Mean depth	Real relative asymmetry	Relative asymmetry	Total depth
First floor entrance	3.12	9.94	1.50	0.05	3677.86	3.00	7.74	1.13	0.04	2863
Third floor entrance	3.10	8.82	1.30	0.04	3264.27	7.00	8.16	1.20	0.04	3018
Meeting room floor	3.09	8.72	1.29	0.04	3226.08	4.00	9.50	1.43	0.05	3533
Whole book spiral	3.16	8.84	1.31	0.04	3272.32	4.00	7.91	1.16	0.04	2927

Area	VGA analysis (larger area)					Point isovist analysis (point of photograph)				
	Mean integration	Mean isovist area	Mean isovist connectivity	Mean isovist visual control	Mean isovist maximum radial length	Point isovist area	Partial isovist area			
First floor entrance	2.02	817.66	826.69	1.49	56.87	527,09	209,76			
Third floor entrance	2.19	1590.50	1458.52	1.87	71.85	1852,86	1463,96			
Meeting room floor	1.91	253.86	251.73	1.01	28.43	244,99	213,06			
Mixing chamber (*not included)	2.52	1391.39	1415.65	1.01	59.95	n/a	n/a			
Whole book spiral	1.93	127.85	131.15	0.99	34.85	155,87	104,52			
Tenth floor (*not included)	2.01	1135.34	1101.87	1.01	51.99	n/a	n/a			
Whole library	1.98	476.00	474.85	1.00	39.74	n/a	n/a			

150 *Saskia Kuliga*

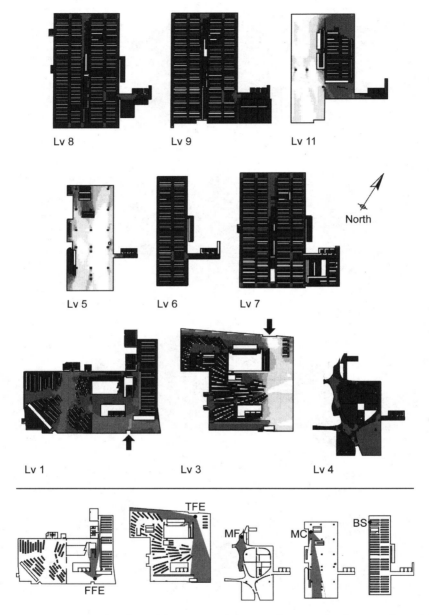

Figure 8.5 VGA for the public spaces of the Seattle Central Library, coloured by isovist integration (high = white, low = black). Below: the locations from which the questionnaire photographs were taken and their respective partial isovists. (FFE = First Floor Entry; TFE = Third Floor Entry; MF = Meeting Floor; MC = Mixing Chamber; BS = Book Spiral).

isovist visual control, and point isovist area did not explain additional variance in this sample's ratings with respect to mean isovist area; and mean isovist maximum radial length, in this sample, did not explain additional variance beyond mean isovist

Table 8.2 Spearman-Rho correlation matrices

Spearman-Rho correlations between item-subset items

	unsafe–safe		narrow–spacious		closed–open		monotone–varied		public–private		inaccessible–accessible	
	r_s	p	r_s	p	r_s	p	r_s	p	r_s	p	r_s	p
unsafe–safe	1.00	n/a	.18	<.05	.31	<.01	.21	<.05	−.33	<.01	.34	<.01
narrow–spacious			1.00	n/a	.75	<.01	.53	<.01	−.48	<.01	.46	<.01
closed–open					1.00	n/a	.62	<.01	−.59	<.01	.53	<.01
monotone–varied							1.00	n/a	−.45	<.01	.40	<.01
public–private									1.00	n/a	−.58	<.01
inaccessible–accessible											1.00	n/a

Spearman-Rho correlations between item-subset and VGA measures (area and photo point)

	unsafe–safe		narrow–spacious		closed–open		monotone–varied		public–private		inaccessible–accessible	
	r_s	p	r_s	p	r_s	p	r_s	p	r_s	p	r_s	p
Mean isovist integration	.19	<.05	.59	<.01	.70	<.01	.58	<.01	−.67	<.01	.52	<.01
Mean isovist Area	.10	.28	.77	<.01	.73	<.01	.53	<.01	−.54	<.01	.49	<.01
Partial isovist area (photograph location)	−.05	.61	.61	<.01	.48	<.01	.33	<.01	−.19	<.05	.30	<.01

Spearman-Rho correlations between item-subset and convex space measures (Area)

	unsafe–safe		narrow–spacious		closed–open		monotone–varied		public–private		inaccessible–accessible	
	r_s	p	r_s	p	r_s	p	r_s	p	r_s	p	r_s	p
Mean connectivity	−.12	.18	.22	<.05	.06	.95	−.12	.16	.19	<.05	−.09	.32
Mean depth	.02	.80	.38	<.01	.26	<.01	.08	.38	−.18	.05	.11	.22
Relative asymmetry	.15	.10	.25	<.01	.29	<.01	.15	.09	−.38	<.01	.17	<.05

Spearman-Rho correlations between item-subset and convex space measures (photo point)

	unsafe–safe		narrow–spacious		closed–open		monotone–varied		public–private		inaccessible–accessible	
	r_s	p	r_s	p	r_s	p	r_s	p	r_s	p	r_s	p
Connectivity	−.05	.54	.19	<.05	.17	.05	.20	<.05	−.02	.85	.15	.08
Mean depth	−.20	<.05	−.04	<.05	−.18	<.05	−.15	.08	.41	<.01	−.16	.07

152 *Saskia Kuliga*

integration (except weakly for safety perception), these variables were dropped from further analysis.

These correlations appeared to form the following descriptive clusters: mean isovist integration (or how visually central was that viewpoint in the library as a whole) was the best predictor for how 'public' or 'private' participants rated the four locations (rs (131) = −.67, r^2 = .45, p<.01); more integrated areas, such as the third floor, felt more public. Mean isovist integration further predicted how monotonous or varied space felt (rs (131) = .58, r^2 = .33, p<.01); the less integrated meeting rooms and book spiral felt more monotonous and private. In addition, mean isovist integration modestly predicted how accessible participants rated the areas (rs (131) = .52, r^2 = .27, p<.01); less integrated areas, such as the meeting rooms, felt less accessible. Accessibility was also strongly captured by mean isovist area (rs (131) = .49, r^2 = .24, p<.01). Mean isovist area (or how large are the views) appeared to be the best predictor for how narrow or spacious (rs (131) = .77, r^2 = .59, p<.01), and how closed or open (rs (131) = .73, r^2 = .53, p<.01) space was perceived, as larger areas were rated safer and more open (spatial openness was also strongly captured by mean isovist integration, rs (131) = .70, r^2 = .49, p<.01; more integrated areas felt less closed). Furthermore, mean isovist integration and mean maximum radial length correlated equally, but weakly, with how unsafe or safe areas felt (rs (131)>.19, r^2 = .04, p<.05); with less integrated areas and shorter lines of sight being rated as less safe. Partial isovist area predicted how narrow or spacious (rs (131) = .61, r^2 = .37, p<.01) and closed or open areas felt (r (131) = .48, r^2 = .23, p<.01), although less than mean isovist integration and mean isovist area. It also correlated with how monotone or varied (r (131) = .33, r^2 = .11, p<.01), accessible or inaccessible (r (131) = .30, r^2 = .10, p<.01), and, weakly, how public or private areas were perceived (r (131) = −.19, r^2 = .04, p<.05).

Spearman Rho analysis between the convex space measures and the subjective participant ratings (Table 8.2) indicated weak correlations: relative asymmetry correlated with how public or private participants rated the areas (rs (131) = −.38, r^2 = .14, p<.01), as areas with lower relative asymmetry were rated more private. Mean depth, relative asymmetry, and total depth were the best indicators for how narrow or spacious (rs (131) = −.38, r^2 = .14, p<.01) and how closed or open (rs (131) = −.26, r^2 = .07, p<.01) space was perceived, as deeper areas were rated more spacious and open. These variables showed similar correlation patterns, so only mean depth is reported here. For the anchor photograph location points, mean depth, real relative asymmetry, relative asymmetry, and total depth also showed similar correlation patterns to how public or private a photograph location was perceived (rs (131)=.41, r^2 = .17, p<.01), and convex connectivity correlated with how monotone or varied (rs (131) = .20, r^2 = .04, p<.05), and how narrow or spacious (rs (131) = .18, r^2=.03, p<.05) areas were rated, while none of the other syntactic measures related to this particular rating scale. In general, the VGA measures provided stronger explanations for the variance in participants' ratings for the four locations than the convex space measures.

Discussion and conclusions

The current study has gathered and analysed user comments about the Seattle Central Library in order to explore how building users describe their aesthetic and emotional judgements of the building, the locations where users identify difficulties in understanding the building, and to what extent space syntax measures correspond to user statements.

First, referring back to the journalist's statement in the introduction of this chapter (Cheek, 2007), study participants also appeared to perceive certain areas in the Seattle Central Library as *confusing, impersonal*, yet *exhilarating*. However, this is not their whole story: while many participants felt a sense of confusion due to the library's complex, unconventional circulation, and unfamiliar and, at times, intimidating style, at the same time, many also adored the library's exceptional 'daring' architecture, its sheer spaciousness, and its creative, stimulating design. Participants indeed felt that the library's circulation was unconventional in terms of unexpected locations of staircases, bypassing escalators, absence of any down escalators, and a missing 'central' location, but they also experienced a curiosity to take an adventurous look and to explore the different floors further. These findings are in line with Zook et al.'s (2012) theoretical argument that the library 'Engenders sort of restlessness, a sense that things are happening somewhere nearby'. As Marković (2012) noted, aesthetic evaluation is a subjective, aroused state of fascination, appraisal, and emotion, which, arguably, can lead to disorientation in space and time. As a result, aesthetic stimulation in the Seattle Central Library might get in the way of functionally accomplishing tasks, and instead excite a need for environmental understanding and exploration.

Second, this chapter also aimed at developing an understanding of how to link qualitative (and often highly emotive) data, to objective spatial analysis. The seven spatial measures selected were, in general, able to account for a large proportion of the variance of six selected, subjective user ratings for the four locations and the whole library. This is a first indicator that the rather mixed user opinions about key locations in the Seattle Central Library are indeed related to the building's spatial structure as quantified by space syntax. In fact, with the aim of assessing *holistic* user experience in a real-world building (thus, with all sensory input, such as other people present, sound, colours, materials, etc.), we found that isovist area and perceived spaciousness and safety were related, specifically that larger areas were rated as safer and more open (similar to Franz and Wiener, 2005). Maybe these areas subconsciously offered more overview/prospect (relating to Appleton, 1975; Herzog and Leverich, 2003). Alternatively, areas with larger views might have offered more environmental information (relating to Kaplan and Kaplan, 1989). However, following these interpretations, we would have expected to find a preference indicator, such as a relation between isovist area and pleasure. However, this was not included in the analysed subset. While isovist area apparently can predict experience of space in terms of perceived spaciousness and possible safety, subjective preferences relating to these concepts in a real building should be further investigated. Summed up, the selected spatial measures could accurately capture part of the experience of a physical environment, and this is an interesting start outside the laboratory. However, several items were included in the study based on the a priori hypothesis that they should be spatial descriptions semantically related to the syntactic measures, such as 'unstable–stable' or 'illegible–legible'. These did not differ significantly between the rooms, and this suggests that lay users (architects or space syntax researchers) rarely use these terms for describing spaces, or that they might simply use different criteria or concepts for environmental evaluation compared to architects, designers, or researchers. Future research needs to examine the interconnections and generalizability of the current findings in more detail.

Relating to Chapter 6, in the view of Zook and Bafna, most of the formal design of the library might be addressing a kind of a user who actively and reflectively thinks

154 *Saskia Kuliga*

about the library's design, and to whom, therefore, any sense of disorientation and sensory input (light conditions, clashing colours, materials) may have a very different implication than for a user who focuses mainly on to what extent the building supports a task (Bafna, personal communication, 2013). Users' experiential ratings may potentially be affected by the context/situation they were in, the tasks at hand, as well as users' individual characteristics (for example, a mindset of reflective thinking, a functional goal-directed motivation, etc.). The context for this chapter was a larger post-occupancy evaluation and wayfinding study. Thus, users probably were highly focused on evaluating wayfinding challenges. Possibly, their feelings about the success or failure during certain tasks may have affected their ratings as well. Future research could address these individual user-specific and contextual differences. The success or failure of a building is not solely determined by constructional and functional issues, but mainly by how a building feels from a situated perspective and how users interact effortlessly and intuitively with their environment. The aim of this chapter is not to judge whether the Seattle Central Library succeeds or fails as a building, but to provide user impressions and explore the link with objective space syntax data. While the building's aesthetics deeply impress many people (and a desire for environmental understanding and exploration could be part of the function of experiencing modern architecture), its unconventional circulation confuses people (which is potentially dysfunctional in a library); leading to an open question: what is the main goal of a building? As Le Corbusier noted, architecture as circulation is

> that symphony which we must experience [which] should not be revealed to us exclusively by functional considerations... but by emotional considerations; for the various aspects only become comprehensible gradually as we follow our wayward feet, moving hither and thither, with our eyes fixed on the walls and the perspectives, meeting expectedly or unexpectedly with doors which reveal the secret of new spaces... Organization must be seen in conjunction with the purpose of the building. Good architecture can be traversed both inside and out.
>
> (Le Corbusier, 1943, quoted in Thiel, 1997, p. 37)

Note

* This chapter is a reprint. It was originally published as: Kuliga, Saskia, Ruth Conroy Dalton, and Christoph Hölscher. "Aesthetic and Emotional Appraisal of the Seattle Public Library and its relation to spatial configuration." Proceedings of the Ninth International Space Syntax Symposium (Seoul: Sejong University). 2013.

References

Appleton, J., 1975. Landscape evaluation: The theoretical vacuum. *Transactions of the Institute of British Geographers*, pp. 120–3.

Appleton, J., 1988. Prospects and refuges re-visited. *Landscape Journal*, 3(2), pp. 91–103.

Architecture Week, 2005. AIA Honor Awards 2005. *Architecture Week*, 30 March, p. 31.

Barnum, C. M. and Palmer, L. A., 2010. More than a feeling: Understanding the desirability factor in user experience. In *CHI'10 Extended Abstracts on Human Factors in Computing Systems* (pp. 4703–16). Atlanta, GA: ACM.

Bartle, S., 2012. Architecture of the Salvation Army, MArch thesis, University of Northumbria at Newcastle (unpublished).

Benedek, J. and Miner, T., 2002. Measuring desirability: New methods for evaluating desirability in a usability lab setting. *Proceedings of Usability Professionals Association*, pp. 8–12.

Benz, I. and Rambow, R., 2011. Sichtbeton in der Architektur: Perspektivenunterschiede zwischen ArchitektInnen und Laien. *Umweltpsychologie*, 15, pp. 112–29.

Brown, G. and Gifford, R., 2001. Architects predict lay evaluations of large contemporary buildings: Whose conceptual properties? *Journal of Environmental Psychology*, 21(1), pp. 93–9.

Cheek, L. W., 2007. On architecture: How the new central library really stacks up. *Seattle Post-Intelligencer*, 26 March, p. C1.

De Kort, Y. A., Ijsselsteijn, W. A., Kooijman, J., and Schuurmans, Y., 2003. Virtual laboratories: Comparability of real and virtual environments for environmental psychology. *Presence: Teleoperators and Virtual Environments*, 12(4), pp. 360–73.

Ericsson, K. A. and Simon, H. A., 1987. Verbal reports on thinking. *Introspection in second language research*. Edited by C. Faerch and G. Kasper. Bristol: Multilingual Matters.

Franz, G. and Wiener, J. M., 2005. Exploring isovist-based correlates of spatial behavior and experience. In *Proceedings of the 5th International Space Syntax Symposium Delft*.

Haq, S. and Zimring, C., 2003. Just down the road a piece the development of topological knowledge of building layouts. *Environment and behavior*, 35(1), pp. 132–60.

Hershberger, R. G. and Cass, R. C., 1974. Predicting user responses to buildings. *Man-Environment Interactions, EDRA*, 5, pp. 117–43.

Herzog, T. R., 1992. A cognitive analysis of preference for urban spaces. *Journal of Environmental Psychology*, 12(3), pp. 237–48.

Herzog, T. R. and Leverich, O. L., 2003. Searching for legibility. *Environment and Behavior*, 35(4), pp. 459–77.

Hillier, B., 1996. *Space is the machine*. Cambridge: Cambridge University Press.

Hillier, B. and Hanson, J., 1984. *The social logic of space*. Cambridge: Cambridge University Press.

Hölscher, C., Brösamle, M., and Vrachliotis, G., 2012. Challenges in multi-level wayfinding: A case-study with space syntax technique. *Environment and Planning B: Planning and Design*, 39, 63–82.

Kaplan, R. and Kaplan, S., 1989. *The experience of nature: A psychological perspective*. Cambridge: Cambridge University Press Archive.

Lacayo, R., 2004. Top 10 everything 2004 – architecture: Seattle Public Library. *Time*, 17 December. Retrieved from http://www.time.com/time/specials/packages/article/0,28804,1999700_1998814_1999 521,00.html.

Leder, H., Belke, B., Oeberst, A., and Augustin, D., 2004. A model of aesthetic appreciation and aesthetic judgments. *British Journal of Psychology*, 95(4), pp. 489–508.

Marković, S., 2012. Components of aesthetic experience: Aesthetic fascination, aesthetic appraisal, and aesthetic emotion. *i-Perception*, 3(1), p. 1.

McNaught, C., Lam, P., and Cheng, K. F., 2012. Investigating relationships between features of learning designs and student learning outcomes. *Educational Technology Research and Development*, 60(2), pp. 271–86.

Murakami, K., 2006. Too many people getting lost in new downtown library: Professional is hired to create directional signs. *Seattle Post-Intelligencer*, 5 September. Retrieved from http://www.seattlepi.com/local/283819_library05.html.

Osgood, C. E., 1957. A behavioristic analysis of perception and language as cognitive phenomena. *Contemporary Approaches to Cognition*, pp. 75–118.

Ramsden, A. and Bate, A., 2008. *Using word clouds in teaching and learning*. Bath: University of Bath. Unpublished.

Thiel, P., 1997. *People, paths, and purposes: Notations for a participatory envirotecture*. Seattle: University of Washington Press.

Turner, A., 2001. A program to perform visibility graph analysis. In *Proceedings of the 3rd Space Syntax Symposium*, Atlanta, University of Michigan, pp. 30–1.

Turner, A., 2004. *Depthmap 4: A researcher's handbook*. London: UCL.

Turner, A., 2007. *UCL Depthmap*. London: UCL.

Viegas, F. B., Wattenberg, M., and Feinberg, J., 2009. Participatory visualization with Wordle. *Visualization and Computer Graphics, IEEE Transactions*, 15(6), pp. 1137–44.

Wiener, J. M., Franz, G., Rossmanith, N., Reichelt, A., Mallot, H. A., and Bulthoff, H. H., 2007. Isovist analysis captures properties of space relevant for locomotion and experience. *Perception*, 36(7), pp. 1066–83.

Williams, W., Parkes, E. L., and Davies P., 2013. Wordle: A method for analysing MBA student induction experience. *International Journal of Management Education*, 11, pp. 44–53.

Zook, J. B. and Bafna, S., 2012. Imaginative content and building form in the Seattle Central Public Library. *Proceedings: Eighth International Space Syntax Symposium*. Edited by M. Greene, J. Reyes, and A. Castro. Santiago de Chile: PUC.

9 Why people get lost in the Seattle Central Library

Amy Shelton, Steven Marchette, Christoph Hölscher, Ben Nelligan, Thomas Shipley, and Laura Carlson

The Seattle Central Public Library has garnered awards for its design, including *Time Magazine's Outstanding Building* (Lacayo, 2004) and the *American Institute of Architects' Honor Award for Architecture* in 2005. There is little question that most people find it impressive in terms of its technical and aesthetic aspects. However, another aspect of design is function, and the Seattle Central Library has received more criticism than credit for its navigability (Carlson et al., 2010), suggesting that the Seattle Central Library may be an informative case for understanding why people get lost in buildings. In this chapter, we will use an existing framework for human navigational variability to try to explore what can be learned by examining this unique case in a naturalistic experiment on human navigational performance.

Variability in human navigation is common (Fields and Shelton, 2006; Ishikawa and Montello, 2006; Schinazi et al., 2013; Wolbers and Hegarty, 2010) – some people just always get lost, others seem to have a keen sense of direction, and some people develop very specific strategies to overcome potential weaknesses. It is also worth noting that variability goes beyond just good or bad. People differ in terms of their ability to navigate in novel environments (Hartley et al., 2003; Weisberg et al., 2014; Wolbers and Hegarty, 2010), their preferences for the format of navigationally relevant information (Pazzaglia and De Beni, 2001), and the types of solutions and strategies they employ (Bohbot et al., 2007; Furman et al., 2014; Iaria et al., 2003; Marchette et al., 2011; Shelton et al., 2013). Places like the Seattle Central Library highlight the fact that the environment also contributes to the ease or difficulty of navigation. To fully understand why so many people feel lost in the Seattle Central Library, we need to think about the influence of both the human navigator and the environment.

Carlson and colleagues developed a framework for understanding the factors that might contribute to the ease or difficulty associated with navigation in buildings (Carlson et al., 2010, Figure 9.1). In this three-factor model, the complexity of navigation lies at the intersection of an individual's strategies and skills, the cognitive map that has been formed, and the structural features of the environment itself. Individual strategies and skills refer to the host of abilities that an individual brings to the table when learning and navigating in an environment. These characteristics include one's preferences for navigational information (e.g., Pazzaglia and De Beni, 2001), one's use of different navigational solutions (Furman et al., 2014; Marchette et al., 2011), and a whole host of cognitive skills that affect navigationally relevant information processing (Gallistel, 1990; Newcombe and Huttenlocher, 2000). Different profiles

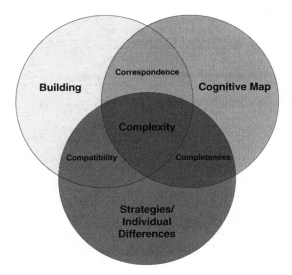

Figure 9.1 Framework for predicting navigational difficulty using a three-factor model from Carlson et al. (2010).

of strategies and skills will differentially affect how an individual approaches a particular environment.

The term cognitive map refers to the internal representation that one constructs (Burgess et al., 1999; Golledge, 1999; O'Keefe and Nadel, 1978; Tolman, 1948), which is determined at least in part by the cognitive processes an individual brings to bear on a navigation task. Cognitive maps can vary with respect to the prioritization of certain features of the environment, such that landmarks or other elements might be more or less robustly represented. The selection of features to encode can contribute to and/or complement the degree to which the representation simplifies or regularizes the environment (e.g., Chrastil and Warren, 2014; Stevens and Coupe, 1978; Tversky, 1981). This selection is akin to what cartographers do when determining how to represent features on a physical map (straightening roads, including or excluding terrain, etc.). Cognitive maps can also vary with respect to the reference frame(s) used to organize the environmental components and how different elements might be coordinated and integrated or be independent and fragmented. For example, in buildings, it is possible to have a good sense of one's orientation within a room or hallway with or without a corresponding sense of orientation with the global reference frame of the building (e.g., Montello and Pick, 1993; Wang and Brockmole, 2003).

The third component of the framework is the environmental features – in this case, the building itself. Buildings can vary dramatically in terms of the characteristics that will affect wayfinding, and these can again be broken down into relevant dimensions (Weisman, 1981). Buildings (and environments more broadly) will offer different degrees of visual access from one part to another, with the critical issue being the ability to readily see the navigationally relevant features. A second major dimension is the architectural differentiation, which refers to how similar or dissimilar different parts of the environment can be – are they easily distinguished or easily confused? This dimension might also affect how readily one can integrate across related elements.

At the intersections of these factors lie different emergent variables that can be evaluated. First, according to the framework, the *completeness* of the cognitive map actually falls at the intersection of the cognitive map itself and the individual strategies and skills. Second, one's ability to successfully navigate the space will depend, in part, on the *correspondence* between the cognitive map one has internalized and the features of the building. Third, the ability to use one's strategies and skills to successfully navigate will depend on whether one's navigational skill profile is compatible with the building features. For example, if one is largely dependent on establishing a set of routes, then having distinguishing features might produce higher *compatibility* than having highly similar features across different areas. Finally, at the centre of all of these components, we can consider the overall *complexity* of the wayfinding problem given that the individual navigator can be in a motivational state that can vary over time as a function of both emotional attributes and current goals (see Chapter 8, by Kuliga, in this book). This individual will also vary with respect to his or her capacity to form a cognitive map, and this cognitive map development will be dependent on the features of the specific environment.

This framework provides a context to consider some of the potential problems that give rise to navigational difficulty in the Seattle Central Library. For example, the high degree of architectural differentiation throughout the building may make it difficult to establish the global structure because the corresponding features may not line up from one floor to another – hallways that are frequently parallel from one floor to the next may be perpendicular or oblique to each other. This might make it difficult to establish correspondence between one's cognitive map and the environment. Similarly, people may perceive that the building allows certain navigational actions that do not match the actual paths or actions available in the environment. This mismatch of perceived and actual affordances challenges the compatibility. In this case, one may see an escalator and plan to use it to ascend to the next floor only to find that this particular escalator skips floors, offering no access to the floors in between. This can be further complicated by cases in which one cannot simply reverse a path to return to a starting point (e.g., when there is a single escalator up, but no corresponding escalator down). These problems along with the overall complexity of the space likely lead to incomplete or fragmented cognitive maps – at worst, people may abandon the effort to even establish a meaningful representation and rely strictly on signage.

With this in mind, we engaged in an opportunistic, one-day, real-world experiment to collect preliminary data on human navigators finding their way to specific targets in the Seattle Central Library. We focused on the building (environmental factor) and the skills of the individual (skills factor) to measure navigational performance in naïve participants (new to Seattle and the library). We did not attempt to systematically incorporate the cognitive map because of the complexities associated with delivering specific experiences, so we focused on utilizing the space as a first-time visitor.

In order to capture the range of human wayfinding behaviours and strategies in an appropriate and representative manner, great care has to be taken in selecting the start and destination locations of wayfinding tasks. Wayfinding tasks for this study were developed jointly in an iterative fashion, with some materials developed remotely and some on-site. First, we analysed the floor plans and identified the location of vertical connections, (cf. Hölscher et al., 2012), which would allow coordination across floors.

We also identified sloped floors, which can be confusing to interpret when examining a map of the building or disruptive when viewed from an egocentric perspective (Holmes et al., 2015; Nardi et al., 2011). Based on the library website and known library functions, we identified a set of potential destinations that represent typical library activities and media types (analogous to a Personas and Scenarios approach; see Dalton's Chapter 3 in this book). Once on-site, we conducted interviews with librarians and volunteers who regularly direct patrons to destinations to confirm and refine selections. We also spoke with a number of patrons to understand their goals and perspectives.

Using the information gathered, two main factors were systematically varied to generate the wayfinding tasks: spatially simple versus complex (based on space syntax analyses) and within versus between floor (see Figure 9.2). The start and end locations for each task as well as the shortest paths are depicted in Figure 9.3. For example, the complex, within-floor task was to find a 'Sherlock-Holmes' novel. This book was located in a corner of the building that was originally planned as a museum shop. The museum shop was later relocated to a more central position, presumably because the original location was identified as being too segregated, which is in line with our syntactic analysis of the building layout. The test destinations were selected so that all locations could be referenced by the (sparse) signage in the building. The paths to these destinations allowed for multiple routes and utilized different structural aspects of the building.

In conjunction with the 2011 meeting of the Psychonomic Society, we invited colleagues to participate in this brief experiment. Participants (n=28) were brought to the library and given the navigational challenges in four different orders. For each challenge, the participant was tracked in real time by an experimenter using a developmental version of PeopleWatcher (Dalton et al., 2012), a custom iPad® app that was developed in the context of this study and that allows an observer to code participant behaviours. The application allowed the experimenter to trace the participant's path through the environment and to code additional events including pausing, checking signs, and reversing directions. We were then able to quantify the performance of individuals on the four different challenges and explore whether the variability in performance might be due to differences in skills and reported abilities/preferences. Broadly speaking we were interested in capturing how efficiently each person moved to each goal location. To this end we recorded how many times they stopped, how long it took each person to get from one place to another, and how much they deviated from the shortest possible path.

When they completed all four challenges, participants returned to the conference hotel and completed a set of questionnaires and measures of spatial skills and experiences. These included measures of mental rotation (MRT; Vandenberg and Kuse, 1978), perspective taking (Spatial Perspective Taking; Kozhevnikov and Hegarty, 2001), sense of direction (Santa Barbara Sense of Direction, Hegarty et al., 2002), spatial anxiety (Spatial Anxiety Scale; Lawton, 1994), and navigational preferences (Questionnaire on Spatial Representation, Pazzaglia and De Beni, 2001). These measures allowed us to profile each individual in terms of their skill in reasoning about spatial relations in small-scale objects that are relevant to navigation (e.g. maps), skill in navigating in large-scale space, as well as navigational strategies (e.g., preference to follow signs or use familiar paths) and emotional comfort or discomfort with having difficulty navigating (being lost). The measures were a combination of objective tests

	Spatially Simple	Spatially Complex
Within Floors	 Restroom	 Sherlock Holmes
Between Floors	 Non-fiction DVDs	 Meeting Room 6

Figure 9.2 Four challenges defined by the complexity and number of floors.

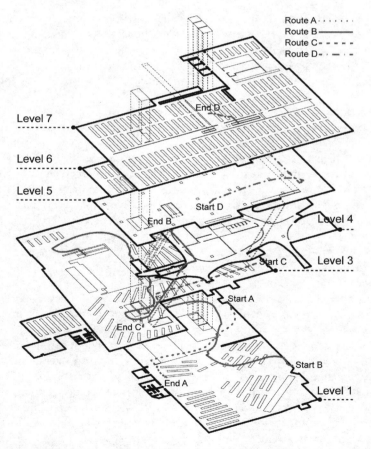

Figure 9.3 Start and end locations for the navigation tasks, connected by the shortest paths.

Figure 9.4 Select quotes from participants (grey = negative comments; white = positive comments).

and self-report measures that have been shown to be correlated with objective navigation performance (see Wolbers and Hegarty, 2010). Finally, we asked participants to rank the difficulty of the four challenges and offer comments on the navigability of the space. Notably, the comments were consistent with the abundant anecdotes from the internet (see Figure 9.4, see also Chapter 10 on using the internet for post-occupancy evaluation or 'POE2.0').

The preliminary results were striking for several reasons. Most prominently, we observed that the complexity of the space as defined by the spatial analysis only for some of the tasks predicted the difficulty that participants experienced when navigating to the goals. In measures of both performance (difference between ideal and actual path length, number of pauses, use of signage, etc.) and in perceived difficulty rankings, the easiest challenge was the spatially simple, within-floor trial (restroom), as predicted. However, the most difficult trial was the spatially simple, between-floor challenge (non-fiction DVDs). In other words, the spatial analysis predicted this would be easier than at least one of the complex challenges, but participants had a grossly different experience. In addition, performance on the four challenges had different relationships with the individual differences measures, suggesting that they depend on different skills rather than being ranked on some single dimension.

Experimenter and participant observations shed some light on this issue (for an in-depth discussion see Chapter 8 by Kuliga). First, experimenters noticed that there were distinct differences among the trial types with respect to how participants corrected their errors in navigation. In the complex, between-floor tasks (meeting room), many participants travelled via the 'wrong' escalator, causing them to overshoot the correct floor. However, they had immediate feedback as they watched the desired floor pass by, so they had instant information about what kind of correction was necessary. By contrast, in the simple, between-floor task (non-fiction DVDs), the error was more semantically driven as they had to determine whether to search for a non-fiction section or a visual media centre. When a participant suspected an error had occurred, there was no feedback on the nature of the error. The participant did not

Why people get lost in the Library 163

know whether it was a local failure (correct floor, wrong specific location) or a more global failure to get to the right part of the library. Moreover, there were not salient indicators for how to correct the error in either a local or global context. In short, finding the non-fiction DVDs was a very complex task but not as defined by the space syntax analysis.

This unexpected twist in the data suggests that a broader interpretation of the individual differences/strategies component than the situational variables such as current goals, emotional/motivational state, and common-sense background knowledge (Frankenstein et al., 2012; Lynch, 1960). For example, patrons of the library come in with their own goals, whether it is to check out a book, to meet a friend, or to find a cosy place to study. These goals may drive their selection of a strategy and dictate their experience in the library. In addition, patrons may differ in their commitment to these goals, which may further impact their navigation strategy. Our participants were given arbitrary (yet plausible) navigation goals, such that their primary motivation might have been to please the experimenters or to explore a new space. We cannot presume that all of our participants were equally motivated, and we have little to go on in terms of understanding how variability in this dimension might affect performance. Finally, individual differences may also provide the common-sense knowledge that participants bring to bear. This would again support the apparent difficulty associated with our spatially easy, between-floors challenge – the non-fiction DVDs, where the expectation was that these should either be in the non-fiction section or in a media centre, depending on the participants' past experience. In fact, the non-fiction media section was distinct from both the non-fiction books and the 'feature film, video, and DVD collection'.

This expansion of individual differences to include a wide range of both locally stable characteristics (e.g., skills that have been acquired over time, motivational styles, etc.) and dynamic situational variables (e.g., current emotional state, goals, etc.) opens up a whole new set of questions about how to characterize the individual entering into a navigational problem. Although it is beyond the scope of the current chapter, it should be noted that within the three-factor framework, each factor may need its own framing, replete with ideas about critical interactions. For individual differences, we likely need to think about how these state and trait variables interact to offer a dynamic profile for any given navigational situation.

We examined the navigational qualities of the Seattle Central Library in light of the Carlson et al. (2010) framework for understanding how people learn and navigate in buildings. The unique design of the library allowed us to push the limits of the model, and we observed that we need to apply broader definitions of individual differences and strategies than are typical in the spatial cognition literature. This preliminary empirical work sets the stage for a comprehensive approach to understanding the critical interaction between building design and the human side of navigation, and serves as an opportunity to examine this interaction in a highly selective group, primarily cognitive psychologists/academics with an interest in space, allowing us to gain more expert feedback from a naïve sample. These participants are not representative of the typical patrons of the Seattle Central Library.

To address these limitations and expand the reach of this line of inquiry, we developed a follow-up study in collaboration with Saskia Kuliga. Using internet advertising in Seattle, the second study recruited from a much broader range of individuals

164 *Amy Shelton et al.*

educationally and a sample more representative of the local population. In this version, we were able to include two additional wayfinding challenges in order to better understand the role of spatial complexity and its relationship to navigational difficulty. In addition, in-depth post-experimental interviews were formally used for all participants to capture information about navigational strategies as well as the participants' subjective experiences and appraisals of the building (see Chapter 8 by Kuliga in this volume). Additional integrative analyses of the two studies together will further inform these issues in the future.

The Seattle Central Library is notoriously hard to navigate for many people, and our results to date substantiate the anecdotes. One might take this to mean that the library is simply a quirk of architectural design with little hope of generalizing to broader issues of human navigation. However, our project demonstrates the power of having a unique set of conditions in which to test the limits of current models. The lack of control over the structures and how to understand them was evident in our inability to accurately predict difficulty. Regardless of one's opinion on the pros and cons of navigating within the library, there is little question that it is an interesting and provocative space.

References

Bohbot, V. D., Lerch, J., Thorndycraft, B., Iaria, G., and Zijdenbos, A. P. (2007). Gray matter differences correlate with spontaneous strategies in a human virtual navigation task. *Journal of Neuroscience*, 27(38), 10078–83.

Burgess, N., Jeffery, K. J., and O'Keefe, J. (Eds). (1999). *The hippocampal and parietal foundations of spatial cognition.* Oxford: Oxford University Press.

Carlson, L. A., Hölscher, C., Shipley, T. F., and Dalton, R. C. (2010). Getting lost in buildings. *Current Directions in Psychological Science*, 19(5), 284–9.

Chrastil, E. R., Warren, W. H. (2014). From cognitive maps to cognitive graphs. *PLoS ONE*, 9(11): e112544. doi:10.1371/journal.pone.0112544.

Dalton, R., Dalton, N., Kuhnmünch, G., and Hölscher, C. (2012). An iPad app for recording movement paths and associated spatial behaviors. *Proceedings of Spatial Cognition 2012*, Springer LNCS Series, pp. 431–50.

Fields, A. W. and Shelton, A. L. (2006). Individual skill differences and large-scale environmental learning. *Journal of Experimental Psychology: Learning, Memory and Cognition*, 32(3), 506–15.

Frankenstein, J., Brüssow, S., Ruzzoli, F., and Hölscher, C. (2012). The language of landmarks: The role of background knowledge in indoor wayfinding. *Cognitive Processing*, 13(Suppl. 1), 165–70.

Furman, A. J., Clements-Stephens, A. M., Marchette, S. A., and Shelton, A. L. (2014). Persistent and stable biases in spatial learning mechanisms predict navigational style. *Cognitive, Affective and Behavioral Neuroscience*, 14(4), 1375–91.

Gallistel, C. R. (1990). *The organization of learning.* Cambridge, MA: Bradford Books/MIT Press.

Golledge, R. G. (1999). Human wayfinding and cognitive maps. In R. G. Golledge (Ed.), *Wayfinding behavior: Cognitive mapping and other spatial processes* (pp. 5–45). Baltimore, MD: Johns Hopkins University Press.

Hartley, T., Maguire, E. A., Spiers, H. J., and Burgess, N. (2003). The well-worn route and the path less traveled: Distinct neural bases of route following and wayfinding in humans. *Neuron*, 37, 877–88.

Hegarty, M., Richardson, A. E., Montello, D. R., Lovelace, K., and Subbiah, I. (2002). Development of a self-report measure of environmental spatial ability. *Intelligence*, 30, 425–47.

Holmes, C. A., Nardi, D., Newcombe, N. S., and Weisberg, S. M. (2015). Children's use of slope to guide navigation: Sex differences relate to spontaneous slope perception. *Spatial Cognition and Computation*, 15(3), 170–85.

Hölscher, C., Brösamle, M., and Vrachliotis, G. (2012). Challenges in multi-level wayfinding: A case-study with space syntax technique. *Environment and Planning B: Planning and Design*, 39, 63–82.

Iaria, G., Petrides, M., Dagher, A., Pike, B., and Bohbot, V. D. (2003). Cognitive strategies dependent on the hippocampus and caudate nucleus in human navigation: Variability and change with practice. *Journal of Neuroscience*, 23(13), 5945–52.

Ishikawa, T. and Montello, D. R. (2006). Spatial knowledge acquisition from direct experience in the environment: Individual differences in the development of metric knowledge and the integration of separately learned places. *Cognitive Psychology*, 52(2), 93–129.

Kozhevnikov, M. and Hegarty, M. (2001). A dissociation between object manipulation, spatial ability and spatial orientation ability. *Memory and Cognition*, 29(5), 745–56.

Lacayo, R. (2004). Top 10 everything 2004 – architecture: Seattle Public Library. *Time*, 17 December. Retrieved from http://www.time.com/time/specials/packages/article/0,28804,1999700_1998814_1999 521,00.html.

Lawton, C. A. (1994). Gender differences in way-finding strategies: Relationship to spatial ability and spatial anxiety. *Sex Roles*, 30(11), 765–79.

Lynch, K. (1960). *The image of the city*. Cambridge, MA: MIT Press.

Marchette, S. A., Bakker, A., and Shelton, A. L. (2011). Cognitive mappers to creatures of habit: Differential engagement of place and response learning mechanisms predicts human navigational behavior. *Journal of Neuroscience*, 31(43), 15264–8.

Montello, D. R. and Pick, H. L. (1993). Integrating knowledge of vertically aligned large-scale spaces. *Environment and Behavior*, 25(3), 457–84.

Nardi, D., Newcombe, N. S., and Shipley, T. F. (2011). The world is not flat: Can people reorient using slope? *Journal of Experimental Psychology: Learning, Memory, and Cognition*, 37(2), 354.

Newcombe, N. S. and Huttenlocher, J. (2000). *Making space: The development of spatial representation and reasoning*. Cambridge, MA: MIT Press.

O'Keefe, J. and Nadel, L. (1978). *The hippocampus as a cognitive map*. Oxford: Oxford University Press.

Pazzaglia, F. and De Beni, R. (2001). Strategies of processing spatial information in survey and landmark-centred individuals. *European Journal of Cognitive Psychology*, 13(4), 493–508.

Schinazi, V. R., Nardi, D., Newcombe, N. S., Shipley, T. F., and Epstein, R. A. (2013). Hippocampal size predicts rapid learning of a cognitive map in humans. *Hippocampus*, 23(6), 515–28.

Shelton, A. L., Marchette, S. A., and Furman, A. J. (2013). A mechanistic approach to individual differences in spatial learning, memory, and navigation. In B. H. Ross (Ed.), *Psychology of learning and motivation* (Vol. 59, pp. 223–59). Waltham, MA: Academic Press.

Stevens, A. and Coupe, P. (1978). Distortions in judged spatial relations. *Cognitive Psychology*, 10, 422–37.

Tolman, E. C. (1948). Cognitive maps in rats and men. *Psychological Review*, 55, 189–208.

Tversky, B. (1981). Distortions in memory for maps. *Cognitive Psychology*, 13(3), 407–33.

Vandenberg, S. G. and Kuse, A. R. (1978). Mental rotations, a group test of three-dimensional spatial visualization. *Perceptual and Motor Skills*, 47, 599–604.

Wang, R. F. and Brockmole, J. R. (2003). Human navigation in nested environments. *Journal of Experimental Psychology: Learning, Memory and Cognition*, 29, 398–404.

Weisberg, S. M., Schinazi, V. R., Newcombe, N. S., Shipley, T. F., and Epstein, R. A. (2014). Variations in cognitive maps: Understanding individual differences in navigation. *Journal of Experimental Psychology: Learning, Memory, and Cognition*, 40(3, May), 669–82.

Weisman, J. (1981). Evaluating architectural legibility: Way-finding in the built environment. *Environment and Behavior*, 13, 189–204.

Wolbers, T. and Hegarty, M. (2010). What determines our navigational abilities? *Trends in Cognitive Sciences*, 14(3), 138–46.

10 Using social media to gather users' feedback of the Seattle Central Library

Ruth Conroy Dalton and Saskia Kuliga

This chapter presents a scoping study in which unsolicited user feedback of the Seattle Central Library was gathered from selected social media and user-review websites to determine the viability of utilising social media as a novel and unconventional approach to post-occupancy evaluation (POE).[1] Fourteen social media/review websites were surveyed and all available review data were extracted. This resulted in a rich dataset of almost 500 reviews, which were subject to further analyses of temporal and geographic patterns, numerical ratings, and the semantic content of the reviews. The study's results suggest building users are quite willing to share, without solicitation, their experiences. The results showed: a high proportion of local reviewers (40 per cent); highly regular, temporal patterns of posting, suggesting a sustained interest in reviewing over a period of seven years; numerical ratings suggesting that comments were not dominated by highly opinionated, extreme reviewers but represented a broad range of views; and geographic differences in the semantic content of the reviews. The chapter suggests that highly valuable information is currently available from peer-to-peer networks and that this forms a new class of POE data which is radically different to current POE paradigms. It concludes that this data might be most valuable through augmenting, and not supplanting, traditional POE.

Background and introduction

What is happening to POE in the era of rising social networks? Might it be evolving into something not only new, but potentially more empowering for building users? This chapter presents a study which begins to explore the value of bottom-up, unsolicited, user-generated building evaluations. 'This [study] is entirely outside the dominant conventions of POE which traditionally is conducted through top-down, highly pre-structured, often fixed-option, questionnaires' (Cooper, 2012).

Academic context of the chapter

This enquiry emerged from an ongoing, parallel research study investigating the wayfinding and navigation problems in the Seattle Central Library in downtown Seattle (please see the preceding chapter by Shelton et al. for an account of this study). The team working on this study consisted of cognitive scientists, an environmental psychologist, a cultural anthropologist, and an architect, all with research backgrounds in wayfinding and spatial cognition. In November 2010 an 'indicative POE' study (term introduced by Preiser, 1995) consisting of walk-through evaluations, photographs, and interviews with key stakeholders of the library (a member of the original architectural team, Head of Communications, Head of Volunteer Services, a library volunteer, the designer of the library's current wayfinding signage system, and a library user) was conducted. This first study was followed up by a 'diagnostic POE' (Preiser's terminology, 1995) in May/June 2012 with an in-depth focus on wayfinding in the building (this study, with 37 participants, consisted of wayfinding tasks, individual interviews, and a card-sorting task – see Chapter 8 for the results of the interviews and the card-sorting task). The Seattle Central Library was selected for this study as it has documented navigational problems; the project architect commented of the building,

> The wayfinding wasn't done perfectly, to put it kindly... When you understand the building, it is very simple – just a series of boxes. But what we didn't understand is, to the uninitiated person, someone not an architect or library staffer, it can be complex if they don't understand that. What we thought is blatantly obvious, isn't.
>
> (Prince-Ramus quoted in Marshall, 2008)

During the preparation stage of the initial 'evaluative POE' study, the authors stumbled upon a number of unsolicited online reviews of the library on review websites such as Yelp.com, which served a valuable function of helping to fine-tune the two, above-mentioned studies of the library. The utility of these unsolicited reviews led to a number of research questions, which this chapter attempts to address: first, how does user-generated, social media-based feedback fit into the standard definitions or toolkits of POE research? Second, how useful are such datasets in augmenting other POE studies? Third, what topics are discussed in social media comments? With these questions in mind, the aim of this study was to rigorously analyse the corpus of available information contained in these review websites (collected in July 2012) to determine the viability of utilising social media as a novel and unconventional approach to POE.

Introduction to POE

There are numerous definitions of POE (including but not limited to Zimring and Reizenstein, 1980; Preiser, 1995; Gill et al., 2010; and Leaman and Bordass, 2001) which are remarkably consistent in their characterisations, proposing that POE covers a broad range of methods employed to rigorously and objectively study the performance of designed environments with respect to their occupants and, in more recent years, also including the physical/environmental performance of a building (for example, its energy consumption). Since the origins of POE in the late 1960s (Preiser, 1995), most occupancy evaluation has typically been conducted by professionals and academics from a number of fields, often in a process of interdisciplinary collaboration. As Bechtel (1996) comments, 'Diverse fields such as psychology, anthropology, architecture, sociology, geography, and landscape architecture are united when they want to evaluate environments'. Furthermore, in an almost contemporaneous paper by Stokols (1995), he, too, suggests that POE 'Reflect[s] its multidisciplinary roots – spanning psychology, architecture, urban planning, behavioral geography, urban sociology, and other fields'. Mirrored by the interdisciplinary origins of the researchers employing them, the methods used to conduct post-occupancy evaluations

Using social media to gather users' feedback   169

also vary (and are frequently characterised by a combination of multiple methods, such as linking interviews, focus groups, questionnaires, manual observations (often conducted as walkthroughs), and research into the design and procurement processes behind a building (Bechtel, 1996).

In order to rationalise such a diverse set of approaches and methods, Preiser attempted to create categorisation of the primary types of POE studies (1995). In this classification, he defines three types of POE: indicative, investigative, and diagnostic. The characteristics, as proposed by Preiser, of these three categories are outlined in rows 1 to 3 of Table 10.1 (row 4 will be addressed later in this chapter).

In recent years, some POE tools have become highly structured and schematised resulting in the key advantage that such structure permits inter-building, inter-organisational, and longitudinal comparisons. 'POEs have evolved from rather simple minded, one of a kind case studies of individual facilities to sophisticated cross-sectional studies of building types with valid, reproducible and generalizable results' (Preiser, 1995). One noteworthy POE process, illustrating these advantages, was the Probe (Post-occupancy review of buildings and their engineering) project/s which ran from 1995–2002 (Bordass and Leaman, 2004). Of relevance to this chapter, is the fact that the Probe approach included a strong emphasis on the role of the user and included an occupant questionnaire. It is suggested, by the creators of Probe, that POE studies, 'Consider the full range of users… staff, visitors, cleaners, security, contractors and passers-by. Do not focus on a subset or an average' (Leaman and Bordass, 2001).

Table 10.1 Characteristics of different POE types (rows 1–3 after Preiser, 1995)

POE categories	Characteristics				
	Activities	*Duration*	*Level of effort*	*Frequency of use*	*Structure*
Indicative POE	Walk-through evaluations, interviews, and inspections	Quick (a few hours)	Least effort	Most common	Top-down and low structure
Investigative POE	Interviews, survey questionnaires, photographic/ video recordings, physical measurements	More in-depth (one week to several months)	Intermediate effort	Moderately common	Top-down and high structure
Diagnostic POE	Longitudinal, cross-section evaluations of specific performance aspects	Highly focused (months to years)	Most effort	Least common	Top-down and high structure
POE 2.0	Ongoing website monitoring and data analysis	Continuous (no defined end point)	Practically effortless	Newly emerging. Potential ubiquity	Bottom-up and low structure

However, despite such exceptional approaches to user feedback, that encompass a truly democratic range of users, as described above, it is still the case that many, highly structured approaches to POE tend to work best for more permanent building occupants (for example the office worker) and less effectively for transient, highly fluid building users such as visitors, who may only enter a building once (airports, hospitals, or recreational/tourist sites all have a high proportion of unfamiliar, first-time visitors). It might be suggested that a different approach could be more suitable for the building 'visitor' as opposed to the 'occupant' or 'inhabitant' (Seamon in Chapter 5 elaborates on these distinctions).

The opposite of the highly structured, top-down approach, are studies that attempt to elicit free-ranging comments from building users. As Leaman and Bordass note, 'Occupants... get fed up with long or repeated questionnaires, and cease to answer them carefully, if at all' (Leaman and Bordass, 2001). This is supported by Cooper, who advises, 'It is necessary to use an approach to collecting data that is sufficiently open-ended to enable [people] to talk about their... environment in their own words' (Cooper, 1985). An excellent example of this approach is Cooper's study of primary school teachers, in which he invited comment, 'By means of a "free description" questionnaire" and asked them to 'Simply write down what they thought about their "working environment"' (Cooper, 1985). However, even this approach was not truly 'open' as Cooper's respondents' comments were still prompted by the provided guidance. It is suggested that to shift from the traditional 'top-down' POE approach to a completely 'bottom-up' approach, the role of social media should be considered; perhaps the future of building usability research lies less with the design professionals or even with academics, but rather with the end users themselves.

A number of reasons prompt this suggestion: first, social media has played a prominent role in recent years in terms of different kinds of (especially social and political) 'grass roots' activism; second, users are becoming more and more used to giving their opinions online (for example when reviewing books on Amazon, reviewing music on iTunes or reviewing places on TripAdvisor), so why not review buildings too?; third, at least in the UK, there appears to be an appetite from the general public for judging buildings. For example, in a television programme entitled 'Demolition' which was aired in 2005, when given a voice, the public nominated over 1,000 individual buildings for demolition (Beney et al., 2005). It is, therefore, the hypothesis of this chapter, that the time is right to propose a new kind of POE (in addition to Preiser's three categories), one that is primarily user-driven and mediated through Web 2.0. In this chapter, it will be referred to as POE 2.0. By means of the Seattle Central Library dataset, this chapter will explore the potential of social media and user-generated content to provide valuable POE information about buildings.

Introduction to the concepts of social media, Web 2.0, and user-generated content

According to Forrester Research (an IT research firm providing data on consumer habits), a significant majority of adults from Europe, North and South America, as well as metropolitan areas of Asia are habitual users of social media. Estimations of the proportions of people who are active users of social media range from around 80 per cent upwards, depending upon the country of origin, the age of the user group, and the date of the survey (since this figure is increasing all the time, surveys of user behaviour become rapidly outdated). Forrester Research has produced the following list of classifications of user-type: 'Creators' (those who produce novel content by writing blogs, uploading videos, etc.); 'Critics' (those who comment upon the content generated by the first group, or those giving ratings/reviews of products or services); the other user types are 'Collectors', 'Joiners', 'Spectators', and 'Inactives'. This chapter, with its concentration on POE, focuses on the group of 'Critics', because the activity of reviewing, or evaluating, a building online is no different, according to this classification, to the act of reviewing, for example, a restaurant or a plumber. (The category of 'Critic' blurs into the category of 'Creator' when a review is augmented by uploaded photographs of the building; 7.3 per cent of this study's contributors were therefore classified as 'Creators' as well as 'Critics'. The effect that this may have on the content of comments submitted (as opposed to traditional POE comments) is influenced by the expectation that they will be read by other visitors, or would-be visitors to the building. Those reading the reviews form the category of users of social media termed 'Spectators' in the above list. According to Forrester Research the group of 'Critics' is the third highest group, the most popular being the 'Spectators'.

So what do these terms, Web 2.0, social media, and user-generated content mean and how are they related? Web 2.0 is essentially a term for all internet-based, enabling technologies that permit users to create and share content (and even modify the content of others) in a highly collaborative fashion. Social media usually refers to specific applications (on the internet or mobile platforms) created to allow networks of friends/acquaintances to exchange communications on a one-to-many or many-to-many basis. Finally, user-generated content can simply be seen as the sum total of all content that has been written, posted, or uploaded onto websites (often using social media applications and on a Web 2.0 platform) by users. This relationship between all three is clarified in Figure 10.1 and is based upon distinctions from Kaplan and Haenlein (2010).

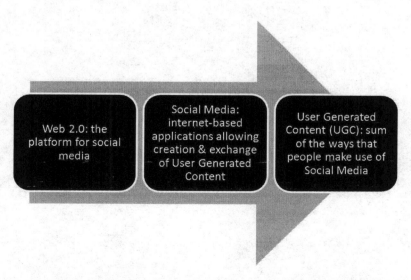

Figure 10.1 Relationship between Web 2.0, social media, and user-generated content (after Kaplan and Haenlein, 2010).

172 *Ruth Conroy Dalton and Saskia Kuliga*

Methods

The Seattle Central Library

The Seattle Central Library is the focus of this study: see Figures 10.2 and 10.3 for the plans of the public areas of the library and its exterior appearance. In 2011 the number of patron visits to Seattle Central Library was 1,903,954 (Seattle Central Library website). It is also a building about which public and critical opinion appears divided, with it being alternatively lauded (e.g., voted *Time Magazine's Building of the Year* in 2004 and recipient of the *American Institute of Architects Honor Award for Architecture* in 2005) and yet, at the same time, being notorious for being hard to

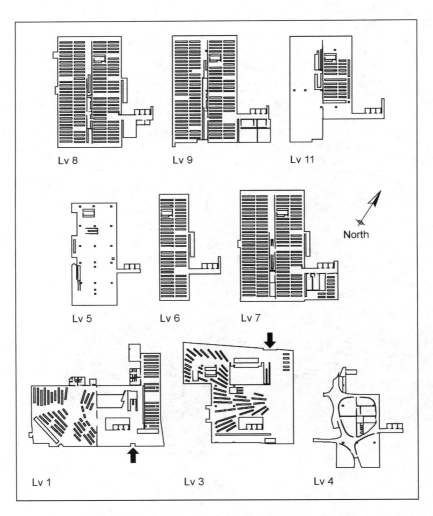

Figure 10.2 Plans of public levels and areas of the Seattle Central Library (arrows indicate the entrances).

navigate (see the architect's quote above and comments by the Chief Librarian, 'The way-finding isn't working. By the second or third day, we had to put up signs to help people' (Jacobs, 2004) and the signage designer, 'It is not without heart-breaking irony that we acknowledge a near-total lack of legibility' (Mau, 2005, p. 242).

Data collection

A number of different websites that contained reviews of the Seattle Central Library were identified. (Returning briefly to Forrester Research's definition of the different types of user of social media, and focusing on the 'Critics' group of users, only websites that provided a framework for people to review, rate, and/or comment upon goods, local services, and places were sought.) At the time of writing, only 14 websites that fulfilled the above criteria and included reviews of the Seattle Central Library were found. These websites could broadly be divided into 'general review' sites (of which Yelp contained the highest volume, see Figure 10.4 for Yelp's interface), 'tourist' websites advising visitors of sights, places, or activities worth visiting (of which TripAdvisor contained the highest volume), and finally, what might be termed, specialist 'architectural' websites, of which Archdaily proved to be the most utilized for reviewing/rating buildings. The information gathered from each website was the name and any indicators of 'social status' of the reviewer, the geographic location of

Figure 10.3 External view of Seattle Central Library. Photograph from author's collection.

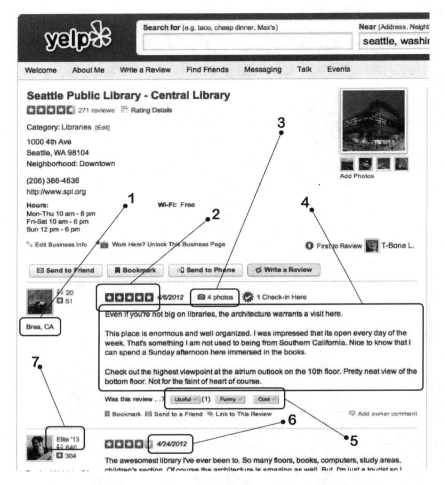

Figure 10.4 Example of an online review page, source: Yelp.com

Notes: (1 = geographic location of reviewer; 2 = numerical rating of building; 3 = numbers of photos uploaded, if any; 4 = textual content of review; 5 = buttons to vote on the review (useful, funny, and cool); 6 = date of posting of the review; 7 = elite status of the reviewer).

the reviewer (if available), the date of the creation/upload of the review, the numerical rating (if any), the text content of any comments provided, if photographs were uploaded with the review, the numbers of photographs added, and other reviewers' ratings of the original review (whether it was found useful, valuable, etc.), if available. In total 494 reviews were amassed and these were primarily, although not exclusively, gathered from only two of the 14 sites, Yelp and TripAdvisor (constituting 53.24 per cent and 37.85 per cent of the dataset, respectively).

Responses are mostly to be found in the general review websites (led by Yelp with 263 reviews). These general review websites were Yelp, Insiderpages, Judy's Book, Yahoo! Local, and Citysearch. The 'tourist' websites were dominated by TripAdvisor, with 187 reviews, and consisting of the following sites: TripAdvisor, Virtual Tourist, and

Lonely Planet. Of the specialist architectural websites, only Archdaily had any notable number of reviews (15 in total); the other websites considered were OpenBuildings, Archiplanet, ArchitectureWeek's Great Buildings Collection, ArchitectureWeek's DesignCommunity, MIMOA: online architecture guide, and ArchDaily. (The authors suggest that one reason why so few reviews were found on such specialist 'architectural' websites is possibly that they are more frequented by architects and that professional etiquette might make architects wary of reviewing other architects' buildings.)

Two potential sources of data that were excluded from the above dataset were reviews commenting upon photographs of Seattle Central Library which had been uploaded onto Flickr (of which there were 33,778 images as of 25 July 2012) and videos of the library uploaded onto the website YouTube. Equally, there are approximately 822 videos on YouTube which are associated with the words 'Seattle Central Library'. One of the most viewed videos is by one of the project architects, Joshua Prince-Ramus (which elicited 22 comments, many of them about the building rather than the video per se). These sources were not included in the dataset as it was ultimately too hard to distinguish the extent to which the comments refer to the primary source (the building) versus the secondary source (the photograph or video).

Finally, in considering social media, both Facebook and Twitter should be discussed. Seattle Central Library has its own Facebook page, created 16 November 2007. The library opened 23 May 2004, so the Facebook page was created almost three and a half years after the opening of the library. It has had 15,355 'likes' (where other users can click onto an icon resembling a 'thumbs up' gesture, indicating a generic, positive response to the page/site/comment or post). At the time of writing this chapter (25 July 2012), 760 users were 'talking about this' (those who have posted any kind of comment mentioning the library on the site). There is also an associated 'Friends of the Seattle Public Library' Facebook site, which has 926 'likes', and was created on Facebook on 23 June 2010, just over two and a half years after the main Facebook site was created and just over six years after the library opened. There are two reasons why these Facebook comments were excluded from the dataset: first, the Facebook sites cover not only Seattle Central Library (the OMA/LMN building) but also other libraries in the Seattle library system and, second, most comments/posts refer to recent or upcoming events taking place in the library. This focus on events rather than the building is equally true of the Seattle Central Library Twitter feed (@SPLBuzz: having issued 1,891 tweets and having 2,943 followers).

Parsing the content of the reviews

The reviews were allocated to a set of pre-defined categories by three human raters. Previous research from the same research group (Brösamle, 2013; Brösamle and Hölscher, 2008) suggests that the terminology used by interviewees in the field of architecture is often too heterogeneous and idiosyncratic to allow for automatic classification or categorisation of small and medium-sized collections of short documents (Brösamle looked at architectural designers as experts in the discourse, and this limitation is likely also apply to lay people in social media contexts).

The pre-defined categories were selected to broadly cover the spectrum of architectural aspects in the high-level categorisation of Preiser (1995) and allowed for capturing comments about orientation and wayfinding issues, which were of specific interest in the context of other studies of Seattle Central Library. Preiser suggests that when POE evaluations are being undertaken, three categories of performance

176 Ruth Conroy Dalton and Saskia Kuliga

Table 10.2 Mapping between Preiser's Levels of Performance categories and this study's semantic categories

Preiser's categories: levels of performance	Study's semantic categories
(1) Health and safety	NA
Security	
(2) Functionality	Functional
Efficiency	Orientation and navigation
(3) Social	Social aspects
Aesthetic	Aesthetics and emotions
Psychological	
Cultural	Architecture and emotion

should be considered (see column 1 of Table 10.1). Almost no reviews gathered discussed issues relating to Preiser's Level 1 category (health, safety, and security) and so Preiser's remaining two categories were used and further unpacked for purposes of disambiguation. The approximate mapping between Preiser's categories and the semantic categories used in this study are shown in Table 10.2.

The pre-defined categories are intended as a means to quantify major themes and to allow for assessing the prevalence of positive and negative comments in these areas. This is identical in approach to Cooper's 1985 study of open-response comments of school teachers. In Cooper's precedent study, the teacher's comments were subjected to two types of thematic analysis, quantitative and qualitative. In precisely the manner utilised here, Cooper's qualitative analysis judged whether comments related to a number of pre-defined thematic categories and whether the tone of the comments were 'endorsive', 'neutral', or 'critical' (he also uses a fourth category that this study does not use, 'prescriptive') (Cooper, 1985). See Table 10.3 for example comments about Seattle Central Library.

Yet these categories cannot, by themselves, detect themes that were not anticipated by the researchers. For in-depth qualitative analysis they can be combined with open-ended, data-driven techniques. A popular approach in the social media context is to visualise dominant terms via tag clouds/word clouds, so-called Wordles (see Figure 10.7). Wordles can be computed both across and with category and support a human analyst in spotting frequent themes and detecting oddities. An alternative approach is to generate a category system based on the verbal dataset. In the Grounded Theory approach (e.g. Corbin and Strauss, 2008; Bryant, 2002) to analysing verbal protocols (Krippendorff, 2004), human analysts carefully develop a category scheme over several iterations of processing the verbal raw data in an attempt to capture the most distinctive and relevant themes while avoiding imposing structures based on their preconceptions.

Automated techniques can also be employed to structure the verbal data set and generate categories. Here the main approach is to cluster documents with similar content into groups (automatic text clustering (Sharma and Gupta, 2012)), based on frequency of words and phrases, and then derive cluster labels (automatic cluster labelling). Techniques like Latent Semantic Analysis (Landauer et al., 1998) can help to reduce the effect of heterogeneous terminology, especially when combined with a

Table 10.3 Examples of positive and negative comment extracts for each of the five Seattle Central Library categories

---

Functionality

Positive comment	'Fantastic Book selection and tons of nooks and crannies to grab a book, read, study and work on your laptop. Ps: Free Wi-Fi'.
Negative comment	'It's noisy in general, also un-library-like. The interior is chaotic, not conducive to reading or studying, which are basic library activities.'

Orientation and navigation

Positive comment	'The library is well kept and easy to navigate'.
Negative comment	'Escalators that shoot up 3 or 4 floors without any off points are completely exclusionary. [The] lack of accessibility is bewildering. I felt like cattle herded down and up the ramps'.

Social aspects

Positive comment	'I'm also impressed by how neat the place is and how diligent the employees working in this structure are when it comes to maintaining silence, helping people, or addressing other concerns'.
Negative comment	'Some of the people here, not staff, are very rude, and a lot of people talk on their phones'.

Aesthetics and emotion

Positive comment	'I've never missed an opportunity to take visitors here and spend an hour or more walking around. And thinking about its beauty simply makes me want to go again.'
Negative comment	'Yes, it's an architectural marvel. Yes, it's sublime, Yes, it stands out. – But it lacks a gut. This library has no soul'.

Architecture and design

Positive comment	'The architecture of this building is stunning, the place is HUGE and the design is very modern. There are 10 floors and I'm amazed that a library can be so edgy in design'.
Negative comment	'The architecture here is just weird, like the red floor really, it's all red, even the ceiling, and the neon-yellow elevator that gives me motion sickness'.

larger reference dataset. Applying any such approach goes beyond the scope of the current chapter, but may prove useful for datasets of varying sizes.

Returning to the non-automated, human categorisation of the reviewers' comments, three raters were trained using sample materials, until they felt comfortable with the instructions and until the trainer judged that the raters understood and could perform the task capably. They were then instructed to read the whole text of each review and use their judgement to allocate sub-sections of the text to the appropriate semantic category (column 2 of Table 10.2). At least two raters reviewed each online comment permitting an inter-rater reliability (IRR) measure to be computed and monitor any individual bias. The SPSS macro developed by Hayes (Hayes and Krippendorff, 2007) was used to assess the inter-rater reliability of the coders for categorizing segments from the 473 user reviews into the five pre-defined categories. Krippendorff's α values greater than or equal to .800 are held as a good level of reliability and values for the smallest acceptable reliability, α_{min}, should be no less than 0.667 to be accepted as reliable (Krippendorff, 2004 p. 242). 'Rater 1' coded 473 comments (100 per cent), 'Rater 2' coded 89 comments (19 per cent), and 'Rater 3' coded 427 comments (91 per cent). The Krippendorff's α values for the different categories were: 'Orientation and navigation' = 0.434; 'Architecture and design' = 0.689; 'Functionality' = 0.719; 'Social aspects' = 0.758; 'Aesthetics and emotion' = 0.599. It is clear that three of these values only just exceed the minimum threshold of reliability, of 0.667, and that two categories ('Orientation and navigation' and 'Aesthetics and emotion') remain below this level.

In addition to the thematic content of the reviews, the raters were instructed to judge whether a themed sub-comment had a positive, negative, or neutral tone (Similar to Cooper's 1985 study). The IRR of the 'tone' exercise shows a higher reliability. The Krippendorff's α values for the different categories were: 'Orientation and navigation' = 0.804; 'Architecture and design' = 0.499; 'Functionality' = 0.696; 'Social aspects' = 0.686; 'Aesthetics and emotion' = 0.738. All of these are reliably rated ('Orientation and navigation' shows a strong level of agreement) with the one exception of the 'Architecture and design' set of comments, which is below the threshold.

Results

Temporal and geographic range of contributions

The earliest comment dated from 10 July 2005, just over a year after the opening of the Seattle Central Library, and the most recent comment found was dated 08 July 2012 (the week of the data-gathering exercises). The comments therefore span a time period of almost seven years. The temporal distribution of the online reviews is remarkably consistent: with a steady posting rate of one review approximately every nine days over these seven years (coefficient of regression (r^2) = 0.9903; significance level (p) < 0.0001; number of persons (N) = 269). There are no identifiable peaks or troughs in the data; neither does the public interest in posting reviews appear to be declining.

Of the reviews gathered, only 390 contained the place of origin of the reviewer (for some review sites it is mandatory while for others it is optional). Of these 390 locations, 128 (33 per cent) reviews originated in Seattle and a further 23 were from

Washington state, which means that 150 (39 per cent) reviewers could be considered 'local' (almost all of the Washington state, non-Seattle reviewers resided less than 20 miles from Seattle). Of the 390 reviews, only 13 (3 per cent) were from outside the USA. The most highly represented group from outside the USA were reviewers from the UK, of which there were five in total (1 per cent). The most geographically re-mote (from Seattle) reviewer was from Greenvale, a suburb of Melbourne, Australia. The 150 'local' reviewers wrote the longest reviews (mean (M) = 580 characters; standard deviation (SD) = 709); the 224 USA, out-of-state reviewers wrote shorter reviews (M = 460 characters; SD = 482), and the 13 non-USA reviewers wrote the shortest reviews (M = 345 characters; SD = 291). However, the Pearson correlation between the reviewer's location (distance from Seattle) and the character length of the submitted review falls just short of the standard 5 per cent criterion. (r^2 = 0.0097; p = 0.0520; N = 389).

Numerical ratings of reviews

Many review websites encourage the submission of a numerical rating of the review object (in this case, the Seattle Central Library). On the review websites surveyed in this chapter, this ranking was on a scale of 1 to 5, where 1 is a low opinion and 5 is a high opinion. One possible hypothesis is that only people with particularly strong opinions, either positive or negative, are likely to post reviews on websites. There was, therefore, an expectation that there would be a high frequency of 4.5 to 5 ratings (out of 5), and also a relatively high frequency of 1 to 1.5s: forming a type of inverse normal distribution, with peaks at each extreme. The results of the frequency distribution resemble a classic decay function, peaking at 5. In other words the majority of reviewers gave the building a rating of 5/5. The proportion of reviewers in each category are 1 (1.9 per cent); 2 (3 per cent); 3 (5.9 per cent); 4 (19.5 per cent); 5 (63.8 per cent).

It is also possible to divide the sample of reviews into sub-samples by considering the 'locals', 'non-locals', and non-USA reviewers separately. Partitioned in this way, the average rating of reviewers from Seattle and the wider state of Washington is 4.4 out of 5, the average rating of the out-of-state reviewers (from USA, but not Washington state) is 4.6 out of 5, and, finally, the average rating posted by international reviewers produces an average of 4.5 out of 5. In other words, there is little difference between the three sub-samples. One hypothesis might have been that 'local' reviewers could be unusually generous out of a type of civic pride (an issue touched upon by Mattern in Chapter 2) or alternatively that the 'local' reviewers might be atypically harsh as they might simply have had more time to become familiar with any shortcomings of the library (in contrast to out-of-state visitors merely being dazzled by the architecture). The fact that no noticeable difference can be detected between the sub-samples pos-sibly indicates an even-handedness of review, by all reviewers, uninfluenced by issues such as civic pride or overfamiliarity (yet, it could also be the case that these factors work in opposing directions and cancel each other out).

Length of reviews

Of the reviews gathered, the average length of the review text was 469 characters, or 88 words. However, there is a high degree of variance, with the sample having a

180 *Ruth Conroy Dalton and Saskia Kuliga*

standard deviation of 95 words (or 490 characters), higher than the sample mean. The longest review consisted of 857 words (4,549 characters) whereas, in contrast, the shortest was just two words (15 characters) long. The distribution of the review lengths (in words) resembles a 'long-tail' distribution, which is extremely common for internet phenomena. There appears no correlation between the location of the reviewer and the review length (as mentioned earlier), neither is there a correlation with the date of posting (it is not the case that people wrote shorter reviews in 2005 and are writing longer ones now or vice versa, $r^2 = 0.0539$; p = 4.63871E-07; N = 461).

Semantic content of reviews

Earlier in the chapter, the IRR was shown to be below an acceptable level for the categories of 'Orientation and navigation' and 'Aesthetics and emotion' and therefore the reliability for these two categories should be noted when reading the results for this section (the implications of this is further discussed above). For the whole sample, the topic most discussed was the architecture and design of the library, this is closely followed by the emotional response to the building and experienced spaces. The least discussed aspect overall are the social aspects of the building. This data can be further examined by dividing it into sub-samples, for the 'locals' (those living in Seattle or Washington state), the 'out-of-state' visitors, and finally the 'international' reviewers and by partitioning the data in this way, interesting differences emerge, see Figure 10.5.

What can immediately be seen from Figure 10.5 is that the locals devote more of their reviews to issues of orientation and navigation and to the social aspects of the library compared to either the out-of-state or international reviewers. Conversely the international reviewers use more words to describe the architectural/design elements of the building as well as their emotional response to and their aesthetic judgement of the building, compared to the local reviewers. The local reviewers spend less time discussing the architectural aspects of the building compared to either of the other two groups. And the international reviews dedicate slightly less text to the review of functional aspects of the building. In terms of the split between positive, neutral, and negative reviews of the library, it can immediately be seen that most reviews are positive in tone, which matches the distribution of the numerical ratings provided by the reviewers. Here, 'Orientation and navigation' and 'Aesthetics and emotion' received the most negative reviews. 'Architecture and design', 'Functionality' and 'Aesthetics and emotion' also receive the most positive reviews (see Figure 10.6).

- In the category 'Orientation and navigation', 44 comments (9.3%) were rated negative, 11 (2.3%) were judged neutral, and 96 were positive (20%).
- In the category 'Architecture and design', 23 comments (4.9%) were rated negative, 10 (2.1%) were judged neutral, and 261 were positive (55.2%).
- In the category 'Functionality', 31 comments (6.6%) were rated negative, eight (1.7%) were judged neutral, and 149 were positive (31.5%).
- In the category 'Social aspects', 17 comments (3.6%) were rated negative, six (1.3%) were judged neutral, and 42 were positive (8.9%).
- In the category 'Aesthetics and emotion', 34 comments (7.2%) were rated negative, eight (1.7%) were judged neutral, and 244 were positive (51.6%).

Using social media to gather users' feedback 181

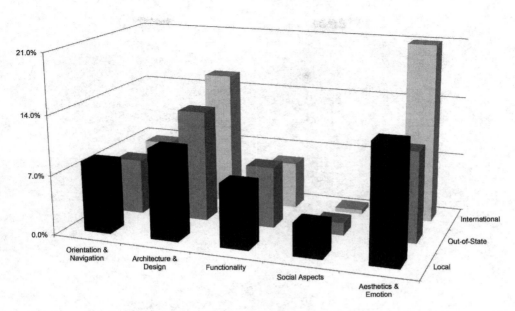

Figure 10.5 Average proportion of review content focus partitioned by geographic location of the reviewer.

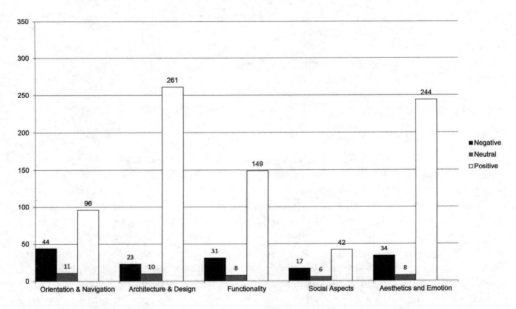

Figure 10.6 Split of positive, neutral, and negative reviews of the library by semantic theme.

If the terms employed by all reviewers are considered, key descriptor words and phrases can be extracted from the reviews and represented as a 'Wordle' in which the frequency of the usage of a word is represented by its size in the resultant word cloud (see Figure 10.7). The majority of the high-frequency words are extremely positive: this reflects the high overall numerical rating found when analysing the sample.

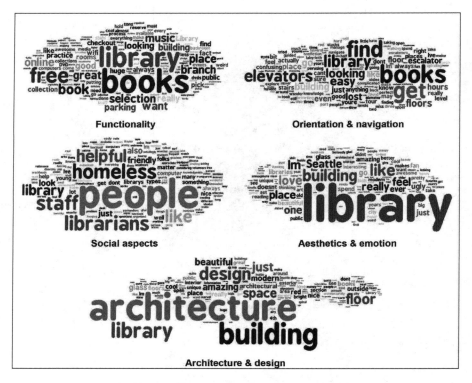

Figure 10.7 Wordles of locals' comments, split by thematic content.

Discussion

Temporal and geographic range of contributions

In this study, 473 online user reviews were identified and analysed in order to explore whether social media has the potential to refresh methods for post-occupancy evaluation. To explore whether online review websites could have the potential to provide durable user feedback, the time span between the first and last comment collected was examined. Analyses showed that posts have been made over the last seven years, at a steady rate (of approximately one review every nine days). This is encouraging for the concept of using social media and user-generated content for POE, as it suggests that, although the volume may not be high, it has the potential to be consistent and have longevity (i.e. be a durable, ongoing way of eliciting feedback).

To answer the question of whether users have an urge to provide comments from their own direct experience, the sample was analysed to determine whether the users in the study were 'local' as opposed to 'visiting' users. The results indicated that a high proportion of the reviewers can be considered 'local' and therefore their comments have the potential to be considered to be those of 'regular users' as opposed to 'visiting users' (although some of the out-of-state reviewers prefix their comments with a statement that they used to live in Seattle and formerly used the library regularly). Almost 40 per cent of the reviewers can be considered 'local'. There is, naturally, a concern that attempting to use social media forums to elicit genuine user feedback might simply invite reviews or comments from people who have very little or no experience of the library. And yet, the high proportion of 'local' reviewers suggests otherwise. It does appear that people are genuinely attempting to provide comments/reviews/ratings from their own direct experience of using the library.

Numerical ratings of reviews

One hypothesis presented in the chapter was that reviewers would tend to be individuals with a strong positive or negative opinion to share and that the numerical rating of the library would therefore be skewed towards both extremes. This hypothesis differs from the typical view, prevalent in POE research, that building users only tend to be aware of aspects of the building's performance when it fails to meet their needs: 'The environment may only impinge and obtrude if and only if and when there is something wrong' (Cooper 1985). In fact, the pattern found in the social media data is subtler, resembling a decay function, peaking at the positive end of the rating spectrum. This suggests a far more considered approach to reviewing than might initially have been expected. The result raises an interesting question of why such a different pattern of responses is being found in this sample and whether this is an artefact of the new medium (a question beyond the scope of this chapter, but a useful topic for future research). Furthermore, if this were proved an artefact of the medium, it could be an advantage to this method (that it elicits a broader range of responses).

Semantic content of reviews

It was in the analyses of the content that most differences between locals and non-locals could be found. A high variation in the length of the reviews posted was found (for POE purposes, this is perhaps less than ideal) and the topics that reviewers commented upon varied in terms of the geographic location of the reviewers. This makes sense, as the kinds of concerns and issues that a local might have (e.g. the social aspect of the library) would not necessarily be the same issues that a visitor would notice and/or comment upon. One question that this does raise, however, is that if there were attempts to 'tap into' this apparent urge by the general public to review buildings online, should the ability to review be constrained to local users of the building, or, at least, should this data (the location of the reviewer) be stored in order to subsequently partition the dataset as performed in our analyses above?

In the methods section, it was shown that the IRR of the raters given the task of assigning the comments to semantic categories proved reliable in only three of the five categories. The difficulty of automating this task was described and therefore one conclusion, given these results, is that both approaches (automatic text parsing and human classification) are problematic. Were further work to be done in this area, and human raters used for the purpose of analysing the semantic content, additional training and pilot tests would need to be performed to ensure the most reliable interpretation of the content.

As well as the thematic content of the text, the human raters also looked at the tone of the comments and whether they were positive, negative, or neutral in tone. (the IRR measures for this were more reliable than the thematic assignments). There are certainly more positive than negative reviews (which matches the decay curve found

184 Ruth Conroy Dalton and Saskia Kuliga

in the numerical ratings), but people do bother to write negative comments (especially when they are disappointed about one particular aspect of the building, e.g. wayfinding, but like another, e.g. the architecture). Again, this is different to some traditional POE work, and it will be interesting to determine how universal this trend is for other buildings reviewed via social media. Another interesting characteristic of this dataset is the low incidence of neutral views. One interpretation is that it stems from the public nature of the online reviewing: there is a supposition that other people will not be interested in reading a neutral review.

Conclusions

The conclusion to this chapter attempts to answer the questions that have been raised in the preceding sections.

(1) *What is happening to POE in the era of rising social networks?* The simple answer to this question is that POE 2.0 is *already* starting to happen. The result of this examination of the Seattle Central Library's reviews suggests that people are already using this medium to give their opinions of and provide information about their daily experiences of using the library. And, if this is the case, then surely the challenge for built environment professionals is to 'fan the flames' of this nascent movement, and potentially find a way to give it some structure or focus (whilst not losing its strengths as a bottom-up, grass-roots movement) as it appears to be a source of valuable information well worth tapping into. Looking towards the future, the key question should be, how might built environment professionals *assist and guide* this already present, already happening phenomenon?

(2) *Might this phenomenon potentially be evolving into something not only new, but potentially more empowering for building users?* This question is also related to a second, important question, *how does user-generated, social media-based feedback fit into the standard definitions or toolkits of POE research?* The results of this chapter strongly suggest that this method of data gathering has the potential to empower building users. The 'POE 2.0' approach essentially has a bottom-up structure, in which the key issues emerge from the sum total of the issues raised by the users themselves, despite that methodological challenge of detecting these issues from the evolving corpus of data. Such a bottom-up approach has the advantage of being able to rapidly and automatically prioritise the key problems or suggestions raised by the users and encourage exchange of ideas between people. It is also useful because it can generate issues that the building owners/managers or POE questionnaire designers were hitherto not aware of. However, there are also a number of disadvantages with such a bottom-up approach: first, it is easy to get lost in the details as people can report on items that are essentially 'out of context', extraneous, or simply inapplicable. Second, there is a potential for the feedback forum to be hijacked by a vocal minority with an issue to promote. Third, people will often misreport issues because they lack the appropriate vocabulary or concepts (so in the case of the Seattle Central Library, users may fail to report the underlying issue of not being able to easily locate the stairs and instead complain that they feel unsafe in the elevators, so a navigational issue becomes disguised as a 'personal safety' issue). Finally, a bottom-up structure produces results that are

Using social media to gather users' feedback   185

hard to summate in the same manner that POE questionnaire responses can be analysed, but, conversely, the ranking or prioritisation of issues immediately 'falls out' of the emergent process.

(3) *Definitions or toolkits of POE research?* The authors suggest that such newly emerging, social media-based feedback does not currently fit into any standard definitions or framework. The final row of Table 10.1 compares the primary characteristics of POE 2.0 to the three different types of evaluation suggested by Preiser (1995) on rows 1 to 3. The main points of divergence between social media-based evaluation and traditional POE methods are that the time scale of this approach is potentially continuous since it has no defined end point, in sharp contrast to traditional POE tools; in many respects, this methodology is practically effortless in terms of data gathering (data gathering can be outsourced to extremely low-cost services such as Amazon Mechanical Turk, although more challenging in terms of data analysis); since this is a newly emerging technology, it is hard to gauge how popular it might be; it does, however, have the potential for full ubiquity (why would any building/facility manager not be open to such a rich source of constant feedback?); as already mentioned, in contrast to Preiser's other types of evaluation, this one is bottom-up, unsolicited, voluntary, and almost unstructured, permitting any structure to emerge from the issues prompted by the users. It is therefore the contention of this chapter that this approach represents a paradigm shift in how building users engage with their environment.

(4) *What topics are discussed in social media comments?* In terms of the content, this study used pre-defined categories of semantic content, and therefore no topics were found that were not already being sought and this question remains outside the scope of the present chapter. An area of future work would be to examine automated methods of text parsing (as discussed above) in order to determine if there is a qualitative difference between the kinds of comments posted on social media websites and the kinds of answers given in response to POE surveys. Ideally, this would be conducted on two datasets (one gathered using traditional POE and one through social media) for the same building or series of buildings. However, one difference that was identified by this study was that the social media-based reviews were generally positive (82 per cent of all comments were judged positive in tone) and with a sensible range of positive to negative ratings. This suggests, as discussed, a fair-minded approach to online reviewing, which might be prompted by a number of aspects, not least of which is the expectation that the review will be read, and potentially moderated (a very unfair review might be publically 'disliked' by a number of other reviewers) by many other people. The more 'upbeat' tone of many of these reviews might also be due to the fact that the reviews are unsolicited and voluntary. This could be one of the more noteworthy advantages to using social media as a POE tool.

(5) *How useful are such datasets in augmenting other POE studies?* In this study, two other post-occupancy evaluations took place, an indicative and diagnostic POE. Having access to the online reviews meant that the planning phase of these two studies could already be informed by the views of some of the library users, resulting in a shorter and more focused design phase. The basic conclusion of this chapter is that despite this method of forming a new type of POE it is not one likely to supplant traditional methods. Rather, it should be seen as something that can augment and complement other work in this area. One way in which it

186 *Ruth Conroy Dalton and Saskia Kuliga*

may be used is to inform the design phase of other POE work, as was used in this study; another way that it may be used is to extend the life of a POE by providing a vehicle for continuous monitoring beyond the duration of a traditional POE.

Note

1 Acknowledgements: to SFB/TR8 Spatial Cognition for co-funding this study. To Dr Nick 'Sheep' Dalton (The University of Northumbria at Newcastle, UK) and to Jana Wendler, David Kühner, and Anselm Geserer (University of Freiburg, Germany) for their assistance in retrieving the data from the websites reviewed in this chapter. Also to Laura Carlson (University of Notre Dame) and Amy Shelton (Johns Hopkins University), and their respective teams, for their work on the aforementioned two studies of wayfinding in Seattle Central Library (also see Chapter 9 of this book).
This chapter is a reprint. It was originally published as: Dalton, Ruth Conroy, Saskia Felizitas Kuliga, and Christoph Hölscher. "POE 2.0: exploring the potential of social media for capturing unsolicited post-occupancy evaluations." Intelligent Buildings International 5.3 (2013): 162–180.

References

ArchDaily website, accessed July 2012, http://www.archdaily.com/.

Archiplanet website, accessed July 2012, www.archiplanet.org.

Architecture Week Design Community website, accessed July 2012, www.designcommunity.com/forums.

Bechtel, R. B. 1996. 'The Paradigm of Environmental Psychology'. *American Psychologist*, 51 (11): 1187–8.

Beney, H., Cooke, L., Dent, C., and Mathur, B. 2005. 'Demolition' (Television series). United Kingdom: Channel 4.

Bordass, W. and Leaman, A. 2004. Probe: How it happened, what it found and did it get us anywhere? Conference paper prepared for Closing the Loop: Post-Occupancy Evaluation: the Next Steps, Windsor, UK, 29 April–2 May.

Brösamle, M. 2013. Sketches of Wayfinding Design: Empirical Studies of Architectural Design Processes. Unpublished doctoral dissertation, University of Freiburg, Germany.

Brösamle, M. and Hölscher, C. 2008. 'The Architects' Understanding of Human Navigation'. *Proceedings of Workshop on Movement and Orientation in Built Environments: Evaluating Design Rationale and User Cognition*, EDRA, Veracruz, Mexico.

Bryant, A. 2002. 'Re-grounding Grounded Theory'. *Journal of Information Technology Theory and Application*. 4 (1): 25–42.

Carlson, L. A., Hölscher, C., Shipley, T. F., and Dalton, R. C. 2010. 'Getting Lost in Buildings'. *Current Directions in Psychological Science*. 19 (5): 284–9.

Citysearch website, accessed July 2016, http://www.citysearch.com/guide/seattle-wa-metro.

Cooper, I. 1985. 'Teachers Assessment of Primary School Buildings: The Role of the Physical Environment in Education'. *British Educational Research Journal*. 11 (3): 253–69.

Cooper, I. 2012. Personal communication, 25 November.

Corbin, J. and Strauss, A. L. 2008. *Basics of Qualitative Research: Grounded Theory Procedures and Techniques*. New York: Sage.

Forrester Research website, accessed July 2012, http://www.forrester.com/home.

Gill, Z. M., Tierney, M. J., Pegg, I. M., and Allan N. 2010. 'Low-Energy Dwellings: The Contribution of Behaviours to Actual Performance'. *Building Research and Information*. 38 (5): 491–508.

Great Buildings website, accessed July 2012, http://greatbuildings.com/.

Hayes, A. F. and Krippendorff, K. 2007. 'Answering the Call for a Standard Reliability Measure for Coding Data'. *Communication Methods and Measures*. 1: 77–89.

InsiderPages website, accessed July 2012, www.insiderpages.com.

Jacobs, D. 2004. Quoted in Pogrebin, R., 'Inside the Year's Best-Reviewed Buildings'. 26 December. Accessed February 2012, http://www.nytimes.com/2004/12/26/arts/design/26pogr.html?_r=0.

Judy's Book website, accessed July 2012, www.judysbook.com.

Leaman, A. and Bordass, B. 2001. 'Assessing Building Performance in Use 4: The Probe Occupant Surveys and Their Implications'. *Building Research and Information*. 29 (2): 129–43.

Kaplan, A. M. and Haenlein, M. 2010, 'Users of the World, Unite! The Challenges and Opportunities of Social Media'. *Business Horizons*. 53 (1): 59–68.

Krippendorff, K. 2004. *Content Analysis: An Introduction to Its Methodology*. Thousand Oaks, CA: Sage.

Landauer, T., Foltz, P. W., and Laham, D. 1998. 'Introduction to Latent Semantic Analysis'. *Discourse Processes*. 25 (2–3): 259–84.

Lonely Planet website, accessed July 2012, http://www.lonelyplanet.com.

Marshall, J. 2008. 'A Moment with… Joshua Prince-Ramus/Architect'. Seattlepi website, accessed February 2013, http://www.seattlepi.com/ae/article/A-moment-with-Joshua-Prince-Ramus-Architect-1284976.php.

Mau, B. 2005. *Lifestyle*. London: Phaidon Press.

MIMOA website, accessed July 2012, www.mimoa.eu.

Open Buildings website, accessed July 2012, www.openbuildings.com.

Oregon: What's YOUR Million Dollar Idea? Website forum, accessed July 2012, http://www.ideas4oregon.org/forums/59917-million-dollar-ideas.

Preiser, W. 1995. 'Post-Occupancy Evaluation: How to Make Buildings Work Better'. *Facilities*. 12 (11): 19–28.

Seattle Public Library website, accessed July 2012, http://www.spl.org/.

Sharma, S. and Gupta, V. 2012. 'Recent Developments in Text Clustering Techniques'. *International Journal of Computer Applications*. 37 (6): 14–19.

Stokols, D. 1995. 'The Paradox of Environmental Psychology'. *American Psychologist*. 50: 821–37.

Santa Barbara Challenge website, accessed July 2012, http://www.noozhawk.com/santa_barbara_challenge.

TripAdvisor website, accessed July 2012, www.tripadvisor.com.

VirtualTourist website, accessed July 2012, www.virtualtourist.com.

Yahoo Local website, accessed July 2012, http://local.yahoo.com/.

Yelp website, accessed July 2012, http://www.yelp.com.

Zimring, C. M. and Reizenstein, J. E. 1980. 'Post-Occupancy Evaluation: An Overview'. *Environment and Behavior*. 12: 429–50.

Zook, J. B. and Bafna, S. 2012. 'Imaginative Content and Building Form in the Seattle Central Public Library'. *Proceedings: Eighth International Space Syntax Symposium*. Edited by M. Greene, J. Reyes, and A. Castro. Santiago de Chile: PUC.

11 Discovering Serendip: Eye-tracking experiments in the Seattle Central Library as the beginning of a research adventure

Clemens Plank and Fiona Zisch

Introduction

Research exploring the relation between humans and architecture has a long history in architectural theory and, more recently, design experimentation. An array of heterogeneous questions has evolved over time and the research journey described in this chapter started by addressing a selection thereof. As the trajectory of the journey unfolded, unanticipated discoveries were made which led to a new strand of questioning. Initially the research was concerned with how humans read and react to architecture, essentially asking questions regarding communication, meaning, and behaviour. As the research progressed, however, the focus started to shift, resulting in a primary interest in the user of architecture – the subject – rather than the architecture – the object – itself. The original question had evolved to analyse whether architecture can be examined via its reading, perceiving subject.

Retrospectively, the journey is reminiscent of the voyages of the three princes of Serendip; the exploration started with a set intention, only to lead to the discovery of an unforeseen realisation and therefore a new objective.[1] The point of departure was an exploration of the relevance and possible application of communication theory to architecture, as well as an interest in the performative realm of architectural space. An experiment was designed to explore the different performative qualities of spaces in the Seattle Central Public Library. The research used an eye-gaze analysis system and select images of spaces in the Seattle Central Public Library; upon completion of the data collection, it became apparent that the gaze was far more pertinent than the space depicted. The research objective was suddenly and dramatically changed from an architectural observation to an epistemological investigation.

One cannot not… perform

> We are setting out late at night on our adventure. Our metaphorical ship is ready to navigate the waters of research. The past weeks have been spent in preparation. Hours and days pouring over books, perusing the shelves of the library, engaging in conversation and debate in search of information. There has been talk of an architectural treasure waiting to be found and it is this treasure we are hunting. Finally, the voyage itself has begun and so we set off into the unknown, armed with an interest, a suspicion, a question. The team, a motley crew of researchers, is highly motivated and full of energy. The linguistic turn is our chaperone and will guide us through the waters, helping us to formulate questions and nudging us in the direction of techniques and experiments.
>
> (Architect's logbook entry 1 March 2006)

The excerpt above is taken from a fictional travel journal, logging the progress of a research project conducted at the University of Innsbruck in 2006. The project was initiated by an interest in how Umberto Eco (1994) relates semiotics to architecture. Predicated on his writing, a research enquiry and an experimental investigation into the correlation of architectural intent and user experience were developed. In essence the research asked the question how architecture – as a sender – transmits information via its form to the user – as the receiver – and what kind of dialogue is established in the process of interaction. Eco posits that a sign, as the carrier of information (signifier), and the informational content (signified) it carries cannot be conflated. He ascertains architecture as a transmitter, which communicates its function by virtue of its formal qualities. When viewed as a sign, architecture not only transmits functional qualities, but – on another layer of information – also connotes deeper meaning. Architects' concepts, ideas, and intent originate and exist on this connoted, deeper layer and are then read and understood or misunderstood by users. The clearly defined aim at the beginning of the project was the assertion of specific connotations elicited by architectural intent designed to accentuate variety in user interpretation and thus functional fluidity. Starting from the basis that architecture acts as a sign, an examination of the review of communication theory was necessary.

In his five axioms of communication the theorist, philosopher, and psychologist Paul Watzlawick famously notes, 'one cannot not communicate' (Watzlawick et al., 1967). He justifies his statement as follows:

> One cannot not behave. Now, if it is accepted that all behaviour in an interactional situation has message value, i.e., is communication, it follows that no matter how one may try, one cannot not communicate. Activity or inactivity, words or silence, all have message value.
>
> (Watslawick et al., 2011)

A range of theories and concepts concerning (human) communication and behaviour have since followed, amongst them for example Marshall McLuhan and his well-known claim 'The medium is the message' (McLuhan, 2011); important to McLuhan's concept is the notion of the form of the medium and how the medium, as the sender, transmits a message via its form to the receiver and in such a way factually influences how the receiver then perceives the message. McLuhan believes that the medium conducts 'the scale and form of human association and action' (McLuhan, 1994). Reflecting on this from an architectural vantage point, the implication is that the conceptual and formal intent expressed by architecture's physical appearance conveys a message, which correlates with spatial affordance and generates corresponding action. By embodying and expressing an intent, architecture not only provides a stage for action, it is a catalyst for the emergence of narratives and the generation of performativity.

Similar to communication theory, the term performativity stems from the linguistic sciences. John Langshaw Austin theorised that language is not only an instrument with which to describe the world, it simultaneously operates as a generative mechanism that literally forms the world. Spoken words alone can achieve transformation; articulating dismissive statements, declaring a sacrament, or passing judgement all provoke change in the conditions of a respective world. Austin's theory of performativity summarises this capability, stating that language has both an assertive and an operative dimension (Austin, 1986; Krämer, 2004). A performative is thus an expression that not only has descriptive power, it also does something. A performative has no external designatum, it engenders change; importantly, however, this relies on an agreement regarding the covenant of an expression. The performative change, while not immediately experienced as such, fundamentally exists alongside its expression. Austin's theory of performativity describes a dependence between language and its influence on human activity. In the present context it is important to ask whether it is viable to assimilate Austin's insight into the realm of the relation between the physical world (e.g. architecture) and human action.

In her, writing, Sybille Krämer conceptualises the corporeal dimension of performativity, corporealising performativity (Korporalisiernde Performativität) (Krämer, 2004). Krämer's corporealising performativity is based on performance art and is reliant on an emphasis of event and presence. The difference to linguistic performativity is marked by the necessity of the physical existence and presence of bodies; corporealising performativity thus exceeds the metaphysical and semiotic nature of linguistic performativity. 'In acts of performance the physical – the actors' bodies as well as all sensually visible attributes – no longer remains a sign for an underlying immateriality which simply appears in the materiality of the exhibited performance' (Krämer, 2004). Corporealising performativity conceives of presence as a way of world making through the senses and the performative qualities evoked by sensual experience. Metaphysical structure is not crucial for the forming of a performative relationship between subject and object. By being physically present, the object axiomatically refers to its function; naturally, this is reliant on cultural circulation and convention. McLuhan conceptualises media as extensions of the senses, where performative relationships depend on an interaction between medium and subject; applying this notion to performativity in corporealising terms infers action and reaction of a subject with and within the physical objects that surround it.

From an architectural viewpoint the importance of Krämer's intellection is evident. The sensual experience of architecture guides subject behaviour by being physically, it causes action and reaction and undeniably has performative characteristics. The corporealising feedback loop between architecture and subject differs from the linguistic concept of performativity, communication, and behaviour: the metaphysical level dissolves and the subject does not simply read architecture, interpret the message, and react, the subject perceives and reacts simultaneously.

Performativity remains a process of communication; a medium, such as architecture, cannot not communicate. The application of Watzlawick's observation to an understanding of architectural space is strengthened by Krämer's argument and asserts that one cannot not react to architecture. Semiotics stipulates that meaning and the carrier of meaning can indeed be separated, which leads to a dualism of sorts. Information of any kind can only theoretically exist detached from a carrier of information. Krämer's performativity merges a presumed virtual layer of meaning with the respective carrier medium, effectively precluding a possible interpretative relationship between subject and architecture. Eco too alludes to an omission of scope for interpretation by way of the respectively denoted function. What, however, would happen if the key conception an architectural space connoted was functional fluidity and flexibility?

The architecture is the massage

> We have reached a critical point on our travels and decisions have to be made. A number of directions are possible, however it is crucial to consider each one carefully and then steer confidently towards a destination. The guiding beacon that will help evaluate each potential turn is the criterion of an architecture based on spatial fluidity. When we identify it and it satisfies our demands, we will steer our vessel of investigation towards it and, once stepped onto the hitherto unknown land, begin a thorough reconnaissance exploration and determine how best to use it in experimentation.
>
> (Architect's logbook entry 2 April 2006)

The methodology of using linguistic concepts for architectural design is well established. Bernard Tschumi, for example, writes about disjunction (Tschumi, 1996), the notion of divorcing meaning from form. The intent is to offer room for a (re)interpretation of function, thus manipulating performative characteristics. The decoupling of conventional correlations of function and form intends to force the user to (re)interpret the built environment. In other words, Tschumi's mode of operation relies on a semiotically dualist understanding of signifier and signified aiming to generate unexpected encounters in user experience. Space without predetermined function purposes to be free of performative qualities and aspires to increase user independence and surprise.

The concept of engendering moments of surprise through unpredictability is used frequently by Rem Koolhaas. Although his motivation differs from Tschumi's, Koolhaas also uses a bipolar design methodology, a method of crisis or irrationality, as a catalyst for design. He assimilates the Surrealist concept of using – and explicitly not avoiding – contradiction as a creative tool for design. In his book Delirious New York Koolhaas borrows Salvador Dali's Paranoid-Critical Method.

'The motto of the Paranoid-Critical Method (PCM) is – The Conquest of the Irrational. (...) The PCM is defined by Dali mostly in tantalising formulas: "the spontaneous method of irrational knowledge based on the critical and systematic objectifications of delirious associations and interpretations"' (Dali, 1969; Koolhaas, 1994). However, not only Koolhaas's design method, but also his built architecture relies on unpredictability and scope for interpretation. A paradigmatic example of a spatial programme formulated by this method is the Seattle Central Public Library. In an interview with *Time* magazine Rem Koolhaas explains his programmatic concept, the distinction between two spatial conditions: 'For me it's a building (Seattle Central Public Library) that accommodates both stability and instability. The things you can predict and the things you can't.'[2]

There are two ways of understanding the concept; first, from the viewpoint of the architect who uses the uncertainty regarding the future development of the building's function as the very motif that drives the design and so leaves parts of the building open for functional appropriation. 'Koolhaas and his design team considered that the two major challenges the library would have to aspire were the unpredictable future growth of new technologies that the library would need to encompass and the new social functions that it may have to serve' (Wired New York, 2003). Second, from the perspective of the library's user the scope for action increases in those areas where function is not predetermined. The differentiation between architect and user is secondary to the research project described here, the primary interest lies on the

192 *Clemens Plank and Fiona Zisch*

differentiation between two spatial concepts. One concept clearly denotes function; the other does not or denotes functional freedom.

The Seattle Central Public Library

> We have landed ashore the Seattle Central Public Library. Everything, which we saw from afar, every resource we hoped for seems to exist in abundance on this island and we can now begin probing and examining in depth. The treasure must surely be close now. We have sent a number of teams out into the field to gather samples and return to the base with the fruits of their search. On-board we await their return and will begin sorting and extracting from the samples as soon as they return.
>
> (Architect's logbook entry 3 May 2006)

The OMA's Seattle Central Public Library is an interesting object for investigation. Offering a variety of degrees of spatial performativity – from functionally fixed to functionally flexible – the design concept led to the question whether the two spatial qualities could be used to explore the performative relationship between user and architecture. Would it be possible to find differing levels of attention in the respective concepts of 'stable' and 'instable', performative and non-performative areas? 'What would motivate or trigger users to respond to the specific offer of an open-function architectural environment, how would this manifest itself?' (Plank, 2010). Put differently, can architecture's respective performative qualities be discerned in users' experience depending on their design designation as stable or instable? Based on the hypothesis that architecture can indeed be examined via experience, the behaviour expressed would be indicative of a currently observed spatial scenario. A stable scenario would therefore fulfil expectations and result, for example, in a predictable movement pattern; an instable scenario which is not imbued with expectations would produce varying and unpredictable patterns. The underlying assumption is that the performative realm of architectural space can be categorised based on design intentionality, sociocultural constellation, or elicited behaviour.

Taking a closer look at the functional organisation of the Seattle Central Public Library, OMA designed five platforms, which form a programmatic cluster that is defined by dedicated function. From the basement level to the upper levels these platforms serve functions such as parking, offices, or meeting space. 'Because each platform is designed for a unique purpose, their size, flexibility, circulation, palette, structure, and MEP (mechanical, electrical, and plumbing) vary' (Koolhaas and Ramus, 2005). These fixed platforms were intended to never change in function or form, regardless of potential future expansion, they were designated as being 'stable', 'Depending on their purpose the stable spaces are distinguished by issues of size, allotment/infrastructure, construction, and building materials' (Koolhaas and Ramus, 2005).

The spaces between the platforms function as trading floors for librarians to inform and inspire and as interfaces between spaces for work, interaction, and play.[3] These 'instable' spaces are intended to accommodate public demand and to exist without constraints and elicit spatial sensations through interaction. Concepts for spaces that aim to initiate unplanned behaviour by means of functional fluidity, thus enabling alternative spatial scenarios to unfold, are not new. Common to all is an ability to engender alternative ways of performing and the creation of myriad spatial relationships between user and architecture (Plank, 2010).

Do you see what I see

> Fieldwork has proven fruitful and we have assembled a rich collection of samples, sorted them, and selected pieces for experimentation. We can now begin to formulate and set up an experiment to see if our assumptions ring true. The crew is working on the experimental setup, installing the testing apparatus (not an easy feat given the rudimentary resources aboard our ship), and recruiting locals to lend a helping eye. I say eye, because we have opted to use a fascinating paradigm for our investigation, where the movement of the eye is tracked as an observer gazes upon a sample, in order to capture what incites attention.
>
> (Architect's logbook entry 4 June 2006)

The technique of tracking eye movement is a research strategy that is used frequently in psychology. The method captures and highlights areas of interest as pictorial representations of a respective object is viewed by a participant.[4] The movement of the eye can provide a certain amount of insight into perceptual faculties. Despite the technique probing only a fraction of human perception, the intrinsic quality of the methodology is that it accounts for both perception (the cognitive process of identification and interpretation of what is 'out there') and behaviour (the behavioural process of eye movement) simultaneously. The depiction of the object of investigation acts as a proxy that generates unconscious information processing. Recognition theory speculates that the nature of a connection between object and subject is echoed in the connection between subject and proxy. This insinuates a causal nature of perception; if the proxy can indeed evoke a response corresponding with the response to the object, it follows that subjective perception is subordinate to information already stored in the brain that represents the object's attributes (Velderman, 2008).

Eye tracking as a research technique has been used since the middle of the last century. Most experiments use a set of preselected pictures, which are shown to participants with the aim of generating distinctive patterns or trails of eye movement. The Russian psychologist Alfred L. Yarbus showed as early as the 1950s that any given image has a large influence on eye movement.

> Records of eye movements show that the observer's attention is usually held only by certain elements of the picture... Eye movement reflects the human thought processes; so the observer's thought may be followed to some extent from records of eye movement (the thought accompanying the examination of the particular object). It is easy to determine from these records which elements attract the observer's eye (and, consequently, his thought), in what order, and how often.
>
> (Yarbus, 1967)

Coming back to user/architecture relationships, the question now arises how the experience of architectural space can be examined solely through viewings of pictorial representations which attenuate bodily movement and thus proprioceptive

194   Clemens Plank and Fiona Zisch

feedback. Yarbus's allusion to thought being mirrored in eye movement finds further support in Kevin O'Regan and Alva Noë's proposition of the 'enactive' or 'sensorimotor' account (O'Regan and Noë, 2001). Previously established intelligence of 'sensorimotor contingencies' enables vision to function as a way of exploring the world. Sensorimotor contingencies in perceptual experience align the (motor) actions of an observer with the elicited fluctuations in sensory input caused by the actions (O'Regan and Noë, 2001).

Taking it as axiomatic that user/architecture relationships can be explored through vision which manifests as actions (eye movement) can then lead to an understanding of spatial experience. Viewing specifically selected pictorial representations of respective spatial situations would provide feedback regarding different eye movements, thus performative qualities and the relation between architecture and user. To investigate this in an experimental setting, different kinds of spatial concepts captured in pictorial representations have to be used. As stated earlier, the Seattle Central Public Library's design emerges from the division of two distinct spatial (performative) conditions; one where the spatial situation communicates a specific meaning and one where meaning is not so readily derived; these two albeit rather broad categories of architectural spaces formed the prime focus for a study on differences in eye movement.

The projected outcome of the study was to identify differences in x-y coordinates mapping areas of interest (such as architectural elements, colours, materials) in the participants' gazes depending on the respective spatial situation being viewed. A mix of 12 colour and monochromatic photographs of library spaces were shown, six depicting 'stable' spaces (e.g. Figure 11.1) and six showing 'instable' ones (e.g. Figure 11.2). Forty participants ranging in age from 20 to 30 were tested, each viewing every photograph for ten seconds (Plank, 2010).

The rushes – raw data

> The testing phase is complete and we can now start comparing predictions with findings. A first viewing of the recordings is scheduled for 5 o'clock this afternoon. The excitement aboard is palpable and I expect the crew are hoping to celebrate late into the night. I too am tense with anticipation.
>
> (Architect's logbook entry 5 June 2006)

The resulting heat maps depicting eye movement and dwelling were superimposed onto each image to highlight those areas that appear to be primary points of attraction. In some cases there was a sole focal point, in other cases there were several. Spatial areas of interest were primarily connected to prominent architectural elements, such as colourful staircases or prominent pieces of furniture.

A closer and more detailed look at the data offered further insight into how the participants had perceived the images. Before settling on certain areas, a very quick 'overview', in which the eyes scan the entire image, is gained; the architectural structure and the depth of the space are gauged at the beginning. The subject first explores the built environment, seeking out safety aspects such as structure, stability, or construction. Then the space is explored more thoroughly and 'interesting' objects are settled upon. However, the predicted trajectory of the investigation never truly ran

Figure 11.1 Stable space. Photograph: M. Kubo and R.Prat, 2005.

its course. It quickly became apparent that a clear differentiation in interest between stable and instable spaces in users' observations was unable to emerge due to the presence of perceptually far more interesting objects. The objects in question, however, transpired to be subjects. What the selection of pictorial representations had neglected to consider was that the majority of spatial scenes photographed were populated by human figures (Figure 11.3).

Retrospectively it seems obvious, however, at the time of the experiment the revelation that the human perceptual apparatus is calibrated to afford other humans higher attention than inanimate objects and architectural space was surprising. Nevertheless, this revelation is crucial to the question of how users relate to architecture and it changed the trajectory of the research immediately. Human figures, corporeal forms that are laden with vicarious expectation and self-projection attract primary attention every time, even when backgrounded and rather hard to spot. Could it be that by identifying other humans in the spatial settings, observers were able to implant themselves into the scene and experience it remotely? Was this a point of access for the emergence of sensorimotor contingencies through the act of seeing? Architectural elements in the pictures attracted less or even no attention. What was initially assessed as a fault in experimental design – resulting perhaps from an openly exploratory and playful mode of research – hindered results which were in line with the research question; however, it proved to be a serendipitous and far more significant discovery.

Figure 11.2 Instable space. Photograph: M. Kubo and R. Prat, 2005.

Serendipitous discoveries

> The events of the past few days have been arousing and highly disorienting. All this time spent on an island whose identity we thought we knew and it appears we were fooled. Where are we? No coordinates at hand, I as the captain have to take decisions based on instinct alone. A sleepless night has led to the conclusion that the only way forward is to embrace the predicament I find myself in, by playing the cards I have been dealt. The operative word is play. I have decided to play, light hearted and open to discovery, and see where the journey takes us.
>
> (Architect's logbook entry 6 October 2006)

To put the matter differently, 'play' (and its associated behavioral variability) is not purely entertainment or a luxury to be given up when things get serious. It is itself a highly adaptive mechanism for dealing with the reality that the context for behavior is always largely unknown.

(Grobstein, 1994)

Certainly characterised by its playful attitude, retrospectively the experiment appears almost overtly destined for the unfolding of serendipitous research mechanisms.[5] Starting as a speculation on different perceptual processes in relation to architectural intent in design method and spatial function and form, the experiment took an

Figure 11.3 Two areas of interest (the white zones) – the escalator and people in the background; test result from eye-tracking observation. Photograph: M. Kubo and R. Prat, 2005.

unexpected turn at the axiomatic revelation that the human perceptual system is principally geared towards living organisms. Under the provision that the human trait of being self-aware and consequently highly aware of similar beings, previous studies of subjects in architecture devoid of inhabitation are essentially problematic. Architecture without inhabitation is a theoretical construct and a study on how lived architecture is perceived can in practical application only be conducted including inhabitation. This insight will help answer the original question asked.

The serendipitous discovery is in essence a new research model. How humans relate to architecture has to be examined in the perceiving subject rather than in architecture. Is it possible to gain insight into the experience of architecture by exploring human anatomy and physiology, and what could this mean for architectural design? The research model proposes a novel user/architecture relationship, where architecture is a profoundly subjective product of the human mind which is based on performativity, perception, and empathy. This is not an entirely new model, but rather an advancement of cybernetic or phenomenological proposals. Considering the trajectory of twentieth-century science, the cognitive turn, and the rise of the sciences of the mind and brain, the century was marked by a shift in the investigative perspective. Established disciplines evolved and new disciplines emerged. Neuroscience focuses primarily on the anatomy and physiology of the nervous system, whereas its offspring

198 Clemens Plank and Fiona Zisch

such as cognitive or behavioural neuroscience, neuropsychology or neurophilosophy incorporate, amongst other concerns, subjective perception and reflection, the interaction of systems, or artificial intelligence studies. By following the neuroscientific model (in the broadest sense) and addressing how an individual experiences and acts in and on the world in her own, unique way, the research focus expands from concentrating exclusively on an observed object to including the interaction with the observer of the object and from the universal to the particulars involved. A study of perception based on interaction and performance means studying the embodied, embedded, and connected nature of observing and observed systems; it is inextricably reciprocal, subjective, and formative.

Where do we go from here?

> We are back at sea and sailing into the unknown. At least this time we know it is unknown. I have logged a number of research proposals from crewmembers and if possible I am sure we will be able to address some. My second in command has voiced an interest in noetics and the brain sciences. Who knows which surprises the journey has in store, but I take comfort in the trust in place in Serendipity.
>
> (Architect's logbook entry 7 February 2008)

Alongside constructing a new, neuro-oriented research model to answer the question asked at the beginning, the experiment yielded a simple and factually logical realisation. When asking questions concerning perception, architectural research has to include the presence of human subjects into any investigation, with all potential challenges involved. The present chapter is concluded with selective reflections concerning human presence and the relevance for user/architecture relationships.

In line with the experiment described, the process of seeing as one way of perceiving serves as one example of sensually relating to architecture. The art historian James Elkins characterises two processes of seeing. 'First seeing' where an observer takes pleasure in seeing in a 'relaxed and languorous' manner and 'second seeing' as 'a restless nomadic way of looking' (Elkins, 1999). The term nomadic here may be interpreted as a mechanism of roaming and searching. One can speculate that in the experiment participants' first sight was the 'relaxed and languorous pleasure' of letting their gaze glide across the image, followed by second sight where the gaze started searching and then identifying and being drawn to a subject and relating to it.

Being able to identify, relate to, and experience vicariously presupposes that humans are able to quickly and clearly offset another human subject from the rest of the environment and equally be able to keep track of and tell apart individual subjects and objects. Modern neuroscience has begun to gain insight into the neural processes underlying this ability. Neurons in the medial temporal lobe are selective in their firing behaviour and will respond exclusively to either human faces, non-human animals, or objects (Quiroga et al., 2005). Emerging research suggests that while these neurons, which were formulated hypothetically as grandmother cells in the late 1960s and are now more often referred to as Jennifer Aniston neurons, respond selectively and preferably to specific faces regardless of viewing angle, or fidelity (there are indications that a comparable set of cells favours buildings). In other words, each of these cells has a specific area – or type – of interest. Architecture as a comprehensive composition will therefore engage a wide number of these neurons (alongside an incalculable number of other neurons across the nervous system) and it is important to account all objects and subjects – and their bodies – that speak to them. The psychologists George Lakeoff and Mark Johnson see the body as a metaphor that enables understanding of the other (Ayuso, 2015). In shape, function, and performance, one's own body positions itself as mediator between the internal milieu and the external world and processes of identification and projection, sympathy and empathy allow relation and connection to other bodies to unfold. Considering how the body – one's own, but also that of the other – acts as a 'way in' and is thus the prime attractor and element of importance in any architectural environment, one question that arises in current debates is how (modern) architectural design neglects to incorporate this into the design process. It appears that the once intuitive inclusion of bodies into design (in conception and built structures) has gone missing. The designer and theorist Alessandro Ayuso (2015) writes beautifully about the status quo of the 'missing body' in design conception and representation. According to Ayuso, the Modernist movement – and contemporary design as its continuation – lies at the root of this omission and exhibits a reluctance to account for lived, bodily experience of humans in its designs. He outlines how both figures in design representation (in the design process and presentation) but also in built architecture (for example as statues that by way of their posture or facial expression guide through the environment) provide the missing 'way in'. The figure is thus at once a 'way in' for the designer as she designs and a 'way in' for the user as she experiences architecture. In order to once again account for embodiment, architecture, Ayuso argues, needs to revisit past design methodologies, as can be found for example in Baroque architecture, and build structures that re-embrace its constituent part, the human body.

Engaging with the other through one's own body is of course an act of empathy. Empathy theory and its term 'Einfühlung' are indeed a steadfast mainstay in architectural theory and design. Heinrich Wölfflin assessed that, 'Unsere leibliche Organisation ist die Form, unter der wir alles Körperliche auffassen' ('Our corporeal organisation is the form through which we experience everything physical', Wölfflin, 1886). While at the end of the nineteenth and the turn of the twentieth century empathy studies and associated areas of interest were in their beginning stages, the twentieth century rise of the psychological sciences and neurosciences resulted in an array of related queries, focal points, and discoveries. In recent years, the neurophilosopher Thomas Metzinger has started to show an interest in empathy theory, contemplating how theoretical examinations may relate to modern neuroscientific knowledge (Metzinger, 2012). The nascent research model described here takes the neurophilosophical model as a starting point to correlate and tie together knowledge from different disciplines. For example, upon closer examination, the neurons mentioned earlier show a number of characteristics that are interesting in the context of design conceptualisation, abstraction, design representation, and design perception. Strikingly, these neurons fire regardless of the specific size, viewing angle, or fidelity of the subject or object perceived; in other words the neurons appear to be coupled to the thing as such rather than merely a visual representation thereof. It has been suggested that the respective percept caused by the thing is transformed into an explicit neural code, which is stored as an abstract memory, and activated and deciphered upon an encounter with the thing itself regardless of the sensory input received from it (Quiroga et al., 2005). Based on the range of sensory input possibilities and an infinite range of never identical scenarios, there cannot be a singular common denominator which underlies the scripting, storage, and activation of this code. This calls to mind Bernard Baars's Global Workspace Theory (2003). Given that it has also been indicated that cells that fire selectively to buildings seem to group buildings into categories (the same cell that favoured the Sydney Opera House also responded to the Lotus Temple in New Delhi (Quiroga et al., 2005), a tentative speculation is that overarching performative processes may be at play. Furthermore, it appears that the cells in fact also respond to abstract representations that are associated with a respective subject or object, such as hearing or reading the name associated with it. The cell's response thus does not correlate exclusively with a visual or auditory percept, but rather the percept is one of many possible sensory mediators between the cell and the perceived object as such. It follows that the perceived object is abstracted and conceptualised by the perceiving subject. From an architectural viewpoint, subjective perception and abstraction lead to the hypothesis that the way architecture is understood depends on the conceptualisation of the architect's subjective intent and on the user's subjective perception and conceptualisation thereof. Gordon Pask (1968) writes:

> Further, when learning to control or to solve problems man necessarily conceptualizes and abstracts. Because of this, the human environment is interpreted at various levels in a hierarchy of abstraction (on the same page we see letters, words, grammatical sentences, meaningful statements and beautiful prose).

Bringing the chapter to a close, the intermittent conclusion of the research journey and the start of the next stage of research can be summarised in these five points:

1. The different layers of information that are associated with a medium correlate with different perceptual and neural processes. The respective percepts, which relate to a medium, therefore correlate with memorised abstractions or concepts connected to recognisable aspects of the medium.
2. Architectural experience cannot be investigated solely as an external detached object but has to be equally investigated from within the perceiving subject, that is to say within the noetic, neural, behavioural, interactive processes of the system composed of architecture and observer.
3. Architecture is a holon[6] and as such cannot be broken up into constituent parts as each part is again composed of parts and all depend on the incorporation into the system and on its own cannot function.
4. Studying a system that includes oneself as an observer is conceivably problematic. An objective understanding can never be achieved when the viewpoint taken is subjective by invariable default. The epistemological gap cannot be bridged but an approximation can be attempted; being mindful of this, an altered but potentially rich and rewarding research approach is the logical conclusion.
5. An inclusive rather than an exclusive research method necessitates collaboration across disciplines.

> We have made significant headway. Based on the realisations made, we have acquired a new ship and named it HAL. I have given orders to fuel the ship with brainpower. The chief officer has taken the ship's tender and is currently collecting samples and recruiting new aids. We feel that there may be interesting lessons to be learnt from inspecting internal worlds, but this time, we are open for true exploration. We are sailing into the open with no predetermined destination; the only guide is the prerequisite to search within as much as in the world out there.
>
> Before we progress, I need to write to Rement and thank him for providing the inspiration to embark on the marvellous journey we are on.
>
> (Architect's logbook entry 8 August 2008)

Notes

1 Serendip is the Persian and Urdu word for Sri Lanka. The story of the three princes of Serendip is a Persian fairy tale. On their voyages the princes repeatedly veer from their set path, only to make an unanticipated but happy and often even silly discovery. The word serendipity was coined by Horace Walpole based on the fairy tale. Voltaire also referred to the story in his novel Zadig, which paved the way for detective fiction and understandings of scientific methods. https://en.wikipedia.org/wiki/The_Three_Princes_of_Serendip#cite_note-1 (accessed 31 August 2015).
2 *Time* (2010) Interview with Rem Koolhaas. Available from http://www.time.com/time/magazine/article/0,9171,993920,00.html (accessed 13 July 2010).
3 See http://www.archdaily.com/11651/Seattle-central-library-oma-lmn/.
4 More recently, mobile eye tracking has allowed researchers to take the paradigm into the real world.
5 The concept of serendipity is not new to scientific investigation. The sociologist Robert K. Merton formulated the 'serendipity pattern' in 1949, an idea that was further developed methodologically by Anselm L. Strauss and Barney G. Glaser in their Grounded Theory. Serendipity as a scientific method is situated in opposition to experimentation with an anticipated and purposeful discovery and is characterised by the observations of the unanticipated, which leads to the development of a new theory or an extension of an existing theory. Serendipity in sociology is both used for the sociology underlying scientific investigation and the investigation methodology itself.
6 A holon is both a whole and a part (Koestler, 1967).

References

Austin, J. (1986) Performative Äusserungen. In: *Gesammelte philosophische Aufsätze*, Reclam, Stuttgart. In: Krämer, S. (2004) *Performativität und Medialität*, Wilhelm Fink Verlag, Munich.
Ayuso, A. (2015) Body agents: Deploying a new figure for design, PhD by Architectural Design Thesis, Bartlett School of Architecture, UCL.
Baars, B. (2003) The global brainweb: An update on the global workspace theory, Guest editorial, *Science and Consciousness Review*.
Dali, S. (1969) The Conquest of the Irrational; appendix of *Conversations with Dali*, Dutton New York. In: Koolhaas, R. (1994) *Delirious New York, A Retroactive Manifesto for Manhattan*, Monacelli Press, New York.
Eco, U. (1994) *Einführung in die Semiotik*, translated by Trabant J., Fink. Verlag, Munich.
Elkins, J. (1999) *Pictures of the Body: Pain and Metamorphosis*, Stanford University Press, Stanford, CA.
Grobstein, P. (1994) *Variability in brain function and behavior*. In: *The Encyclopedia of Human Behavior*, Volume 4 (V.S. Ramachandran, editor), Academic Press, New York.

202 Clemens Plank and Fiona Zisch

Koestler, A. (1967) *The Ghost in the Machine*, Hutchinson, London.

Koolhaas, R. (1994) *Delirious New York, A Retroactive Manifesto for Manhattan*, Monacelli Press, New York.

Koolhaas, R. and Ramus, J. (2005) *Seattle Central Public Library*, Archplus 174, OMA Projekte, ARCH and Verlag, Achen.

Krämer, S. (2004) *Performativität und Medialität*, Wilhelm Fink Verlag, Munich.

McLuhan, M. (1994) *Understanding Media: Extensions of Man*, MIT Press, Cambridge, MA.

McLuhan, M. (2011) *The Medium Is the Massage: An Inventory of Effects*, Gingko Press, Berkeley, CA.

Metzinger T. (2012) Keynote lecture at Spatial Thinking 2 Symposium, University of Innsbruck.

O'Regan, K. and Noë, A. (2001) *A sensorimotor account of vision and visual consciousness, Behavioral and Brain Sciences* 24, 5, 883–975. Further developed as the 'enactive approach' in Noë, A. (2004) *Action in Perception*, MIT Press, Cambridge, MA.

Pask, G. (1968) A Comment, a Case History and a Plan. Cybernetic Serendipity exhibition.

Plank, C. (2010) The Conscious User of Architecture, A conceptual framework for the exploration of the relationship of architecture and its user based on the current neuroscientific debate, PhD thesis at the University of Innsbruck.

Quiroga, R. Q., Reddy, L., Kreiman, G., Koch, C., and Fried, I. (2005) *Invariant visual representation by single neurons in the human brain, Nature* 435, 1102–7 (23 June).

Time (2010) Interview with Rem Koolhaas. Available from: http://www.time.com/time/magazine/article/0,9171,993920,00.html (accessed 13 July 2010); https://en.wikipedia.org/wiki/The_Three_Princes_of_Serendip#cite_note-1 (accessed 31 August 2015).

Tschumi, B. (1996) *Architecture and Disjunction*, MIT Press, Cambridge, MA.

Veldeman, J. (2008) *Reconsidering pictorial representation by reconsidering visual experience. Leonardo* 41, 5, 493–7.

Watzlawick, P., Beavin-Bavelas, J., and Jackson, D. (1967) Some Tentative Axioms of Communication. In: *Pragmatics of Human Communication: A Study of Interactional Patterns, Pathologies and Paradoxes*. W. W. Norton, New York.

Watzlawick, P., Bavelas, J., and Jackson, D. (2011) *Pragmatics of Human Communication: A Study of Interactional Patterns, Pathologies and Paradoxes*. W. W. Norton, New York.

Wired New York (2003) Rem Readings. Available from: http://www.wirednewyork.com/forum/showthread.php?t=3778

Wölfflin, H. (1886) *Prolegomena zu einer Psychologie der Architektur*, Buchdruckerei von Dr. C. Wolf und Sohn.

Yarbus, A. (1967) *Eye Movement and Vision*, Plenum Press, New York, http://www.archdaily.com/11651/Seattle-central-library-oma-lmn/.

Epilogue
Drawing together the multiple perspectives of the Seattle Central Library

Wilfried Wang

The built fact: literally

Characteristic of contemporary architectural criticism is the absence of concrete and direct analysis of the built fact.

The reasons for this are manifold: firstly, the danger that a literal reading of a building as a physical fact might render conclusions that are not only unpalatable to the clients, the public, the adulating fans of the building's architects but to the architects themselves; secondly, a literal reading of the building might reveal the architects' compositional approach with the possibility of disappointing those who all thought that there was more to it. Thirdly, many people who talk about buildings are unable to 'read' them; instead they use less or more related constructs as foils against which they project what they think they would like to see in the buildings in question. Sadly, as an architect, one has to admit that there are even architects and architectural historians who are unable to read plans and sections, let alone identify components of buildings. And then there are quite a few architectural commentators who disparagingly consider the scrutiny of buildings by the analysis of their spatial, formal, and material facts to be hermeneutics, simply personal, subjective interpretation. Many commentators only feel secure in their 'judgements' if they can base these on texts, preferably written by the architect of the building in question, but failing evidence of this kind, then by other supposed authoritative individuals, first and foremost 'famous' writers. Models, sketches, and drawings, that lead to the physical reality of a building, are regarded by these commentators to be unreliable sources. Most importantly, for these people, the building itself is regarded as being full of doubt and merely the source of idiosyncratic guesswork.

There are of course other points of view. There are people, including architects and those interested in built reality, who understand this constructed reality as embodying ideas and values, and that this built reality divulges these ideas and values if, and only if, it is carefully read and thoroughly investigated. These investigations can take a number of routes, use a number of techniques of enquiry, employ a variety of methodological probes and scientifically structured research. As is in the logic of analysis, phenomena are taken apart in the process using tools that have been designed by the question that frames the enquiry in the first place.

Analyses can focus on the nature of publicness of a public building; on the ease of accessibility for the users of its front of house and its deeper interiors; on the way people obtain their sense of orientation within the edifice; on the ambience of the smaller spatial situations; on the degree of conduciveness for casual encounters.

Analyses could also review the relation between professed concepts and ideals by client and architect prior to the building's realization and the degree to which these ideals and concepts have been realized in the finished phenomenon.

Analyses could check on the environmental performance of each component of the building and its overall life expectancy in a comprehensive life-cycle analysis: how long will the floor finishes last in comparison to the cladding system; will the ordering system of the books be outdated faster than the embedded electronics? Analyses could test the library's potential for future changes, its degree of readiness for internal adaptation or whether it is at all capable of being extended. Analyses can include the cost in use, the heating and cooling costs in relation to the number of users, the efficiency of the staffing to visitor numbers; that is, the financial sustainability of the operational regime.

The set of essays contained in this book thus brings together a number of ways of seeing the world of one built artefact: the Seattle Central Library. The conclusions, as far as the authors in this collection of papers have dared to take their analytical approaches, are less assuring of the quality of the Seattle Central Library than most architectural critics have expressed. The reason for this disparity rests on the logic of architectural hagiography: few editors are prepared to publish comprehensive criticisms that include negative aspects for fear of losing the chance to publish the next project by the inevitably upset architects; and few writers are independent enough to clearly state a building's successes and failures and to call out the shortfalls of the architects' discourse. In architectural journalism there are some basic rules. Number one: don't criticize famous architects; number two: choose to write on a building by a famous architect; number three: write positive criticisms of works by famous architects to increase your own fame; number four: if you do write negative criticisms of works by famous architects, be sure to have all the facts at your disposal and be aware of potential ostracism by the establishment (all of this probably does not only apply to the field of architecture).

There are some buildings that do not deserve any attention; some that are not even worth ignoring. Given all the international hype around the Seattle Central Library, it is clear that this building deserves the review that is laid out in this collection of essays. Beginning with the way design participation was promised, manipulated, and in fact ultimately not realized (Albena Yaneva), readers will learn that the architects of the Seattle Central Library embraced their rhetorical skills to ensure that their concept be realized regardless as to whether it would hold what they had promised (Shannon Mattern). The architects' claim to uphold the importance of the users is found to be lacking as far as the users' ease of orientation within the building is concerned (Ruth Conroy Dalton); something that members of the architectural team were aware of during the course of the design but were unable to correct, given the sacred-cow nature of the architectural concept. However, this apparent sanctity of the architectural concept of the Seattle Central Library is found to lead to a deliberate 'one-way street', indeed to a 'one-way building' (Kim Dovey), that treats users as useful automatons mainly adept at satisfying the architectural concept, mechanical units apparently devoid of a desire for exploration and lacking in the desire for freedom of choice.

Looking at the experiential dimension of the building, a set of probes into the Seattle Central Library's spatial and formal elements reveals the range of successes and failures of the building (David Seamon, using, in part the analytical methodology of Thomas Thiis-Evensen). Equally, understanding the building as stage for the

Epilogue 205

presentation of the self in a phenomenal as well as social dimension can bring forth its relative accomplishments and shortcomings, depending on the type of user, their needs, and their points of view (Julie Zook and Sonit Bafna). Such multi-perspectival points of view – whether taken as an occasional visitor attending a meeting in the library, a regular user, or an architectural sightseer – like a cubist painting, provide a more comprehensive understanding of the phenomenon that is the Seattle Central Library and reveal the true beneficiaries of the architects' concept: the attentive architectural sightseer. In other words, the building stages itself as the protagonist to the consuming sightseer.

Post-occupancy evaluations are typically used to both compare the claims and predictions of the clients and architects with the users' experience. Using the interview format and subsequent statistical evaluations, visitors and readers of the Seattle Central Library can provide insights into their reading of the building and its components as well as their emotional response (Saskia Kuliga and Ruth Conroy Dalton). However, with contemporary technology and websites such as social media, the impeding nature of interviews can be avoided. At the same time, there are limitations to the evaluation of voluntary comments as the manner in which this data comes about cannot be verified. Not every user of a building is able or willing to express her or his opinions. Nevertheless, the voicing of extreme positions can be useful in subsequent designs.

Finally, the 'reading' of the literal reading of the Seattle Central Library (as conducted by Clemens Plank and Fiona Zisch) through the tracking of eye movements of a sample of volunteers moving through the building may draw the conclusion that the 'gaze' of the subject is far more important than the observed object or space. The limitation of such an approach lies in the placement of the experiment in the here and now, that is to say, in the separation of the cultural context from the knowledge of the observer.

Architectural analysis as performed by architects, architectural historians, and architectural critics, however, does not take place in the separation of the here and now from the socio-cultural context, but is intimately tied to the continuous universe of architectural discourses. For architects may design for clients' purposes and users' expectations on the one hand, on the other some architects design for themselves, for their peers. In concluding this collection of interdisciplinary research papers on the Seattle Central Library, the following comments are an attempt at providing an architectural context to the library's conceptual and compositional (formal and spatial) epistemology.

The design of the Seattle Central Library: the compositional technique

From neoplasticism to the picturesque stacking of boxes

In the search to leave the rationalist box, OMA departed from the compact space planning seen in their competition entry for the Bibliothèque de France (1989). OMA began the picturesque assembly of orthogonal parallelipipeds with the Casa da Musica (Porto, 2005) and the Seattle Central Library. What the French architect Dominique Perrault had undertaken for the Fondation François Pinault pour l'Art Contemporain at Boulogne-Billancourt (project, 2001), that is, the stacking of relatively autonomous boxes of different dimensions and shrouded by a tensile metallic membrane, OMA

206 Wilfried Wang

developed in the two variations using a concrete skin for the concert hall in Porto and a steel and glass cladding system in Seattle.

The genealogy of this compositional technique can be traced back to at least the Dutch neoplasticists Cornelius von Eesteren and Theo van Doesburg of the 1920s. Whereas these two architects confined their picturesque plasticity to the compositional elements of the tectonic components (walls and floors), Perrault and OMA extended this picturesque composition to the spatial units of individual compartmental volumes (galleries, halls, etc.).

To what end this picturesque composition was used can be related to the general anti-authoritarian attitude popularized by the early modernists such as the Swiss architect Charles-Éduard Jeanneret-Gris, later on known as Le Corbusier, who subverted orthodox compositional conventions by the so-called *Five Points*, placing columns or *piloti* and the recessed ground volume against the traditional rusticated base; the open plan or free plan against the cellular room composition; the free façade against the composed; the horizontal strip window against the upright; and finally the roof terrace against the double-pitch roof. Such anti-authoritarian posturing has been especially popular amongst young design students, who have thus been able to live out their late puberty, believing that going against the orthodox, the conventional, the normal is per se 'cool' or 'modern'. Undoubtedly, such anti-establishment resentment towards convention continues to accompany architects even in their more mature years, leading to their continued attempts at subverting orthodoxies for the sake of it. One might consider this late-pubescent attitude to be a constituent part of the modernist tradition (with my emphasis on the word 'tradition', given that this approach is nearly a century old now).

Inversion as a symbol of anti-authoritarianism

While Le Corbusier pretended to 'liberate' the task of composition by his five-point rule, he also drew on the ancient system of proportional relations (root 2, Golden Section, etc.) as a disciplinary compositional device. Such disciplinary devices have not been relevant in late twentieth- and early twenty-first-century architectural composition. Instead, OMA and subsequent Dutch architects such as their offspring MVRDV have pursued with reluctant servility the translation of programme requirements into a three-dimensional assembly (to most neomoderns the term 'composition' is unacceptable, in the same way as the words 'hierarchy' or 'order') of boxes with the correct areas. While MVRDV's Dutch pavilion for the 2000 EXPO in Hannover was a deliberately diverse stacking of mixed programme along the lines of their subsequent not-so-tongue-in-pork's cheek vertical farm, otherwise known as *Pig City* (2001), OMA fundamentally changed course with regard to the compositional tactic of containing diverse functions within a tight geometric envelope and chose to diversify configurational expressions along the lines pursued by Herzog and de Meuron with their unsuccessful competition entry for the extension of the Laurenz building of Basel's Kunstmuseum (2001). Herzog and de Meuron at that time were infatuated by the traditional Chinese scholar's stone, the latter is a small rock of a particular sculptural shape possessing innate configurational associations, however, Herzog and de Meuron turned this into an inflated irregular polyhedron, giving it an inhabited, multi-story segmental floor subdivision that in its scalar and detailed

Epilogue 207

translation had lost any associative powers otherwise found in an 'as-found' natural rock.

The autonomous irregular polyhedron

Herzog and de Meuron were among those Swiss architects who departed from the 1990s era of the right-angled box that had dominated the architectural discourse. The so-called avant-garde architects had become tired of these orthogonal boxes and were looking to other sources of formal articulation, including those that might be applicable to a building's overall form.

In this regard Dominique Perrault's late projects of the 1990s, culminating in the proposal for the Fondation François Pinault, shows the trajectory of the collective search for the irregular polyhedron. This irregular polyhedron owes its existence to the undercurrent of the picturesque tradition (an ancient compositional and aesthetic development with sources, amongst others, in ancient Chinese courtyard gardens) and less to occasional modern instantiations such as Konrad Wachsmann's studies of complex nodes or Louis Kahn and Anne Tyng's *City Tower* for Philadelphia (1952–7). The latter were based on a constructional logic, including the logic of the main structural components. The Fondation François Pinault, the Seattle Central Library, and the Casa da Musica were designed from the point of view of their configurational appearance rather than from the point of view of their inherent structural logic. Structure, as one possible primary source for a compositional logic, is irrelevant to those architects who are obsessed with the creation of icons. In this, they follow the principle of the Statue of Liberty on Ellis Island: sculptural form is autonomous of the internal framework that merely has the role of supporting the skin.

The collage

The idea of superimposing boxes on top of each other also follows the ancient tradition of the collage. With collage is meant the possibility of freely associating elements with one and another to achieve a compositional whole. Thus, for example, we see in the tradition of western painting artists such as the prolific Giovanni Pannini (1691–1765) who produced oil paintings of ancient and modern Rome showing objects that are ideally united in a painting that in reality are miles apart. This early form of a souvenir was sought by the first tourists, who bought such paintings in the same way as postcards used to be bought in the post-Second World War period. Similarly, James Stirling (1926–92) and Aldo Rossi (1931–97) were masters at the drawn and built collage. While these two architects were educated in the classical tradition of architectural composition, OMA's shows neither signs of interest in such abilities nor sensibilities for subsequent compositional challenges. The only formal discipline that corsets the Seattle Central Library is the picturesqueness of the irregular polyhedron. Formal associations with known architectural elements have been consciously excised for fear of being considered old fashioned (itself a widespread phobia cultivated in architectural academia ever since the Bauhaus pedagogy has been canonized).

Thus, while in such large buildings as Erik Gunnar Asplund's Stockholm City Library users are left in no doubt as to the location of the main entrance and the main

208 Wilfried Wang

organizing space, OMA and other architects prefer to solve the task of providing orientation for the users by means of so-called 'wayfinding systems', or super graphics. The quasi-democratization, in this case dumbing down, of the readability of architecture to two-dimensional typography and escalators, an architecture that believes that it is no longer permitted to refer to conventional, archetypal, or even abstracted formal and spatial typologies, has produced the forced mechanization of the Seattle Central Library. Visitors are brought to what the architects consider to be the 'centre' without any recourse to any semblance of what that centre might be in formal or spatial terms: it just is willed to be the centre.

Coupled with the rationalistic, quasi-incontrovertible application of the Dewey Decimal System and a continuous ramp, the architects and the librarians have abrogated their responsibility for structuring knowledge as printed in a book and shelved in a building to such an idiosyncratic order. Consistent with this abrogation of responsibility is the architects and the librarians' application of an unarticulated and relentless repetition of shelves on the upper levels. The layering of spaces in the library is thus equivalent to the paratactic array of book shelves.

Another public library

If we compare the Seattle Central Library with other modern libraries such as Hans Scharoun's State Library in Berlin (1964–78), we begin to understand the distance that the Seattle building has covered to move away from a public building serving readers in their quest for knowledge, the intimate interrelation between medium and the monumental collective act of reading to one that is primarily concerned with the realization of a concept that 'avoids' the phobias of the modernist profession and that permits the realization of a rationalistic concept. Scharoun's library is a large, national, yes, monumental in a modern sense library on the interior. From intimate to grand spaces, from reading desks in open halls to cubicles, the variety of reading environments upholds the character of a library. Seattle Central Library departs from this certainty and from this notion of the collective. Its character is more like a department store with some seating facilities. In this sense, it is closer to 'Main Street'. The loss of decorum and the denial of the collective appears to be taken for granted by both client and architects. This loss stands in the tradition of modernism: no to representation, away with conventional certainties, but welcome to appropriated and abstracted 'street-cred' aesthetics, itself in the long-standing tradition of early twentieth-century fine art's embrace of *objets trouvés* to Denise Scott-Brown and Robert Venturi's *Learning from Las Vegas*.

The redeeming qualities of the Seattle Central Library, its location in the city's downtown area, its extended opening hours, its free access, its air-conditioned interior, its provision of free internet, are all qualities with which the architects had little to do. Any box could have been erected on this location with these facilities and it would have been popular amongst the locals. But that would only have been part of the story. The other part, the international hype, Seattle's strategy to overcome its notorious lack of self-esteem (a phenomenon by no means limited to Seattle, this is a widespread phenomenon: a sense of inferiority principally suffered by wannabe-famous local politicians), led to the excess called starchitecture and all of its collateral benefits and damages, that is, the irregular polyhedral configuration and internal shenanigans. Globalization, and its side effects, has thus given us an irregular polyhedron with horizontal floor plates on the lower levels and a ramped surface on the upper levels, variously connected by escalators and elevators, ramps and stairs, that currently is being used as a library.

Who knows, in a few years' time, when neoliberalism strikes back with full force, the library will have closed due to excessive costs to the tax payers; the lower levels might be given over to some Seattle-based, international beverage company with its newest range of food products and a sorely needed downtown public car park on top.

Index

access to libraries 126–7; *see also* disabled access
aesthetic experience 138
Agnew, John 116
Allen, Paul 21; *see also* Microsoft
Allen, S. 55
American Institute of Architects 27, 38, 139, 157, 172
analytical study of buildings 95, 203
Archdaily website 173, 175
archetypes, architectural 74
architect-selection process 5, 24
architects and architecture: relationships with buildings and their users 4–5, 42–4, 47, 189, 197–8, 204–5
Architecture journal 90
Asplund, Erik Gunnar 207–8
assemblage theory 53, 57, 65
attention, psychology of 99
Augst, Thomas 114
Austin, John Langshaw 189
awards, architectural 3, 26–7, 38, 49, 139, 157
Ayuso, Alessandro 199

Baar, Bernard 200
background consciousness 100, 103–5
Bafna, Sonit xii, 5–6, 40, 48, 138, 153, 205; *co-author of Chapter 6*
Barnum, C.M. 142
Basso, Keith H. 113
Beaches Toronto Branch Library 114
Bechtel, R.B. 168
Bender, Thomas 22
Berlin State Library 208
Bill and Melinda Gates Foundation 24
Block, Marylaine 114
Boatman, Edward 4
bond measure to finance SPL 23–4
'book spiral' design 34, 40–1, 46–7, 49, 59–63, 105, 117, 120, 141, 146
Bordass, B. 170
Bourdieu, Pierre 57
branch libraries 23–4, 26, 33, 63, 129

'breadth' themes with building examples 76–8
Brewster, David 22, 25
Brösamle, M. 175
buildings, puposes of 108
Bush, James 27, 35

Carlson, Laura xii, 6–7, 157–8, 163; *co-author of Chapter 9*
Carnegie libraries 28, 31–2
Castleberry, Elizabeth 29
centrality, spatial 105; *see also* space syntax analysis
Cheek, Lawrence 27, 70, 86, 89–91, 139
closed functions of buildings 97
cognitive processes and cognitive maps 157–9
Coliton, Sue 29
collage 207
Colomina, B. 64
communication theory 188–9
community, sense of 123–4
concrete, use of 14, 81, 103, 120, 139, 143–7
Conroy Dalton, Ruth xii, 5, 7, 47, 86; *author of Chapter 3, co-author of Introduction and Chapter 10 and co-editor*
contextuality of design 32–3
Cooper, A. 46
Cooper, I. 170, 183
Corr, Casey 24
Coyne, Richard 26
Cresswell, Tim 115–17, 128, 130
Curry, Ann 113

Dain, Phyllis 114
Dali, Salvador 191
Davis, M.H. 42
daylight 33, 48, 108, 114
De Kort, Y.A. 140
'deep' buildings 57
Deleuze, G. 57–8
Department of Justice, US 34
Depthmap software 98, 148

Index 211

descriptors of a building 71–4
design process 4–5, 11, 17, 22–4, 32, 42, 48, 95
Dewey decimal system 60, 62, 208
Dietrich, William 7, 38–9, 47
disabled access 34, 46–7
'disjunction' (Tschumi) 191
disorientation 63, 90; *see also* lost in the Library building
double hermeneutic 92
Dovey, Kim xii–xiii, 5, 40, 204; *author of Chapter 4*
Durrance, Joan C. 114

Eco, Umberto 189–90
Edwards, Phillip M. xiii, 6; *co-author of Chapter 7*
Eesteren, Cornelius von 206
Einfühlung see entropy
elevators *see* lifts
Elkins, James 198
emotional responses to buildings 137–54, 180
empathetic insideness 89–92
empathy, concept and theory of 7, 42, 47, 199
English as a second language (ESL) facilities 33–4, 122
entropy (*Einfühlung*) 199
environmental psychology 6, 47, 137–41
escalators 60–3, 90, 106, 108, 146, 159, 162
ethnic diversity in Seattle 22
ethnography 5, 11
existential insideness and *existential outsideness* 89
Experience Music Project 21
experiential qualities of a building 5, 67
experimental psychology 7
eye tracking as a research technique 7, 188, 193–4, 197, 205

Facebook 175
Faye G. Allen Children's Centre 29
Feld, Steven 113
Feldstein, Lewis M. 116, 129
field conditions 55
first-time library visitors 101, 159
Fisher, Karen xiii, 6, 114; *co-author of Chapter 7*
Flick house, Zurich 15–16
foam used in modelling 11–16
Fondation François Pinault 207
Forrester Research 170–1
Forward Thrust programme 22
'frame' motifs 81
Frankl, Paul 99
Franz, G. 138
Frasca, Zimmer Gunsul 24

free association as a research method 117–18
free speech 125
functionality 4, 139

gamma analysis 55–6; *see also* space syntax analysis
Gates, Bill 29; *see also* Bill and Melinda Gates Foundation; Microsoft
Gehry, Frank 21
genotypes of buildings 56–7
Gestalt psychology 1–2
glass floors 27, 31
glass walls 31, 71, 80, 120
global workspace theory (Baar) 200
globalization 208–9
Goffman, Erwin 97
Gorman, Michael 114
Graafland, A. 54, 64
'grandmother cells' 198
graphics, use of 30
Grobstein, P. 196
grounded theory 176
Guangzhou Opera House 12–13
Guattari, F. 57–8

habitual library users 103–5
habitus 57
Haenlein, M. 171
Hanson, Julienne 53–8, 88; *see also* space syntax analysis
Harris, Alexandra 25, 27–8, 31, 34
Harvey, David 22
'height' themes with building examples 79
Heisenberg, Werner 2–3
hermeneutic phenomenology of architecture 91–2
hermeneutics 6, 67–70, 86, 91–2, 203; compared with phenomen-ology 68–9
Herzog, T.R. 206–7
Hillier, Bill 53–8, 88; *see also* space syntax analysis
Hinshaw, Mark 21–2
Hirasawa, Louise 27
Holl, Steven 24
Hölscher, Christoph xiii, 3, 6, 47; *co-author of Introduction and Chapter 9 and co-editor*
Hopkins, Jeffrey 114
hours of operation of libraries 128

Ikea 57
information, concept of 116–17, 130
'inner spatial experiencing skills' 43–4
'inside-outside' relationship of a building 76–7
interaction with buildings 137
inter-rater reliability (IRR) 178, 180, 183
interviews, semi-structured 142
isovist-based measures 98–9, 147–53

212   *Index*

Jacobs, Deborah 22–5, 28–31, 34–5, 38–9, 173
Jameson, F. 55
Jaso, Nora 25
Jean, Jill 24, 40–1
Jeanneret-Gris, Charles-Éduard 206;
   see also Le Corbusier
Jennifer Aniston neurons 198
Johnson, Mark 199
journalism, architectural 204

Kahn, Louis 207
Kane Hall (Washington University) 124
Kaplan, A.M. 171
Kelbaugh, Douglas 21
Kipnis, J. 53–4, 64
Koolhaas, Rem 12, 18, 25–35, 48–9, 53–60,
   63–5, 69–74, 79, 81, 90, 109, 191–2
Krämer, Sybille 190
Kranich, Nancy 114
Krippendorf, K. (and Krippen-dorf's
   α-values) 178
Krukar, J. 47
Kubo, M. 44
Kuliga, Saskia xiii, 6–7, 47, 163; *author of*
   Chapter 8 and co-author of Chapter 10
Kunsthal museum 96

Lakeoff, George 199
Le Corbusier 53, 154, 206
Leaman, A. 170
learning, places for 127
Leckie, Gloria J. 114
Leder, H. 138
librarians and other library staff 24–5, 32,
   34, 89, 124–7
libraries, perceptions of 118, 130
library and information science (LIS)
   literature 113–14, 117, 128
'lifeworlds' 5–6, 67–8, 92
lifts 48, 90
Lippard, Lucy R. 113
lived experience 92
Loschky, Marquardt and Nesholm (LMN)
   architects 2, 5, 24, 27, 39
lost in the Library building, people's sense of
   being 3, 7, 39, 63, 137, 139, 144, 157–64
Lukermann, Fred 113
Luscombe, Belinda 29

McCook, Kathleen de la Pena 115
McLuhan, Marshall 189–90
McNaught, C. 142
Mai, Jens-Erik xiii, 6; *co-author of Chapter 7*
Marchette, Steven xiii–xiv, 7; *co-author of*
   Chapter 9
market ideologies 26
Marković, S. 138, 153

Markus, T. 56
Martin, David 26
materials, development of 14–16
Mattern, Shannon xiv, 5, 39, 42–8, 71;
   author of Chapter 2
Mau, Bruce 30, 39, 173
meeting rooms 48, 59–60, 141, 148
metaphors, use of 25–6
Metzinger, Thomas 199
Microsoft (company) 141
mission statements 122
mixed-methods research 2, 6
mixed-use developments 26
'mixing chamber' design 30, 59–60, 146
mock-ups 17, 46–9
models, architectural 12–18, 46
Modernism and the Modernist Movement
   198, 206
modernization 32, 199, 206
Molz, Redmond Kathleen 114
Moore, Michael 125
Multnomah County Library 114
Muschamp, Herbet 38
MVRDV 206

NATO headquarters 15–16
navigation around buildings 97, 101,
   108–9, 140, 146, 157–64, 180; *see also*
   disorientation; navigation
navigational aids 39–40, 60–2, 139; *see also*
   Mau, Bruce
Near North Branch Library, Chicago 116, 129
Nelligan, Ben xiv, 7; *co-author of Chapter 9*
Nelson, Douglas 118
networks 58
neuroscience 197–9
New York Public Library 114
newspaper critics 24, 27–8
Nielsen, Susan 27, 31
Noë, Alva 194
Norberg-Schulz, C. 63
'Northwestern-ness' 27, 33

Ochsner, Jeffrey 27
Office of Metropolitan Architects (OMA)
   2–3, 5, 11–19, 24–30, 35, 42–9, 53–4, 60,
   96, 192, 205–8
Oldenburg, Ray 114–17, 128–30
Olson, Sheri 27, 29
'one-way streets' and 'one-way buildings'
   62–4, 204
O'Regan, Kevin 194
outsideness 89

Palmer, L.A. 142
Pannini, Giovanni 207
paranoid-critical method (PCM) 191

Index 213

participation, definition of 29
Pask, Gordon 200
passers-by 126
Pastier, John 23
pattern-seeking instinct 1–2
peer-to-peer networks 167
performativity 189–94, 197
Perrault, Dominique 205–7
personas 45–7
perspective-taking 42–8
Perspex 12, 14
phenomenal staging in buildings 95–9, 103, 106, 109–10
phenomenology 5–6, 67–70, 74, 85–92; compared with hermen-eutics 68–9; of Seattle Central Library 85–6
photographs, use of 30, 142–3
Piaget, Jean 42
place: conceptualization of 113–17; definition of 116, 130 ;phenomenology of 70; theories of 6; *see also* sense of place
place experience 89, 92
Plank, Clemens xiv, 7, 42, 48, 192, 205; *co-author of Chapter 11*
post-occupancy evaluation (POE) 7, 86, 137, 139, 162, 167–71, 175–6, 182–5, 205; definitions of 168; types of 169
Preiser, W. 168–9, 175–6, 185
Prince-Ramus, Joshua 41, 168, 175, 192
Pritzker Prize 26–7
Probe project 169
public opinion 28, 35
public process 34–5
public realm 58
public relations 28–9, 35
public spaces, characteristics of 64, 114
publicness, sense of 98
Putnam, Robert D. 116, 129

Queens Borough Public Library 114

Rainer Beach branch library 26
Ramus, Joshua *see* Prince-Ramus
reaction card task 141–6; results from 145–6
reading rooms 39, 48, 60, 63, 91
'realist' and 'realistic' architecture 18
recognition theory 193
reference strategy scenarios 45–6
Relph, Edward 89–92, 113
research on buildings: methods applied in 2–4; publication of 7; reasons for 1–2
reviews of library facilities and buildings 167–85; semantic content of 180–4
rhetorical skill and rhetorical aggrandisement 29–32

'rising' motifs 82–3
Rossi, Aldo 207
Rowe, Colin 99

Saxton, Matthew xiv, 6; *co-author of Chapter 7*
Sayeki, Yutaka 43–4
Scharoun, Hans 208
Schell, Paul 24
Scott-Brown, Denise 208
Scully, Vincent 99
Seamon, David xiv–xv, 5–6, 85, 204; *author of Chapter 5*
Seattle, city of 21–5, 31–3, 90–1
Seattle Art Museum 21
Seattle Central Library 2–4; design technique employed for 204–9; emotional responses to 137–54; field study of 113; first proposal for a new building 5; Koolhaas's view of 191; and library norms 97; model of 15; nature of staging in 100; perceptions of 70–2, 118, 147; photographs of 13, 72, 75–6, 173, 175; as a place 85–91, 119–29; public involvement in design of 21–5, 28–9, 33–5; public presentations at 123; public reaction to 139; reasons for coming to 122–3; reviews of 173; seen as a space 113–30; strengths and weaknesses of 38–43, 48–9, 91; as a subject of study 3–4, 96, 110, 172, 192–4; as a symbol 119; user trajectories in 101–8
Seattle Commons (park) 21
Seattle Design Commission 25–6, 31–3, 72
Seattle Public Library: democratic nature of 23; shop in 160
Seattle Public Library Foundation 29
Seattle riots (1999) *see* World Trade Organization uprising
segmentarity 57–8
semiotics 190–1
Sennett, R. 64
sense of place (SoP) 32–3, 115–17, 130
Shelton, Amy xv, 6; *co-author of Chapter 9*
Shipley, Thomas xv, 6; *co-author of Chapter 9*
short stories as a literary genre 11
sightseeing 106–8
signage 39–40, 90, 139, 146, 159–60, 173
'sinking' motifs 77, 80, 82
Slinkachu 44
Snodgrass, Adrian 26
social capital, *bonding* and *bridging* 129
social functions of libraries 122–5, 128, 180
social media 7, 85–8, 167–71, 176, 182–5, 205
social staging in buildings 95–9, 103–9

214 *Index*

socially oriented functions of buildings 97
space syntax analysis 53–8, 137–8, 147,
 153–4, 160, 163; *see also* Hanson,
 Julienne; Hillier, Bill
spatial experiences 138
Speaks, M. 55
Spiegelberg, H. 70
'squeezed' motifs 82–4
stable and *instable* spaces 194–6
Stadler, Matthew 28–30, 35
staging of experience 95–9, 103–10
Stirling, James 207
Stockholm City Library 207–8
Stokols, D. 168
stories, common features of 11
'strangers' at Seattle Central Library 89
structuring of knowledge 208
studio events 14–18
studio practice constituting the architect's
 world 18
Stupid White Men 125
Sundberg, Rick 31

Tenbrink, T. 42–3
text clustering 176
Thiel, P. 139
Thiis-Evensen, Thomas 6, 70, 74–83, 92, 204
'third place' concept (Oldenburg)
 115–16, 128–30
Thomas, Nancy Pickering 114
Tiensvold, Dennis 4
'time-body' of a building 92
Time Magazine 38, 139, 157
Toronto Central Library 114
tourists 88–90; *see also* sightseeing
trajectories of design 11, 14, 16, 18
TripAdvisor 173–4
Tschumi, Bernard 191
Turner, Alasdair 98; *see also* Depthmap
 software
Twitter 175
Tyng, Anne 207

urbanity, definition of 64
usability as distinct from *user experience* of
 buildings 47–9
user-generated content 170–1, 182
users of library facilities 6–7, 25, 42–7, 86–9,
 113, 118, 126–7, 138–40, 147, 152–4;

as disinct from visitors 86–8; 'knowledge
 acquirers', ' information gatherers' and
 'hang-outers' 44–7; various types of 46–7,
 88; *see also* habitual library users

van Doesburg, Theo 206
Vancouver Central Library 114
Venturi, Robert 21, 208
Vetruvius (and the Vetruvian Triad of
 architectural qualities) 4
visceral reactions to a building 70–4, 78,
 81–5, 92
visibility graph analysis (VGA) 147–50
visitors to Seattle Central Library 86–9, 183;
 see also first-time library visitors
visual environment/ambience, changes in
 101, 103, 108–9
visual exposure 98, 103, 105

Wachsmann, Konrad 207
Waiting for Godot 96
Wang, Wilfried xv; *author of Chapter 12*
Watzlawick, Paul 189–90
wayfinding 7, 39, 41, 90, 101, 139–40,
 146–7, 154, 158–60, 164, 167–8,
 172–3, 208
Web 2.0 technology 170–1
Wheat, Leonard 117–18
Wiegand, Wayne A. 114
Wiener, J.M. 138
Wölflin, Heinrich 199
word association 120–7
word clouds 142
'Wordles' 142–3, 176, 181, 182
World Trade Organization uprising
 (Seattle, 1999) 30–1

Yaneva, Albena xv–xvi, 5, 42, 46, 204;
 author of Chapter 1
Yarbus, Alfred L. 193–4
Yelp 85–9, 92, 173–4
YouTube 175

Zamperlini, Augusto 4
Zisch, Fiona xvi, 7, 42, 48, 205; *co-author of
 Chapter 11*
Zook, Julie xvi, 5–6, 40, 48, 138, 153, 205;
 co-author of Chapter 6